PROMOTIONAL CULTURE AND CONVERGENCE

The rapid growth of promotional material through the Internet, social media and entertainment culture has created consumers who are seeking out their own information to guide their purchasing decisions.

Promotional Culture and Convergence analyses the environments necessary for creating a culture of collaboration with consumers, and critically engages with key areas of contemporary promotional development, including:

- promotional culture's primary industries, including advertising, marketing, PR and branding, and how are they informed by changes in consumer behaviour and market conditions;
- how industries are adapting in the digital age to attract both audiences and advertising revenue;
- the evolving dialogues between 'new consumers' and producers and promotional industries.

Ten contributions from leading theorists on contemporary promotional culture present an indispensable guide to this creative and dynamic field and include detailed historical analysis, in-depth case studies and global examples of promotion through TV, magazines, newspapers and cinema.

Helen Powell is Programme Leader for Media and Creative Industries at the University of East London where she teaches Advertising and Consumer Studies. Her previous publications include *Stop the Clocks! Time and Narrative in Cinema* (2012) and *The Advertising Handbook* (3rd ed, 2009).

PROMOTIONAL CULTURE AND CONVERGENCE

Markets, Methods, Media

Edited by Helen Powell

Routledge
Taylor & Francis Group

LONDON AND NEW YORK

First published 2013
by Routledge
2 Park Square, Milton Park, Abingdon, Oxon OX14 4RN

Simultaneously published in the USA and Canada
by Routledge
711 Third Avenue, New York, NY 10017

Routledge is an imprint of the Taylor & Francis Group, an informa business

British Library Cataloguing in Publication Data
A catalogue record for this book is available from the British Library

Library of Congress Cataloging in Publication Data
Promotional culture and convergence : markets, methods, media / [edited by] Helen Powell.
p. cm.
Includes bibliographical references and index.
1. Internet advertising. 2. Interactive marketing. 3. Branding (Marketing)
I. Powell, Helen.
HF6146.I58P76 2013
658.8--dc23
2012037242

ISBN: 978-0-415-67279-5 (hbk)
ISBN: 978-0-415-67280-1 (pbk)
ISBN: 978-0-203-13032-2 (ebk)

Typeset in Bembo
by Taylor & Francis Books

CONTENTS

PART II
Media in Context

LIST OF FIGURES AND TABLES

Figures

Table

LIST OF CONTRIBUTORS

Chris Hackley is Professor of Marketing in the School of Management, Royal Holloway University of London. His PhD from Strathclyde University entailed a study of the creative advertising development process in top London advertising agencies. He has published research on a range of topics connected to consumption and cultural policy, including UK alcohol policy and young people, media regulation, advertising and promotion management, media ethics, management education, consumer cultural identity, creativity and advertising, and marketing theory.

Rungpaka Amy Hackley née Tiwsakul is Lecturer in Marketing at Queen Mary, University of London. She was previously Lecturer in Marketing at the Universities of Durham and Surrey. Her PhD, a cross-cultural study of television product placement, was awarded by the School of Management, Royal Holloway University of London. Dr Hackley's research in consumption, identity and marketing communication has appeared in various publications, including the *Journal of Business Research, Journal of Marketing Management* and *International Journal of Advertising*.

Jonathan Hardy is Reader in Media Studies at the University of East London and teaches political economy of media at Goldsmiths College, University of London. He is the author of *Cross-Media Promotion* (Peter Lang, 2010), *Western Media Systems* (Routledge, 2008) and co-editor of *The Advertising Handbook* (Routledge, 2009). He teaches and writes on political economy of media, media and advertising, communications policy and regulation, and international and comparative media. He is secretary of the UK media reform group, the Campaign for Press and Broadcasting Freedom (www.cpbf.org.uk).

The day **Tim Holmes** started on his first magazine the management decided to close it down. Fortunately he found a better job on a bigger title, working with talented people who taught him all he needed to know to start his own publishing company. He is now a Senior Lecturer at Cardiff University, where he runs the journalism school's magazine courses and publishes in the field of magazine studies. His most recent book is *Magazine Journalism* (Sage, 2011).

Searle Kochberg is a maker and writer on cinema and other performing arts. He has an academic post at the University of Portsmouth where he teaches film history, film production and scripting (fiction and non-fiction). He is currently pursuing a PhD in the essay film and self-representation.

Daniel Lee has worked as a print and web writer and editor for *The Guardian*, *The Times*, *Time Out*, the *New Statesman*, Channel 4 and other organizations since 1989. His writing includes several non-fiction and fiction books, including a children's novel, *Finding Dad* (illustrated by Korky Paul, launched at the Hay Festival in 2005 and later performed by Michael Palin for an audio CD). He has appeared on Sky News and BBC Radio discussions and helped to launch a number of publications. He is a lecturer on several undergraduate and postgraduate courses at City University London and is director of the consultancy Being Media in Oxford (http:// www.beingmediaoxford.com). He continues to write and practice as a journalist.

Cheryl Martens has lectured in Branding and Brand Communications and Digital Communication Strategies as Senior Lecturer at Bournemouth University and was previously Senior Lecturer in Advertising, the University of the Arts, London. She holds a PhD from the University of Manchester and has published work on the politics of global branding and corporate social responsibility, the branding of HIV/ AIDS communication, as well as cross-sector social partnerships. Cheryl currently teaches methodology and communications courses in the Latin American Faculty for Social Sciences (FLACSO), Ecuador.

Jeremy Orlebar is an experienced radio and television producer, director and lecturer. He has over 25 years of experience with BBC Television and Radio, producing and directing factual programmes. He now works as a freelance writer, consultant and lecturer in media. His publications include *The Television Handbook* (Routledge, 2011), *The Practical Media Dictionary* (Bloomsbury, 2004) and *Digital Television Production* (Arnold, 2002).

Helen Powell previously worked in advertising before joining the University of East London where she now teaches advertising and consumer behaviour in the School of Arts and Digital Industries. She gained her PhD in 1999 from the London Consortium (Birkbeck and the British Film Institute) and has published research on a range of topics including advertising and the elderly, temporal structures of reality TV programmes, emotional branding and the role of nostalgia in advertising during times of economic uncertainty. She is the co-editor of *The Advertising Handbook* (Taylor and Francis, 2009) and in 2012 published *Stop the*

Clocks! Time and Narrative in Cinema (I. B. Tauris), an interdisciplinary text that brings together ideas on temporality, visual culture and storytelling.

Heather Yaxley is a hybrid public relations practitioner–academic, with over 25 years' experience working in-house and as a consultant. She is a Chartered Institute of Public Relations (CIPR) Fellow and Accredited Practitioner as well as an honorary member and director of the Motor Industry Public Affairs Association Ltd. A lecturer at Bournemouth University where she is studying for a PhD, Heather is also course director for the CIPR qualifications with Cambridge Marketing Colleges. She established Applause Consultancy in 2000 and has worked with clients including Nissan, Bentley Motors, Coca-Cola, npower renewables, Tata and General Motors. She is a PR pioneer in social media and can be found as Greenbanana on Twitter and other social networks.

INTRODUCTION

Promotion in an Era of Convergence

Helen Powell

Over two decades ago Andrew Wernick's seminal text *Promotional Culture* (1991) examined not only the impact of the rise of promotion upon the culture in which it was situated, but noted how every aspect of life began to be informed by and adopt promotional strategies in order to gain attention. This infusion of publicity was to seep seamlessly into a plethora of new promotional spaces, both physical and virtual, and was framed by increasingly neo-liberal policies taking hold in the UK and the US from the 1980s onwards. At the heart of this political agenda lay the marketization of everyday life. In order that consumers might begin to identify with this agenda, to recognize consumption as the solution to any problem, promotional tools and strategies were put in place, enhanced by two inextricably linked developments within the sphere of information communication technologies (ICTs). Firstly, the rise of the Internet changed not only the accessibility to consume by containing the time and space between promotion and consumption but it also, as this book will examine, potentially empowered the consumer by making markets more transparent and businesses more answerable. As Anderson (2007: 53) identifies, markets were reconfigured online, challenging the accepted practices of the Pareto Rule by allowing access to 'a culture unfiltered by economic scarcity'. By connecting suppliers directly with consumers, new markets or 'aggregations' are assembled and speak to a range of taste cultures made accessible through the 'demand dynamics of networked, informational economies that distinguish Web 2.0 media and e-commerce firms' from mass markets and traditional media (Spurgeon 2008: 27). Secondly, for promotional industries comes the realization that in terms of the new demand curve assembled out of niche markets and audiences 'the tail ... can be cumulatively more valuable to advertisers than the head' (Spurgeon 2008: 27).

However, as markets evolve in the wake of these new technologies, so a 'new consumer' arises, documented in Chapter 1, characterized by a revised attitude towards consumption that is fundamentally more demanding and less accepting than their modern counterpart. Short of 'time, attention and trust' (Lewis and Bridger 2001: 6), they rely less on traditional promotion and instead positively seek out information regarding their future purchases, gathering opinions through social media and scanning online reviews. Social commerce company Reevoo.com, for example, carries 3 million reviews and peer-to-peer recommendations posted by owners of electrical products purchased from 120 retailers, including Sony and PC World. As a result of these new attitudes towards consumption, the contributors to this book will argue, one significant element of change that promotional strategies must now consider is how to adapt to this culture of co-dependency and collaboration.

The central aim of this book is to explore the changing relationship between the media and promotional industries, currently under revision against a backdrop of a culture of convergence informed by accelerated change across the communications landscape and driven by the proliferation of new technologies. Changes within one facet of the creative industries will therefore produce a symbiotic effect in another – particularly in terms of how audiences are constituted and how marketing communication is delivered. A central theme arises which draws attention to the dialogic relationship between old and new media, rather than the simple replacement of one by another, although the utilization of these terms and their appropriateness are also made problematic. In this context, the book explores a reconfiguration or 'remediation' of media forms, producing greater complexity in relation to traditional conceptualizations of how media are produced, distributed and consumed and, of particular importance, how traditional media texts present themselves as suitable vehicles of promotion in the digital age. The embracing of a multiplicity of new platforms by the media under consideration here – television, newspapers, magazines and cinema – comes as a response to a marketing model that moves away from the 'push' of messages onto a large mass target market, to the evolution of new, more personalized, customized approaches that 'pull' the consumer in through what the brand has to offer. As a consequence, consumers are no longer marketed 'at' but rather engaged in conversation in order to nurture a personalized relationship with the brand. To what extent this additional participation by the consumer actually directly benefits them, or whether this is simply another tool to persuade through collaboration, is questioned throughout.

This book also wishes to address the question raised by Aeron Davis (2006: 149) when he asked: 'What is the significance of the rise of promotional culture in contemporary society?' In response to this question, Davis draws our attention to the different strands of promotional culture that require our consideration. The range of industries and professionals involved is certainly one dynamic, but he elaborates on this to encompass many of the central themes of the book. He observes:

> In effect promotional culture has become much more than the means by which sellers promote their products to buyers. The promotional professions

have become involved, to a greater or lesser extent, in the creation of products, values, ideas, political and market trends, and even markets and
democratic processes themselves.

(Davis 2006: 150)

The industries represented in this book, both traditional mass media (newspapers,
magazines, television and cinema) and promotional (branding, advertising, marketing and public relations, or PR), are connected through their location and
participation within the broader church of the 'cultural' or 'creative industries' and,
hence, their responsibility towards the production and circulation of culture. While
'culture industries' dates back to the work of Adorno and Horkheimer (1944/
1997), the repositioning of media production within the 'creative industries' can be
attributed to the British Department of Culture, Media and Sport (1998) and seeks
to 'reconcile the emergence of increasingly individual and small-scale, project-
based or collaborative notions of commercial and non-commercial media production with institutionalised notions of cultural production as it exclusively takes
place within the cultural industries' (Deuze 2007: 249). What these industries share,
either in a promotional capacity or as an attractive vehicle through which promotional work might be made active, is a sensitivity and susceptibility to the changing
nature of consumer engagement within the media landscape. As a result, traditional
relationships between these industries, audiences, consumers and markets and the
methods employed to interconnect them are, at present, subject to seismic shifts,
which this book seeks to document and reflect upon. The outcome is a revision of
fundamental intrinsic practices: how audiences might be assembled; which platforms are now available for promotional purposes; what kinds of competition do
traditional media industries face; what does the consumer want from promotion
and how can they be reached accordingly? Furthermore, these are no longer isolated questions specific to certain factions of the creative industries. Rather, both
aesthetic and technological deliberations circulate for 'we are living at a moment of
profound and prolonged media transition: the old scripts by which media industries
operated or consumers absorbed media content are being rewritten' (Jenkins and
Deuze 2008: 5).

So how are these promotional industries responding on a practical level to these
changed market conditions? One example of the kinds of response addressed is
articulated by MacRury (2009: 243), who recognizes that 'promotion, culture and
commerce have become integrated spheres of activity' and predicts that in the
future we will talk nostalgically of the 'ad break' from a position of immersion in
promotional content. This permeation of promotion into non-traditional spaces in
an attempt to engage with consumers 24/7 characterizes much contemporary
brand activity. Branding involves the construction and communication of 'the set
of associations held in people's minds about a particular product or service. Those
associations are created by the sum of experiences that a person has had with that
brand. Clearly, many of those experiences are beyond the direct influence of the
marketer', which therefore makes it important that the elements that can be

controlled do leave a consistent impression (Devon and Kerr 2010: 11). In recognition of the role that brands can play in the lives of the time pressured, brand value becomes enhanced as these semiotically and emotionally charged icons function as shortcuts to both meaning-making and decision-making in burgeoning market sectors, especially that of FMCGs (fast moving consumer goods). Yet, in times of austerity when clients' budgets are constrained and spectacular marketing campaigns trimmed back, PR has come to the fore within the marketing mix. From once being in a position where it was seen as 'specialised and limited', PR is now perceived as a highly creative and influential tool (Shimp 2010: 536). Rarely used alone, however, it speaks to the necessary interrelationship of promotional forms, for as consumer motivations are recognized as increasingly complex and attempts to track down their attention becomes a greater challenge for any media planner, so more tailored and nuanced communication responses are required.

As the second half of this introduction will explore, convergence requires responsive changes to be made not only by the promotional industries, but also by the media in which their promotional messages are positioned. Media convergence challenges traditional models of assembling and delivering commercially viable audiences to advertisers specifically due to their displacement across a plenitude of screens, stationary and mobile. Dwyer (2010: 2) defines media convergence as 'the process whereby new technologies are accommodated by existing media and communication industries and cultures'. That is to say, he draws attention to a complex process based around adaptation and transition and, indeed, 'co-evolution' (Dwyer 2010: 32). In order to find an audience, traditional media must work with new digital platforms in order to remain profitable and current. As a result, to a large degree the concept of 'new media' is already outdated as new and old work together symbiotically to keep audiences entertained and informed. Simon Dalglish, group commercial director of ITV in the UK, exemplifies this when he observes: 'TV can now be accessed on every platform, but the experience goes well beyond just "catch-up" or video on demand. We've seen a massive take up in second-screen interaction via mobiles and tablets, especially when experiences are built around brands' (Dalglish 2012: 19).

Such observations echo and affirm the opinions of those commentators (Hesmondhalgh 2007: 249; Mendelsohn 2011) that we are not speaking of the replacement here of old with new media, but rather its complementation: while the advantage of the Internet is its ability to offer customized audiences to advertisers, it consequently places even more of a premium on reaching mass audiences, as the Super Bowl and other major sporting events testify. Interestingly, it is around the Super Bowl that we begin to see a number of themes emerging in terms of the relationship between old and new media that will become a central narrative of this book. For example, the car manufacturer Volkswagen seeded its 2011 *Star Wars* 'Darth Vader' ad on YouTube ahead of the Super Bowl in order to drum up a word-of-mouth 'you must see this' buzz. Doritos, the snack brand, on the other hand, have used this media spectacle over several years as a vehicle to encourage public participation in their brand promotion. It is this concept of 'planting the seed' and seeing what happens online that has brought PR into the heart of marketing practice. Furthermore, this co-existence of old and new media, rather than the replacement of one with another, was further confirmed following my own discussions with a digital planner at JWT's digital arm who heralded not the end of the 30-second spot but rather saw TV taking on a new role. He felt that television would now be used increasingly to launch integrated marketing communications (IMC) brand campaigns, functioning to arouse interest and make emotional connections with audiences which would then be followed up with online activities that could deliver both factual content and experiential interaction. Such an observation is supported by MacRury (2009) who recognizes a qualitative shift in the content of television advertising as a result of the impact of IMC. 'Relieved of the burden of information communication' which can be carried out elsewhere, particularly online, and indeed in a peer-to-peer context devoid of the agency's input, television advertisements now seek to generate instead a 'sensory impact' (MacRury 2009: 225). As a consequence, one could argue, going forward 'the ongoing merging of communication technologies makes demarcations between media circuits arbitrary and raises a need for new media concepts' (Fornäs et al 2007: 51).

The Internet has significantly informed not only what constitutes valuable promotional media space, as the discussions of the initial public offering (IPO) of Facebook will later explore (see Chapter 3), but the activities of media planning and media buying have also been significantly reconfigured as a result of new technologies affecting how media more generally are consumed as a product. In this context, Deuze (2007: 246) believes that convergence culture produces a particular 'media ecology', whereby large media corporations explore opportunities to deliver content over a more varied range of platforms while also hoping to tap into a new consumer base. Within the magazine industry, *Heat*, the celebrity gossip magazine, for example, has utilized radio (Heat Radio), online content (Heatworld.com) and Twitter to extend the reach of the brand with the aim of reinforcing sales of the core product. The magazine itself has witnessed a progressive drop in readership which at its peak in 2006 had an ABC figure of 598,623 (Maden 2011: 23). Other strategies used by magazines to draw attention to the brand include holding events such as fashion shows and award ceremonies to attract PR attention. One specific example of this is film magazine *Empire's* 13-day movie event at the 02 in London Docklands in August 2011 and September 2012. Yet, there is still some inherent emotional quality about print media, non-producible in digital form, that makes it difficult to see the end of magazines in their traditional format. In August 2011, the Audit Bureau of Circulation figures for magazines found that of just 16 titles put forward for audit, *Men's Health* had the highest digital circulation with just 1,746 (Darby et al 2011: 18). *Total Film* magazine had amassed 500,000 downloads for its app by November 2011, which allows consumers to sample the magazine. And yet conversion rates, those that go on to pay for content, are around 5 per cent or lower (Spanier 2011: 46). Furthermore, how we access our media changes with the time of day. The *Financial Times* newspaper has recorded that between 9 pm and midnight more of its readers are accessing the paper digitally, via tablets, which affects how advertising revenue is generated. For as John Slade, the *FT*'s global digital advertising sales director indicates, tablet click-through rates are more pro-lific than on a desktop computer: 'it is around five to 10 times higher (as) people are more engaged' (Slade cited in Spanier 2011).

However, perhaps the single most difficult challenge for print media is the acceleration of the amount of free content available. This will become heightened as the 'digital natives' grow older and simply will not be prepared to pay for it (Bashford 2010: 7). As Anderson (2010: 5) notes: 'This is the Google generation, and they've grown up online simply assuming that everything digital is free.' At present, different models circulate the newspaper industry, hit hard by the amount of free news available in print (e.g., *Metro* and the *Evening Standard*) and online (such as *The Huffington Post*). Rupert Murdoch's response on 2 July 2010 was to begin charging for online access to *The Times* and *The Sunday Times*. In contrast, *The Guardian* has adopted a model of 'open journalism', examined below through a case study of *The 3 Little Pigs* advertisement and which draws attention to this revised approach to news reporting.

At the heart of this book is the recognition that 'media convergence is more than simply a technological shift. Convergence alters the relationship between existing technologies, industries, markets, genres and audiences' (Jenkins 2008: 15). The impact of convergence upon the form and content of television is significant. As Chris Locke (2012: 26), UK trading director at Starcom MediaVest Group iterates, 'of course, most viewing happens live every night, but in a lot of cases – especially on digital channels – the collective scale of the cumulative reach is greater than the live moment'. So 'screens', and not TV, are the new language. Screens and not TV are what we watch. Television is no longer situated, as pre-viously noted, as the automatic medium towards which adspend gravitates, as an examination of the recent media budget of Procter & Gamble (P&G) will testify. While television audiences *per se* are not in decline, viewers are spread across channels fuelled by increased choice and, indeed, niche programme content, and therefore eyeballs have dispersed and fragmented to the point where a large audi-ence bringing in high returns for advertisers is difficult to assemble. In response to such competition the BBC, for example, has introduced on-demand usage through its iPlayer in the hope of increasing loyalty. The digital switchover in the UK in 2012 brought with it more information on the screen, higher resolution and therefore more detail, and because it uses less bandwith more channels become available, including brand extensions: BBC1–4, for example, or the advertiser-funded ITV1–4. In the latter case there is also a 'plus 1' channel which reruns the main schedule an hour later.

Cinema, too, has not gone unchallenged in terms of the variety of viewing opportunities now available. Where once its main challengers were television and then Blockbuster, the video and DVD rental store (in administration as of January 2013), now new pretenders are capable of offering on-demand viewing of films due to significant changes in technological delivery services. Netflix, for example, was founded in 1998 as a DVD-by-mail service but recognized early on in its history the potential for the amalgamation of TV and the Internet. Love Film (owned by Amazon) and digital streaming through providers such as Sky and Virgin Media all speak to the demands of the 'new consumer', allowing them, for a fee, the opportunity to watch what they want, when and where. Emphasis shifts towards consumer as media planner, owning the schedule, personalizing viewing choices rather than being reliant on something fixed and determined. This is the world of choice 'on demand'. In this context Netflix operates on the basis of customization and recommendation: not by offering you everything in store, but by offering you choices based on past selections. 'As you make more choices and the computer algorithm that watches what you do gets better, the selection should be ever more perfect' (Appleyard 2012: 18) As a result, 'the direct distributor–consumer relationship has repositioned cinema as an optional mediation' for the consumption of film (Harbord 2006: 264). Yet any examination of box office figures produces interesting reading (see, for example, Powell 2012: 163). While the number of Facebook members grows globally with 526 million daily active users on average in March 2012 (http://newsroom.fb.com/), which might, indeed, indicate a turn towards more solitary leisure practices, accessed either stationary through a computer or via a mobile device, youth, in particular, still yearn to be part of a mass spectacle. Indeed, Charlie Yeates, associate director and head of cinema at Media-Com, also points to the continued growth in UK cinema audiences and believes this is attributable to the fact that 'going to the cinema is an experience that a device cannot offer' (Yeates 2012: 21). For cinema fights back, seeking out new markets through alliances with, for example, mobile phone network Orange, and owning a day of the week, Orange Wednesdays, when cinema-going can once again become ritualized for those who can take advantage of these mid-week offers.

What links the media industries considered in this book – television, print media and cinema – is that they all are facing the same challenges in responding to new forms of competition from online services: both in terms of their potential to assemble an audience attractive enough for advertisers and simultaneously to compete in a market where access to media content becomes proliferated and is increasingly free. So how is the traditional relationship between media and promotion changing 20 years or so after Wernick (1991) initially drew our attention to this highly challenging problem?

Media convergence

The term 'convergence' first circulated the literature in the mid-1990s; but it was following the work of Henry Jenkins from 2004 onwards that it took a distinctive cultural turn and became popularized in relation to recognition of both fundamental changes to the media industries and the content they produced. Jenkins's contribution is significant in terms of his ability to contextualize the convergence 'not just as intertextual, economic, and technological linkages at the site of production, but as the shifting cultural relations and reception practices that emerge around and exploit those linkages' (Kackman et al 2011: 5). Principally, convergence has occurred at three levels: in relation to technologies, industries and media content (Sayre and King 2010: 23). As a result, Jenkins's work documents convergence as process, engendering cultural transformation and impacting the realignment of the relationships between the promotional industries and the markets they serve. The proliferation of digital technology in everyday life allows for new ways of representing the world and also offers up new relationships between subjects and media technologies that consequently engender divergent means of media production, distribution and use across a range of platforms and devices, all of which, this book will argue, place interactivity at the core.

In 2004 Henry Jenkins gave the Keynote Address at the New Media Consortium (NMC) Summer Conference, where he drew attention to the empowered consumer in an age of media convergence. Convergence, argued Jenkins, centres on the flow of media across national boundaries, across platforms and across the bridge between producers and consumers, and is realized physically through a plethora of technological devices and mentally through our thought processes. As a result, convergence informs not only the structures of the creative industries (media convergence) but also their products (cultural convergence). Jenkins (2004) conceptualized the impact of convergence culture as replicating that outlined by Walter Benjamin in his seminal essay of 1935, 'The Work of Art in the Age of Mechanical Reproduction', in terms of the decline of a specific aura that is weakened not this time by mechanical reproduction but rather by the dissolution of the means of production in the digital age. As a result of this paradigm shift in terms of the ways in which media is produced and consumed, it provides a lens through which we might examine the changing relationships between the technological, industrial, cultural and social elements of the world in which we live. Digitalization, for example, fosters new practices and engenders new cultural forms based on participation and interaction.

As a process rather than an endpoint, convergence informs what media industries produce, how audiences receive what they see and what they do with it beyond its immediate reception. As processes evolve so commensurate changes ensue. Nowhere is this more visible than in the advertising industry, which was slow to embrace digitalization and has responded more successfully of late as young graduates, *au fait* with the parlances of social networking, are employed by agencies such as Wunderman's digital arm (owned by Young & Rubicam), which nurtures talent through its Zed Academy. Over time advertisers have begun to understand Web.2.0 as a media space with new opportunities and models for revenue generation, often on sites where the content is produced outside the agency itself by media consumers. This encapsulates Jenkins's (2008: 18) observation that 'convergence requires media companies to rethink old assumptions about what it means to consume media'. In an era of convergence, media industries, such as advertising, witness and are subject to an increased amount of mergers and acquisitions (M&A) activity, with the aim of amalgamating media portfolios via horizontal integration, allowing for the implementation of products to be distributed across a wider variety of media platforms. The first half of 2012 alone saw significant M&A activity: BBH have been bought by the French Group Publicis (July 2012); the British group WPP bought digital agency AKQA in an estimated £350 million deal (June); while in May Omnicom paid around £55 million for Adam & Eve, the agency behind the John Lewis advert discussed in this volume (Spanier 2012: 51).

But as this book will examine, media convergence is more than media mergers at the level of the corporation letterhead: it speaks to convergence of content, technologies, job roles and skill-sets (Huang et al 2006). This is observed, for example, in the UK where we are witnessing a pseudo return to the concept of the 'full service' advertising agency (Powell 2009: 16) as increasingly creatives and technologists are working together for brands, constructing multiplatform strategies to both inform and engage the consumer. This point is elaborated upon by Laura Jordan Bambach (2010: 52), executive creative director of Lost Boys International, London, and it is worth noting her observations in detail:

> By their nature, digital projects require a great deal of collaboration. Whether in-house or outsourced, the complex production processes involved can't be separated from the conceptual stage as cleanly as with older formats. The killer idea could just as easily be a technical solution as a traditional advertising concept. So digital innovators are interacting with one another in new ways, acting as suppliers and partners to get the job done and calling on one another's expertise and point of view.

These new alliances and the pooling of knowledges that emanate out of such partnerships challenge the once shared perception that user-generated content fuelled by Flip cameras and Mac Books would herald the end of creativity as a professional paid-for practice (Keen 2007). Instead, creativity has extended its sphere of influence to all facets of the promotional industries, provoking thought not just around creative content, but how and why media is used.

A complementary approach, in terms of recognizing convergence as a paradigm shift for media and technology, has been proffered by Bolter and Grusin (1999), who introduced the concept of 'remediation' to examine the impact of new digital technologies upon traditional media. Spawned from audiences' drive for immediacy and instantaneity, Bolter and Grusin identify that each new medium initially replicates old media in both form and content. In the quest to deliver the 'real', they examine how affect is attained, especially through the inter-play of media forms. In this way, a 'dialectical interplay' (Fornäs et al 2007: 50) emerges as, for example, digital culture looks back at the main objectives of previous media forms and, in particular, how through the act of mediation, a sense of connection with the viewer was achieved via a sense of denial of the medium itself. Yet, at the same time, attention is drawn subversively to its points of difference from traditional mass media. Such 'remediation' is heightened in the digital age due to the frequency of new media devices and platforms. So while the news might be delivered to mobile devices via RSS feeds, the more traditional format of news broadcasting adopts the layout of the PC screen, with the ticker tape of breaking news and split screens injecting a sense of immediacy to events as they unfold. As Han (2011: 7) argues: 'remediation is not only a means of looking at technological change or evolution but also a way of identifying a logic of contemporary media culture'. As a result, the ways in which we experience all facets of the promotional and entertainment industries – indeed, even the elision between them – is changing.

Bolter and Grusin (1999: 225) recognized early on the 'black box fallacy': that no one technology will dominate to the point of eliminating all others. That is to say: 'Convergence is often misunderstood to mean a single solution, but in fact, as these technologies appear, they remediate each other in various ways and in various rations to produce different devices and practices' (Bolter and Grusin 1999: 225). So despite the surge in opportunities to access film-on-demand, traditional cinema going remains robust. Indeed, as noted, UK consumers spent more than £1billion on cinema tickets between April 2011 and April 2012 (Yeates 2012: 21) and, as a result, cinema remains a potent advertising medium. This has recently been supported by John Hegarty, worldwide creative director and co-founder of advertising agency Bartle, Bogle, Hegarty (BBH), who also does not believe that digital will replace traditional media as an advertising platform. Rather, he argues, what digital provides is a wider range of platforms to choose from and therefore purports that the key question advertising should be asking is: 'How do we link the powerful world of broadcasting to the incredibly efficient developments of digital?' (Hegarty 2011: 107).

Another dynamic one can identify relates to the convergence of media content. 'Transmedia entertainment' is a key concept when unpacking convergence culture and addresses the coordinated flow of stories, characters and images that enhance the consumer's experience of a brand. It is no longer sufficient for any media product to generate profitability through a single distribution channel; rather, its malleability into an interactive experience, for example, gives it competitive advantage from the commissioning stage onwards. How a product might become 'transmedial' – that is to say, its ability to generate 'revenue across a range of audiences and platforms linked by Internet marketing and distribution' (Lister et al 2009: 165) – is a consideration for all media producers. The capacity to transform users into fans who will seek out and share all further opportunities to acquire both the tangible and intangible elements of any media product becomes a highly profitable marketing tool. It is also interesting in this context to explore the concept of intertextuality in relation to form as well as content. Borrowing heavily from the construction of 'paratexts' (Kackman et al 2011: 2) within the film industry, whereby a key rationale to buy the DVD is the additional material it includes, advertisers now produce their own 'the making of' shorts for their own websites or YouTube. One example of this is the John Lewis Christmas ad (2011) that Orlebar explores in Chapter 9 on television. This is a specifically new feature that comes with digitality as no other appropriate distribution mechanism is obviated and the motivations here seem twofold. Not only does it teasingly provide the viewer with a window into what has been, to date, a very secret world in terms of the derivation of creative inspiration (and these shorts do nothing to distil this; in fact, they seemingly enhance the 'magic'); but for the client and the shareholders it justifies the adspend, demonstrating that, in essence, what is being created is a mini-movie. Whatever perspective one adopts, this is simply a new promotional vehicle: one built on the recycling of existing footage, edited together by words from those 'in the know' and on the set. As the degree of intertextuality, both in form and content, across media increases, so it encourages new degrees of media literacy that work across platforms with, Cardoso suggests (2011:119), television and the Internet functioning as the primary hubs in this set of transformations.

So what are the drivers of media convergence? Of critical importance is the rise of Web 2.0, heralding a fundamental shift in Internet practices. Where previously it had been utilized in a unidirectional manner for the garnering of information, it now functions as a vehicle for information production and sharing, allowing for the establishment of communities of users. From around 2005, the mediascape of the web became fundamentally social (Han 2011: 5) and inextricably informed a new dynamic of social life whereby the need to remain connected became for many a sign of their very existence. Of significance was the impact of digital forms of creative content that can be delivered to a range of static or portable devices. This is then taken up by consumers who learn how to use these different media technologies to bring the flow of media more under their control and to interact with other users, creating greater degrees of interdependency, one could argue, between previously highly independent sets of actors. This participatory culture speaks to the kaleidoscopic array of points of interaction that consumers now have with media content: its production, distribution, interpretation and evaluation. Therefore, for convergence culture to become functional it requires the consumer's participation. Rather than working on previous models of transmission based on reaching the isolated viewer, new models tap into communities of users who share in the evolution of the programme through their participation in a multiplicity of ways. Reality TV, for example, draws its appeal and success as a programming strategy through the degrees of interactivity it can channel: voting, comments on the micro-blogging site Twitter, etc. However, formats are constantly under review; as in the entertainment economy, nothing stays fresh for long and new forms of 'emotional capital' (Jenkins 2004) are required to sustain any sense of audience connectivity. Once attained, however, fan communities are assembled around programmes, especially those whereby camps of followers of particular actors or participants can be channelled, allowing for an 'affective economy' (Jenkins 2004) around programme as brand to channel revenue-raising away from the programme *per se* towards off-air sales of associated merchandise. *The X Factor* has capitalized on this, for example, through track downloads via iTunes of your favourite competitors on a week-by-week basis. Further affect can be generated post-TV via the

PR interest that the programme generates: we see the finalists at film premieres enhancing their star quality and column inches.

The more time the consumer invests in participation, so the emotional bond is enhanced, especially within the context of a transmediated media environment which allows for an emotional deepening with the brand. As a result, 'in contrast to the pre-determined 30 second ad, if online content is good enough users will engage for as long as it holds their interest' (McStay 2010: 198). The novelty of the combinations of media utilized not only adds value to the brand experience but shapes the identity of the brand more holistically and innovatively. This was the case with a forerunner in this category, Wieden + Kennedy's (Amsterdam) 'Coke Side of Life' (2006), which appeared on TV but which, through its global website, allowed consumers to engage more with the characters at their leisure. 'The brief that the brand gave the agency was simple – "Happiness in a bottle"' (Williams 2012: 62) – and gave birth to the creative concept of a world within a vending machine that we never get to see. The advertisement takes us inside this interior universe which comes to life as it is made operational by a man putting a coin in the slot. And yet our immersion in that world is curtailed by the limited time that TV allows. Online, each of the animated characters, whose global appeal resonates through their archetypal traits, is brought to life as we engage with the role that they play in the production and delivery of the bottle: chilled by the Penguins and sealed with a kiss by the Love Puppies, for example.

The next question to focus on is how do the creative industries, media and promotional, seek to keep up with these 'new times' based on an increasingly participatory culture? The traditional model that is being deconstructed here is one whereby traditional media functioned as audience aggregators, producing programmes that would speak to specific target groups that advertisers sought to address. However, assembling such an audience has become increasingly problematic through a series of economic, social and technological changes and challenges. Mark Deuze (2007) articulates how this participatory turn demands a response from the traditional mass media, and yet he recognizes that this kind of collaboration between producers and users of media is not new: letters to the editor in a newspaper being one such example. What has changed is that we are now living in an age of 'amplified interaction (whereby) the process of media production and dissemination also becomes more transparent and open to external intervention, giving users increasing powers of access both outside and within corporate industrial contexts' (Deuze 2007: 246). Deuze believes that media content today is produced in a post-Fordist manner, utilizing small batch production that is subject to much pre-testing in 'determining what kind of messages would be welcomed most' (Deuze 2007: 244), with many of the messages comprising a fusion of individual consumer creativity delivered through platforms provided by big business, as the Doritos 'Crash the SuperBowl' campaign exemplifies. This more piecemeal type of strategy is also recognized by Springer (2009: 297), who argues that rather than the implementation of a predetermined roll-out campaign, the promotional strategies of brands need to remain both media neutral and flexible enough to accommodate the kinds of experiences consumers want from brands, communicating through honed channels of interest and garnering feedback wherever possible.

Case study: *The Guardian's 3 Little Pigs* (2012)

Cardoso (2011: 119) argues that 'the newspaper is no longer one of the two central nodes in the network communication model'. Rather, in the age of the 'informed citizen', these spots are held by TV and the Internet due to the fact that not only can they deliver content more effectively in the age of immediacy, a central theme of this book, but also, he argues (Cardoso 2011: 119), what is valued more in contemporary society is not news but information. News tells us what happened: information prepares us for what might happen. Social networks therefore gain their currency through this sharing of information and the generation of knowledge around things that matter in our lives. The rise of the blog is testament to this and, as a result, digital natives are 'constantly in dialogue with the world, as content fuels more content and yet more content' (Bashford 2010: 7).

The reworking of the tale *The 3 Little Pigs* which launched on Channel 4 at 10.10 pm on 29 February 2012 was *The Guardian* newspaper's first TV ad in relation to brand positioning for more than 25 years, the last being its street chasing 'Points of View' ad of 1986. The ad, which won a gold lion in the Film category, one gold and five silver lions in the Film Craft category and silver in the Titanium and Integrated category at Cannes Lions Advertising Awards (June 2012) examined the newspaper's response to the rise of citizen journalism, crowd-sourcing and open platform collaboration. As Alan Rusbridger, editor-in-chief, commented: 'open is our operating system, a way of doing things that is based on a belief in the open exchange of information, ideas, and opinions and its power to bring about change' (Sweney 2012). Functioning as intermediaries between the producers of news and its consumers, bloggers put their own spin on the news and therefore offer up a multiplicity of viewpoints around which debate on a story within a participatory culture might take place, the story building through the collective intelligence of the contributors. *The Guardian* recognized this and through its online site seeks to channel such activities under its own brand name. In so doing it pays witness to a 'ubiquitous media' (Featherstone 2009: 2) precipitated by multifunctional portable devices that allow the recording, production and sharing of content. 'Ubiquitous media' is also providing challenges to the PR industry as an ever-increasing number of opinions circulate, all of which can impact upon a business's credibility and future. This advertisement for *The Guardian*, therefore, taps into the new ways in which stories are produced, circulated and then reproduced, shifting the model of news production away from a unidirectional linear model to one that more closely resembles a Möbius strip, continually turning on the basis of that which feeds and informs it. In this way, Featherstone (2009: 2) comments, 'the media can no longer be considered to be a monolithic structure producing uniform media effects'.

Jason Gonsalves (2012), head of strategy at BBH London, explains the context behind the ad:

> Nowadays eye witness accounts are shared instantly with the world through Twitter, whilst Google Alerts or new destinations like Gawker and Huffpo offer an alternative to traditional news brands. What's more, we all know the broader Newspaper industry is struggling. Print circulations and revenues keep falling, and for most the business model simply isn't working ... . Where does that leave a newspaper like *The Guardian*?

In this 120-second TV commercial, advertising agency BBH reworked the story of *The 3 Little Pigs* for postmodern times and imagines how the media today would cover these events. A melange of fairy-tale imagery mixed with gritty realism, the ad opens with a close-up of a boiling cauldron which quickly cuts to a newspaper headline emerging on screen: 'Big Bad Wolf boiled alive'. The story breaks across all news channels and formats as the Little Pigs' house is raided and arrests made. A voiceover online from a *Guardian* reporter informs us that the third Little Pig has now been taken into custody. In response, opinions form via blogs and tweets: should the Little Pigs have done what they did to defend their home from the Wolf? However, new evidence emerges that the Wolf, in fact, had asthma and a new line of enquiry follows: it was an 'inside job'. This is then corroborated by an expert in house construction who reveals that the house should have been robust enough to sustain any levels of huffing and puffing. In court, the Little Pigs confess to framing the Wolf; behind on their mortgage payments their actions came out of desperation. Public opinion seizes the moment, empathizing that in an

FIGURE 0.1 *The Guardian* open journalism: *Three Little Pigs* advert
Source: Guardian Media Gallery; image used courtesy of the Bartle Bogle Hegarty Agency

economic climate where defaulting and repossession are all too common occurrences, policy reform is required to ameliorate situations such as this. 'The whole picture', how it is gathered, reported and commented on across a multiplicity of channels, 24/7, is therefore rendered both aesthetically stunning and emotionally charged.

Gonsalves (2012) unpacks the client brief. 'Our brief was to help cut through preconceptions, and engage new readers by bringing to life *The Guardian*'s remarkable transformation over the last ten years from a left-wing, British newspaper to a global digital news hub.' The ad opens evidencing the traditional form, the newspaper headline 'Big Bad Wolf Boiled Alive', but recognizes that through open journalism, which the paper itself adopts, scientific evidence from housing specialists and medical input has the capacity to take that initial headline in a series of different directions. The headline, therefore, functions as a starting point: comment subsequently effuses through *The Guardian* blog and extends outwards into the Twittersphere. The newspaper is represented as far more than 'simply an aggregator of opinion and comment' (Gonsalves 2012): rather, it is a living entity. As a result, the advertisement builds on the newspaper's belief that:

> In the modern world no single organisation can possibly claim to be sole arbiter of truth, with expert journalists working in isolation to pass down the day's news to the masses. Instead, for *The Guardian*, modern news is a dynamic, participative and open dialogue in which the public and other news sources enrich and expand stories, inviting response and opinion. It's open and mutual rather than closed and didactic. It's iterative and alive rather than final and definitive.
>
> *(Alan Rusbridger,* The Guardian'*s editor, cited in Gonsalves 2012)*

In essence, the advertisement demonstrates how convergence is changing the way in which journalism is practised. However, rather than the Internet displacing what has gone before, the message is one of a 'continuum between the online and off-line worlds that exists in a relationship of mutuality and interdependence' (Fenton 2012: 557). As a consequence, the generation and circulation of news becomes more of an on-going process, with stories evolving and developing over space and time; for the value of online space is that it is infinite, allowing for reflection and comment to be made well beyond the immediate point of the newspaper's reception.

Outline of the book's themes and chapters

The overarching aim of this book is to both document and interrogate the changing face of promotional culture. As the promotional landscape evolves and is informed by significant changes, including the technological, globalization and, at present, economic instability in Europe, so we must ask what does this landscape now look like and what issues, debates and, indeed, innovations emerge as a response? In principle, the book will argue that one of the fundamental changes experienced in the last 20 years is a shift in the nature of promotion from one based on interruption to one informed by engagement. The *first* theme, therefore, examines how promotion, in terms of its creative content, must now compete to get noticed. With so many other forms of entertainment available, promotion reviews and appropriates the form and content of its competitors. Such observations were documented earlier in the discussion of 'remediation' where Bolter and Grusin (1999: 55) recognised over a decade ago that 'no medium, it seems, can now function independently and establish its own separate and purified space of cultural meaning'. With promotion no longer unidirectional but based on the audience's wish to be spoken to, debates need to address 'what kinds of advertising content consumers will actually be willing to seek out and receive?' (Donaton 2004: 10). As a result, we have seen in the last decade of the twentieth century, for example, the injection of the 'E-factor' (Wolf 2000: 54) into many facets of marketing; but this cannot simply be subject to any formulaic input. Rather, brands are increasingly using entertainment to build relationships with their target audience, predominantly through social networking sites, and, as a result, evolving content based on a tried-and-tested approach – that is to say, adopting a more experiential stance towards promotion and existing in sharp contrast with the former didactic approach based on product demonstration (Clarke 2010: 102).

However, the *second* theme of the book recognizes that promotional content must become sensitive to how, where and when consumers wish to be engaged. Jim Carroll, chairman of advertising agency BBH, addresses this detailing that 'time and attention have become our most precious commodities … and … must be earned and rewarded' (Carroll 2005). Therefore, creativity as a concept cannot remain tied to the aesthetics of campaigns; it is now also integral to media planning strategies. The rise of integrated marketing communications (IMC) made it increasingly difficult and, indeed, superficial to think in terms of different promotional forms acting in isolation, and instead introduced convergence planning with the 30-second TV commercial functioning as one item on a menu rather than adopting the role of the *plat du jour*. Above all, IMC heralded a greater cooperation across the different promotional industries and recognition of a common goal that centred on the creation and delivery of the client's message to an identified target audience with the intention of precipitating behavioural or attitudinal change. Mapping 'total communications' in relation to the various promotional methods employed lies at the heart of the book's agenda.

How these messages are received is made more complex by the concomitant changing relationship the audience has to media as it increasingly converges and produces revised viewing conditions. The complexity of 'media convergence' comes through if we stop and define what is understood by the term 'media' and consider the interconnected set of elements that have the potential to be transformed by technological change. 'If culture is based on communication, media as vehicles of meaning and tools for signifying practices are the material technologies and institutional apparatuses of culture' (Fornäs et al 2007: 47). As a result, how audiences are assembled (the *third* theme) is evolving with an increased turn towards 'networked individualism' (Dwyer 2010: 68); consequently, revised structures for assembling audiences for profit are evident. As the ensuing chapters will document, convergence itself (the *fourth* theme) represents more than just technological change. Rather, it 'alters the relationship between technologies, industries, markets, genres and audiences' (Jenkins 2008: 15). In this context the *fifth* and final theme of the book explores the markets and marketplaces in which consumers are active and their changing relationship to both producers, as the suppliers of goods and services, and promotional industries, functioning as the conduits through which messages about these goods and services are formulated and articulated.

In order to present these five themes cogently, noting that they will, indeed, become inextricably linked as the text unfolds, the book has been subdivided into *two parts* and a series of chapters. *Chapter 1* seeks to provide the contextual under-pinning around the need for promotion and examines the culture of convergence in terms of both the construction and characteristics of contemporary markets and the various consumer typologies, including the 'prosumer', that marketers need to engage with in order to effectively target their communication messages. The rationale here is to provide a platform for the 'Methods' in Part I in that it seeks to investigate and understand the diverse motivations that function as the drivers of contemporary consumption and the multiplicity of opportunities spatially afforded, both off- and online, to meet these demands. As a result, *Chapter 2* addresses a specific question: what are the primary industries composing promotional culture today and how are they informed by changes in consumer behaviour and market conditions? This is then followed by more specialized chapters that examine these industries using case study material to illuminate key themes and points raised. In *Chapter 3*, Hackley and Hackley née Tiwsakul examine the implications of con-vergence for the management of marketing communications, on work processes and its wider cultural impact. Specific reference is made to the introduction of inte-grated marketing communications as a largely theoretical ideal and its development towards a more reactive and pragmatic managerial approach to technology-driven media convergence, with consideration of campaign planning and content in the new media landscape. The chapter closes with emphasis placed on convergence in the context of the entertainment economy, with specific reference to product placement. Martens, in *Chapter 4*, discusses brand communication in the digital age. The chapter begins with a discussion of brand value and brand positioning as dis-tinguishing features of brands within the context of promotional culture. Con-sideration is then given to the impact of convergence culture upon the branding process, with specific reference to case analyses of the branding of MTV's Staying Alive and Viacom's HIV/AIDS campaigns. Finally, Yaxley, in *Chapter 5*, provides an in-depth insight into the history and development of public relations as a promo-tional industry, while recognizing that to locate it within such a field is in itself contestable. Situated within the framework of IMC, Yaxley explores the symbiotic relationship of PR tactics on other promotional strategies and, conversely, its specific points of difference, attributes and capabilities.

Part II on 'Media in Context' opens with an illuminating chapter (*Chapter 6*) by Hardy in which he maps key changes in media, focusing on media–advertising relationships. It asks what have the transformations of digital media convergence meant for the relationship between media and advertising and how are advertiser-funded business models adapting to new media contexts? The changing relationship between media and marketing is examined in relation to the promotion of media brands themselves and the increasingly multimedia promotion of content and services. The chapter concludes by considering some of the critical issues and problems identified in the interaction and integration of media and promotion. In *Chapter 7*, Lee opens by posing the interesting question: 'Convergence and the Internet offer more newsgathering and publication opportunities than ever before, but how can one take advantage of these openings without running away from the core business – newspapers?' In response, the author takes us through the history of newspaper production with specific reference to the role of advertising in providing its financial support. He considers the challenges that newspapers face in the digital age in terms of how news is garnered, reported and received across a multiplicity of platforms, and against which print has to compete. Taking these issues into consideration, potential future business models are surveyed, as is the future of journalism as a profession. In *Chapter 8*, Holmes draws attention to the role magazines play in relation to self-promotion and sees this as an essential driver of their continuing popularity. In this context he examines the resilience of the magazine industry and, in particular, the strategies employed to both cultivate and develop unique sets of relationships between the magazine as brand and its readers. Holmes explores the different paths that magazines, both mainstream and independent, are taking to secure their futures, often diversifying away from the core product offering in order to protect it.

This takes us on to Orlebar's study of television advertising (*Chapter 9*) in which he examines its history and engages with the challenges posed by contemporary viewers' habits and practices. He predicts a future in which TV advertising will continue to remain a valuable and distinctive format, as exemplified through the John Lewis Christmas ad (2011) case study, but suggests that, going forward, it will become more firmly embedded within the context of integrated marketing communications, often taking on an 'afterlife' experienced across a range of digital platforms. Finally, Kochberg, in *Chapter 10*, maps how a promotional culture has been endemic to cinema history since its early years. Through a series of illuminating case studies, the author charts the evolving nature of how the film industry has promoted itself through to the digital age. Kochberg explores the challenges faced by the impact of video-on-demand (VOD), prompting the repositioning of the industry within the entertainment business and the subsequent adoption of cross-platform marketing and brand promotion, as exemplified through the worlds of Harry Potter.

A final note or observation: it might seem contrary that a book on convergence should be ordered so particularly when, in fact, the subject matter in question inherently produces so much cross-fertilization of ideas, issues and introspection. How this could be countered was subject to much discussion both with the book's reviewers and the editorial team at Routledge. As it stands, the form adopted addresses a need for clarity and cogency and, as a result, thanks to the comments and guidance received, is sectioned and chaptered accordingly.

Bibliography

Adorno, T. W. and Horkheimer, M. (1944/1997) 'The Culture Industry: Enlightenment as Mass Deception', in *The Dialectic of Enlightenment*, John Cumming (trans.), London: Verso.

Anderson, C. (2007) *The Long Tail: How Endless Choice Is Creating Unlimited Demand*, London: Random House.

——(2010) *Free: How Today's Smartest Businesses Profit by Giving Something for Nothing*, London: Random House.

Appleyard, B. (2012) 'The Beginning of the End for Live Television', *Sunday Times: Culture*, 1 January, pp18–19.

Bambach, L. J. (2010) 'Would the Last Person to Leave Please Turn out the Enlightenment?', in D. Fiandaca and P. Burgoyne (eds) *Digital Advertising: Past, Present, Future*, London: Creative Social.

Bashford, S. (2010) *Fluid: PHD on Harnessing the Rising Speed of Influence*, Foreword by Mike Cooper, London: PHD.

Bolter, J. D. and Grusin, R. (1999) *Remediation: Understanding New Media*, Cambridge, MA: MIT Press.

Cardoso, G. (2011) 'From Mass to Networked Communication' in S. Papathanassopoulos (ed) *Media Perspectives for the 21st Century*, Abingdon, UK: Routledge.

Carroll, J. (2005) '10 Principles for Marketing in the Age of Engagement', *Admap*, February, issue 458, pp20–22.

Clarke, C. (2010) 'Your Brand Is an Ape', in D. Fiandaca and P. Burgoyne (eds) *Digital Advertising: Past, Present, Future*, London: Creative Social.

Dalglish, S. (2012) 'What Can the Merging of TV and Online Bring?', *Campaign*, 18 May, p19.

Darby, I., Lee, J. and Maden, S. (2011) 'Mags Face Digital Crossroads', *Campaign*, 26 August, pp18–19.

Davis, A. (2006) 'Placing Promotional Culture', in J. Curran and D. Morley (eds) *Media and Cultural Theory*, Abingdon, UK: Routledge.

Deuze, M. (2007) 'Convergence Culture in the Creative Industries', *International Journal of Cultural Studies*, vol 10, no 2, pp243–263.

Devon, J. and Kerr, G. (2010) 'The Art of Serial Brand Arson', in 'What Next in Digital?' (Supplement), *Campaign*, 25 June, p11.

Donaton, S. (2004) *Madison & Vine: Why The Entertainment & Advertising Industries Must Converge To Survive*, New York, NY: McGraw-Hill.

Dwyer, T. (2010) *Media Convergence*, Maidenhead, UK: Open University Press.

Featherstone, M. (2009) 'Ubiquitous Media: An Introduction', *Theory, Culture & Society*, vol 26, no 1, pp1–22.

Fenton, N. (2012) 'News in the Digital Age', in S. Allan (ed) *The Routledge Companion to News and Journalism*, Abingdon, UK: Routledge.

Fornäs, J., Becker, K., Bjurström, E. and Ganetz, H. (2007) *Consuming Media: Communication, Shopping and Everyday Life*, Oxford: Berg.

Gonsalves, J. (2012) 'How *The Guardian* and the 3 Little Pigs Hope To Keep the Wolf from the Door', 2 March, http://bbh-labs.com/how-the-guardian-and-the-3-little-pigs-hope-to-keep-the-wolf-from-the-door, accessed 21 May 2010.

Han, S. (2011) *Web 2.0*, Abingdon, UK: Routledge.

Harbord, J. (2006) 'Digital Film and "Late" Capitalism: A Cinema of Heroes?', in J. Curran and D. Morley (eds) *Media and Cultural Theory*, Abingdon, UK: Routledge.

Hegarty, J. (2011) *Hegarty on Advertising*, London: Thames & Hudson.

Hesmondhalgh, D. (2007) *The Cultural Industries*, 2nd edition, London: Sage.

Huang, E. et al (2006) 'Facing the Challenges of Convergence: Media Professionals' Concerns of Working across Media Platforms', *Convergence*, vol 12, no 1, pp83–98.

Jenkins, H. (2004) 'Spoilers, Bloggers, Moders, and Thieves: Empowering Consumption in an Age of Media Convergence', *Keynote from NMC Summer Conference*, accessed via iTunes Podcasts.

——(2008) *Convergence Culture: Where Old and New Media Collide*, New York, NY: New York University Press.

Jenkins, H. and Deuze, M. (2008) 'Editorial: Convergence Culture', *Convergence*, vol 14, no 1, pp5–12.

Kackman, M., Binfield, M., Payne, M. T., Perlman, A. and Sebok, B. (eds) (2011) *Flow TV: Television in the Age of Media Convergence*, Abingdon, UK: Routledge.

Keen, A. (2007) *The Cult of the Amateur: How Today's Internet is Killing Our Culture and Assaulting Our Economy*, London: Nicholas Brealey Publishing.

Levine, R., Locke, C., Searles, D. and Weinberger, D. (2000) *The Cluetrain Manifesto: The End of Business as Usual*, Harlow, UK: Pearson Education Ltd.

Lewis, D. and Bridger, D. (2001) *The Soul of the New Consumer*, London: Nicholas Brealey Publishing.

Lister, M., Dovey, J., Giddings, S., Grant, I. and Kelly, K. (2009) *New Media: A Critical Introduction*, Abingdon, UK: Routledge.

Locke, C. (2012) 'The Year Ahead in Television', *Campaign*, 13 January, p26.

MacRury, I. (2009) *Advertising*, Abingdon, UK: Routledge.

Maden, S. (2011) 'Force of Nature Has Big Plans for *Heat* Brand', *Campaign*, 7 October, p23.

McStay, A. (2010) *Digital Advertising*, Basingstoke, UK: Palgrave Macmillan.

Mendelsohn, N. (2011) 'The Mad Men We Love To Hate: Our Changing Relationship with Advertising', *RSA Lecture*, 8 July, accessed via iTunes podcast.

Powell, H. (2009) 'Advertising Agencies and Their Clients', in H. Powell et al (eds) *The Advertising Handbook*, 3rd edition, Abingdon, UK: Routledge.

——(2012) *Stop the Clocks! Time and Narrative in Cinema*, London: I. B. Tauris.

Sayre, S. and King, C. (2010) *Entertainment and Society: Influences, Impacts and Innovations*, 2nd edition, New York, NY: Routledge.

Shimp, T. A. (2010) *Integrated Marketing Communication in Advertising and Promotion*, international/ 8th edition, London: Cengage Learning.

Spanier, G. (2011) 'Keep Taking the Tablets in Search of App-iness', *Evening Standard*, 28 November, p46.

——(2012) '"Mad Men's" Ad Agency BBH Sells to Publicis for £100m', *i*, 6 July, p51.

Springer, P. (2009) *Ads to Icons: How Advertising Succeeds in Multimedia Age*, London: Kogan Page.

Spurgeon, C. (2008) *Advertising and New Media*, London: Routledge.

Sweney, M. (2012) '*Guardian* TV Ad Kicks Off "Open Journalism" Campaign', *The Guardian*, 29 February, http://www.guardian.co.uk/media/2012/feb/29/guardian-tv-ad-open-journalism/print, accessed 21 May 2012.

Wernick, A. (1991) *Promotional Culture*, London: Sage.

Williams, E. (2012) *How 30 Great Ads Were Made: From Idea to Campaign*, London: Laurence King.

Wolf, M. J. (2000) *The Entertainment Economy*, London: Penguin.

Yeates, C. (2012) 'How Is Cinema Meeting the Digital Challenge?', *Campaign*, 4 May, p21.

PART I

Methods in Context

1

CONSUMERS, MARKETS AND MARKETPLACES

Helen Powell

Knowing the consumer

Introduction

The contemporary consumer is fundamentally Janus-headed. On the one hand, the amount of choice now available and the means to access it points towards a highly individualistic, authentic consumer who sees themselves as the architect of their own consumption patterns. And yet, as Simmel observed back in 1904, we continue to use fashion and trends as a mechanism by which we may secure group belonging. The majority of e-commerce sites, for example, allow us to rank search results by the 'most popular' in terms of other consumers' previous choices or the 'like' facility on Facebook, which allows users to independently display their allegiance to a brand and which functions as a purchasing security blanket in terms of managing adherence to the taste cultures of those closest to us.

A second paradox that this chapter will address is that of the issue of consumer empowerment. Jenkins (2008: 3) addresses how technological changes inform consumption, specifically the ways in which 'consumers are encouraged to seek out new information and make connections among dispersed media content'. And yet, one could argue that while we may be more informed in terms of making choices, those choices are always framed within the context of a capitalist system, with the pursuit of profit remaining that system's *raison d'être*. Today consumers are no longer simply seen as 'a market' to sell into (Jenkins and Deuze 2008: 9), but rather as the principal drivers of what is supplied and, ultimately, consumed. Furthermore, they are also active in shaping the marketplaces, physical and virtual, in which such transactions take place. However, while evidencing such activity, this chapter also considers whether consumer participation is engendering a sense of belonging as information is shared online, thus enhancing the decision-making process; or is it turning the consumer into a market researcher, working for free in the cultivation of a more transparent marketplace with businesses then drawing upon this information to provide themselves with a more competitive edge based on consumers' comments and findings? In this context, the chapter asks, is the rise of online 'prosumer' activity a positive outcome of convergence culture in that the fusion of participatory culture and collective intelligence now allows the marketplace to be shaped for the benefit of all, or only for the enhancement of a minority?

Convergence in the context of a neoliberal agenda

Under the traditional marketing paradigm, the producer and the consumer were positioned as complementary entities brought together in business through the intervention of the promotional industries. Communication flowed through a chosen set of media to a consumer who would be informed as to what was available, where it could be purchased and why such purchase was necessary. In the case of the latter, throughout the last decades of the twentieth century we witnessed a significant cultural turn away from the functionality of material goods towards their symbolic value, coupled by their promotion in more creative and potentially abstract ways. In the twenty-first century, the promotional industries are acutely aware that much promotion commences with the construction of the consumer as a desiring subject who makes purchases in order to fulfil the lifestyle choices made available to them through marketing and advertising. In this way, advertising creates sign value to enhance the use and exchange value of every product, conjuring up degrees of personalization and differentiation within the context of a mass market. Developing Raymond Williams's (1980) argument that advertising functions as a 'magic system' (1980) through the symbolic imagery that connotes a whole range of additional qualities that the product can seemingly bring to the consumer (e.g., 'Happiness is a cigar called Hamlet'), McAllister (2011: 152) argues that the ability of the magic system to construct commodity signs located within complex referent systems is now enhanced by digitality. The 'blurring' (McAllister 2011: 152) of commercial messages into social network pages, coupled with the degrees of interactivity made available between the consumer and the brand online, makes the Internet an enhanced promotional environment.

How, why, what and where we consume have all significantly been shaped by an increasingly neoliberal agenda that began in the latter decades of the twentieth century and has seeped through into the early decades of this millennium. Constituted on the basis of the deregulation of markets and the adoption of the monetarist policies of economist Milton Friedman as a means to both curb public spending and harness inflation, it took shape on the back of the Thatcher–Reagan alliance of the 1980s and offered itself as a new paradigm for late twentieth-century capitalism. Following the floatation of publicly owned enterprises such as British Telecom and British Gas, further attempts were made to cultivate new markets in the belief that the 'commodity market is the best way of distributing resources and to that end as many goods and services must be available for trading, and at as many sites and in as many markets as possible' (Lister et al 2009: 180) nationally and internationally. In essence, neoliberalism blossomed as the marketization of everyday life, with consumers finding their daily shopping forays enhanced by the introduction of new technologies, and more recently the introduction of apps that allow 24/7 shopping to become a reality (even if the delivery of those goods remains, at present, somewhat problematic and at odds with a culture of instantaneity). Transactions increasingly take place based on greater amounts of information accrued − not just from traditional advertising but from online research and peer-to-peer reviews. Trust is highly valued and consumers have concomitantly become highly sceptical of the opinions of experts. To gain their trust, brands must be sensitive to these trends but also remain highly transparent in their activities: 'fake blogs' or 'flogs' are very quickly detected, as was the case with Sony, L'Oreal and Wal-Mart, and are only ever met with derisory comments once the lack of authenticity has been made public.

Andrew Wernick's (1991) *Promotional Culture* sought to explore through a postmodern lens the strategies adopted by the promotional industries − namely, plundering all of culture for their own gain and developing inter-textual references across their range of communications. As noted, promotion becomes more important following the turn to sign value as the predominant means through which consumers tap into the value of goods, with functionality no longer being a primary reason to consume or a mechanism through which competitive advantage can be gained. As consumers look to construct their identities through marketplace adventures, so Wernick (1991: 188) draws our attention to a new phase of capitalism and a concomitant promotional turn: 'From the clothes we wear, to the parties we vote for at election time, wherever in fact a market of some kind operates, everything mirrors back the same basic signifying mode.' Yet, it is the ways in which the concept of promotion permeates the interstices of our daily being that fascinates Wernick (1991: 192), as a result, engendering a culture of self-promotion: 'from dating and clothes shopping to attending a job interview, virtually everyone is involved in self-promotionalism which overlays such practices in the micro-sphere of everyday life'. In this context brands become 'symbolic resources for the construction and maintenance of identity' (Elliott and Davies 2005: 155). This commences and is most prolific in youth when brands, as carriers of cultural meaning, are utilized to manage friendships, and to demonstrate points of similarity with and difference from other subcultural groupings. And, yet, it is up to brands 'to fit into the complex identity of youngsters today rather than the other way around. Brands aren't dictating styles or image anymore' (Van den Bergh and Behrer 2011: 23).

As the teenage years progress, so brands move in and out of vogue, speaking to different stages of adolescence and utilized as one moves from a position of '"who I am" to "who I want to be"', but more often than not a third position emanates − namely, '"the self in-between"', emphasizing the lack of stability and certainty involved (Elliott and Davies 2005: 167–168). Indeed, Generation Y (aged 13 to 29) are insecure and 'seek reassurance for what they perceive to be a chaotic world' (Van den Bergh and Behrer 2011: 33). Global brands such as Coca-Cola appeal in this context and they are prepared to pay more for them 'because they have proven to be able to survive' (Van den Bergh and Behrer 2011: 33). Another brand that has used social media effectively to tap into the 'ordinary' 16- to 24-year-old male seeking reassurance is Lynx, who use it to engage with young men on their own terms by creating a persona for the brand that the target market can identify with. In this way, Lynx embeds itself within the project of identity construction, which increasingly is taking place online within the youth market. Through promotion, brands more widely position themselves as facilitators in the construction of an 'autobiography of the self' (Giddens 1991) that consumers work through via the choices they make, evidencing as they mature a more individualistic turn in relation to its maintenance. But choice is not without its detractions, producing anxiety around the decision-making process (Schwarz 2004; Elliott 2008), with the brand as confidant and the arm of reassurance stepping in here.

However, the notion of consumption as inextricably tied to identity construction and manifesting itself only as an integral part of the neoliberal agenda is challenged by Trentmann (2009: 211), who argues that 'people's attachments to things are older than the post-war age of affluence and fixation on growth'. He draws attention to the sixteenth century, for example, and the development of trade which engendered both a reflexive interest in other cultures and a turn towards self-fashioning. As a result, he argues, we should acknowledge:

> ... that a consuming lifestyle is far more deeply entrenched than often thought, and for reasons that are often ignored or misunderstood in mainstream critiques of consumerism. To target primarily external agencies as responsible for the creation of new desires – be they corporations, or governments calling on citizens to be patriotic consumers – is to miss the internal attractions that have led people to use, want and find themselves in things in the past. Our material self has been growing for a long time.
>
> (Trentmann 2009: 211)

The new consumer

While the 'consuming lifestyle' may have taken many guises over time, it is in relation to the identification of a specifically 'new consumer' that this chapter now turns, and which becomes prevalent, not coincidentally, I would argue, within the literature of consumer studies at the same time as *The Cluetrain Manifesto* (Levine et al 2000) was published. It is worth taking the time to map the emergence of this specific subject position, with the first wave of writers under discussion here recognizing a 'new consumer' whose identity was being shaped by the Internet, allowing for more informed choices within the marketplace to be made. As a consequence, there arose a responsive recognition that how such consumers are marketed to, going forward, needs to change.

Writing a decade ago, Frank Shaw, then director of the Centre for Future Studies, identified a new type of consumer that at that point made up 35 per cent of the adult population of the UK (Shaw 2002: 5). They comprised a cohort with 'higher educational qualifications; who lives in a household with discretionary income; who has access to new technologies' (Shaw 2002: 5) and, as a result, constituted a new category in the typology of consumer subjectivities based on how they utilized the information made available, predominantly online, to inform their purchasing decisions. They had become notable, argued Shaw, as the increase in number was promulgated by more and more young people going to university and using their education to make commercial decisions. He began to map particular characteristics of this 'new consumer' that would impact future communication strategies between brands and their target markets. The 'new consumer' would:

1 Prefer choice: they will examine a wide range of choices when making purchasing decisions.
2 Demand tailored information and communications: time-starved consumers look to dedicated sites that provide the information that they need. Quality not quantity of information is important here.
3 Sceptical of brands: due to their ability to carry out research, a brand name is not enough to warrant purchase. Brand value becomes a critical steer on choice. If better value is attached – for example, to a supermarket own brand – then they will switch to that label.
4 Willing to experiment: cash-rich but time poor, new consumers will test products that they feel have the potential to allow them greater control over their lives.
5 Value convenience: they are also prepared to pay for services that give them more leisure time.
6 Expect superior service: new consumers value their time and are not prepared to put up with poor service.
7 Skills for catering to the new consumer: the new consumers will challenge traditional marketing thinking over the next decade. Uncertainty levels will rise as it becomes increasingly challenging to meet individual customer expectations and needs.

(Shaw 2002: 7)

The shift from purchasing on the basis of needs to that of wants is perhaps the most prevalent characteristic of this 'new consumer'. Increasingly, material goods and the forays into the marketplace to buy them become one of the mainstays of leisure time and a principle mode, as noted above, of self-actualization. The emotional investment that comes with both the anticipation and realization of the experiences that are inextricably linked to consumption is not to be underestimated, as is the disappointment when expectations are not met and when the perceived psychological benefits (happiness, popularity, belonging) are not realized (Dittmar 2008).

Much of this disappointment emanates from the scarcities of the New Economy, for while 'Old Consumers' were 'beset by scarcities of cash, choice and availability, those confronting the New Consumer are shortages of time, attention and trust' (Lewis and Bridger 2001: 6). In contrast with 'Old Consumers', dictated to by manufacturers and suppliers, in order to ameliorate disappointment, 'New Consumers dictate not only what they buy but how and where those purchases are made' within a marketplace that is increasingly fragmented (Lewis and Bridger 2001: 2). As a result, in terms of how their wants are satisfied, they seek out 'original, innovative and distinctive products and services ... that can claim to be in some way authentic' (Lewis and Bridger 2001: 4). This explains the growth of the 'long tail', discussed in depth later in the chapter, and the use of objects to establish a point of difference; but it also accounts for a growing distrust in traditional (mass) advertising.

In 2006 and 2008, Yiannis Gabriel and Tim Lang returned to the consumer typologies that they had originally mapped out in 1995. During the intervening period, they recognized that it was virtually impossible to generalize about the consumer, seeing the consumer now as 'unmanageable' both as 'concept' and 'entity' since 'no one can pin it down to one specific conceptualisation at the expense of all others, and as an entity, since attempts to control and manage the consumer lead to the consumer mutating from one impersonation to another' (Gabriel and Lang 2008: 325). As the previous authors considered had recognized, why we consume is highly complex: the dualism of true and false needs is rendered somewhat redundant. The symbolic resonance of any object is testament to this. However, what can be identified as an emerging theme is increasingly that of consumption as work, as drawn attention to by Nava (1996: 48) with specific reference, in this context, to consumer behaviour in the early department stores and 'consumption and consumer expertise as activities that were as gendered as production'. Here Nava was keen to map out female consumption as labour that required particular knowledge and skills within a definitive retail setting but which now, I would argue, can be applied to both genders following the introduction of the Internet. With the pressures to 'get it right' made manifest across a variety of media, as Gabriel and Lang (2008: 326) comment, consumption now involves 'patient or breathless searches through high-streets, shopping malls or Internet sites; it involves minuscule comparisons and painstaking choices; it demands

TABLE 1.1 Initial mapping of the emerging features of the new consumer

Old Consumers	New Consumers
Seek convenience	Seek authenticity
Synchronized	Individual
Less often involved	Involved
Conformist	Independent
Less well informed	Well informed

Adapted from Lewis and Bridger (2001: 19)

continuous updating and vigilance'. This notion of the consumer as a complex being extends further if we begin to question 'the extension of the status of consumer' to include 'cultural audiences and public service users' (Keat et al 1994: 1). Under the neoliberal agenda, competition effuses into an ever-increasing range of services, even those publicly funded, and students, hospital patients and TV viewers are all reconstituted under this new subject position.

To bring the consumer typology up to date, in 2009 Gottschalk concurred with Gabriel and Lang that the 'new consumer' is motivated by a complex set of factors that are difficult to categorize. Havas Worldwide (formerly Euro RSCG) (2010) sought to map out these motivations and identified that choice is largely informed by reference to and guidance from peers, coupled with a significant degree of research, predominantly online. However, anxiety levels around making the right decision remain high: some '54% feel more anxious in general compared with a few years ago' (Havas Worldwide, 2010). Added to this sense of heightened intensity around the decision-making process comes a new challenge – namely, a reconfigured relationship to time that widely informs our behavioural practices. Elsewhere (Powell 2009, 2012) I have begun to map the ways and means by which we seek to 'time squeeze', packing as much as we can into every minute through strategies such as multi-tasking, time-deepening and stacking. In essence, it is not so much that we have less time to do what we want to do, but rather the potential to do so much means that strategies must be put in place to allow every moment to be filled to the maximum.

One of the most significant ways in which this new relationship to time affects the promotional industries concerns the nature of viewing practices and the possibility that at any one moment the target audience is engaged in a number of activities, interacting with a series of screens as they strategically try to time-deepen their leisure. This then amounts to recognizing that full attention cannot be guaranteed and certainly supports a move to integrated marketing communication, discussed later in this section. In this context, television advertising, for example, functions to seed the brand in the consumer's mind, while other brand touch points are then mobilized to deepen that relationship, especially through the interactive capacity of online promotion where greater attention is required to get the most out of what the brand has to offer. The role of online advertising has also become important with the move towards more individualized and personal schedule-building, creating a culture of 'daily me' as we shape media around us on demand. As a result, consumers not only have greater choice as to what they watch, but how and when they watch it:

> They can obtain a synchronic versus asynchronic timetable, they can control time flow directions (by means of rewind, pause, start over), and they can accelerate viewing rates (by means of fast-forwarding, zapping). One way or another, media time squeezing promotes the deconstruction of temporal hegemony.
>
> *(Moshe 2012: 79)*

In a highly engaging essay in the advertising trade journal *Campaign*, Sarah Morning of the agency Republic examines the impact of an accelerating time-centred culture upon the promotional industries. The consequences of the quest for immediate gratification, she argues, have had a significant effect on brand promotion, especially in relation to a commensurate decline in consumer trust, specifically because 'the building of trust necessarily required a long-term approach to media' (Morning 2010: 16). In this way, Morning sees one of the key qualities of the inter-relationship of brands with social networking sites as lying in the opportunities to obviate short attention spans through brand messages embedding themselves within the content of pages that users choose to visit and around which a whole series of personal social interactions are conducted. This approach also provides for the brand additional opportunities for data mining, what Lury (2011: 153) terms 'transactional data, data collected as a by-product of doing something else' and allows for a more accurate way of measuring both effectiveness and return on investment (ROI).

The role of research

The idea that to be successful in their aims and objectives employees of the promotional industries must 'know' the consumer and what they want from the goods on offer can be traced back to the America of the 1920s and 1930s when advertisers were positioned as 'captains of consciousness' successful in implanting 'brand names into the idiom of daily expression' (Ewen 2001: 203). However, it was in attempting to steer consumer demand in the post-War rebuilding of the economies on both sides of the Atlantic that advertising really grew as a significant promotional industry. 'Combining the social and technological developments of the twenties with the component of economic boom that characterized the fifties, the postwar era was one in which mass consumption erupted, for increasing numbers, into a full-blown style of life' and where 'TV became a vehicle for a consumerist mentality' (Ewen 2001: 208). Of critical importance in both the identification of new markets and tools for their promotion was Ernest Dichter. Dichter appropriated Freudian psychoanalysis in the development of 'depth research' which involved continually 'probing' the consumer beyond the mere acceptance of their first response to questions posed, as adopted in survey techniques. Through the appropriation of such methods Dichter became aware that consumer behaviour was often irrational and products were consumed in an attempt to fulfil unspoken desires and wishes. These findings were of interest to senior figures in the US promotional industry at the time who sought to adapt these 'interpretative, qualitative and explorative approaches to the dynamics of the consumption process and the communication between products and consumers' (Schwarzkopf 2007: 221). By probing the unconscious in seeking to understand people's desires and their possible relationship to the material world, undiscovered motivations to consume, often of a highly irrational nature, were identified and incorporated within future adverting campaigns. The idea that consumers be given a space to speak freely and interact with others around products and product choices later informed the focus group, still widely used in advertising today. Ultimately, Dichter's legacy is that the starting point of any contemporary advertising campaign must be with the consumer: to research and understand why they might wish to purchase and the benefits they feel they will acquire through purchasing, albeit often highly intangible in nature.

While the turn to embed research at the heart of its business model was increasingly adopted by agencies in an attempt to professionalize advertising in the post-War years, it was perhaps, ironically, the critic Vance Packard who did most to change the nature of advertising practice. In his book *The Hidden Persuaders* (Packard 1962), it was not advertising *per se* that Packard sought to challenge, but rather to warn consumers of the dangers of the subliminal tactics employed: 'many of us are being influenced and manipulated – far more than we realize – in the patterns of our everyday lives' (Packard 1962: 11). As Schudson (1981: 4) has commented: 'Packard has no essential complaint with advertising or capitalism or persuasion – only with persuasion that sneaks up on us.' But if one delves deeper into Packard's text the realization dawns that Packard fails to take on board any sense of consumer 'needs' that the market is actually responding to and that Dichter was beginning to identify. It is interesting that Rory Sutherland, vice-chairman of Ogilvy Group UK and former president of the Institute of Practitioners in Advertising (IPA), argues that the impact of Packard has been lasting, specifically in terms of how the industry measures effectiveness. He believes that the advertising industry has struggled to truly understand how advertising changes consumer behaviour and that this is down to the shadow cast by Packard half a century ago. As 'rattled by books such as *Hidden Persuaders*, people such as Rosser Reeves ... were so fearful of accusations of advertising being an underhand influence that they insisted on naïve and hyper-rational models of how it worked' (cited in Forrest 2009: 7).

Many subsequent attempts have been made to 'know' the consumer more effectively, and, significantly, such pontificating led to the introduction of the role of 'advertising planner' positioned, in essence, as the voice of the consumer in the agency. While Stanley Pollitt, of Boase Massimi Pollitt, is traditionally regarded as the founder of the discipline, much credit is also attributable to Stephen King of JWT and Tony Stead also of JWT who coined the term back in 1968 (Tungate 2007: 88). By extension, with reference to media planning, in its recent study of 37,600 Internet users aged 15 to 64, advertising agency Universal McCann (2011: 5) summarized its findings across 54 countries, arguing that 'a deeper understanding of consumer needs and motivations is the key to unlocking a real understanding of social media and its users'. For brands to take full advantage of a burgeoning participatory culture they must understand the complex sets of rationale behind this participation, for 'it's not merely a question of identifying the best places to target – the classic media planning/buying approach – but truly knowing what motivates them to be a part of it' (Universal McCann 2011: 18).

To return to Sutherland, it is this quest 'to know' and how that knowledge may then inform promotional strategies that led Sutherland to become such a positive advocate of nudge economics as applied to marketing techniques. 'Until the mid-1700s, the word "economy" was mostly used in politics and law. But Adam Smith gave the term its modern meaning when he defined economics as the study of markets, in particular what we now shorthand as "the science of choice under scarcity"' (Anderson 2010: 181). Behavioural economics has arisen as a more recent specialism within economics, but when applied to marketing it becomes a useful tool to both understand and influence consumer behaviour through focusing upon the ways in which people make decisions. It takes as its starting point the concept of a 'choice architecture' (Thaler and Sunstein 2009) which centres on the management of choice in any given situation or context. As a result, the 'choice architect has the responsibility for organizing the context in which people make decisions' (Thaler and Sunstein 2009: 3). For example, how items are arranged on a menu or laid out in a store is deemed to have a positive effect in enabling choice through a more considered approach to how information is presented to the consumer. In this way, a change to small details may be enough to attract our attention, allowing us to perceive something differently and therefore 'nudge' behaviour accordingly.

Such an approach sits well within the discourse of advertising, which for decades after Dichter has recognized that consumers are not rational actors and that it is important to study how they actually behave in any purchasing scenario. All too often the consumer stays with the same brand choice simply because it is perceived as 'safe'. It is this status quo bias that keep markets stable. Sutherland (2012) has championed the potential of the adaptation of behavioural economics to advertising practice. He juxtaposes its approach to '1950's packaged goods persuasive techniques', which at that point in time accounted for two-thirds of an agency's income stream. Today, two-thirds of advertising budgets come from outside the realm of packaged goods, and therefore advertising is now making a much greater 'behavioural ask': which broadband service provider should I go with, for example? The role of persuasion is smaller here, Sutherland argues, in that tiny details will make the difference as to the provider chosen. In essence, therefore, promotional strategies can be used to deconstruct the problems associated with choice into a series of steps that are deemed by the consumer to become more manageable and less daunting. That is to say, promotion can be used to 'nudge' the individual along a particular decision-making path (Simms 2010: 18). Communicating these small differences requires the opportunity for engagement and interaction, and new media and new technologies provide the necessary platforms to allow this to materialize.

One business that has overtly utilized the philosophy of nudge in its marketing activities is that of Lovefilm. Simon Waldman (2011), the group product director, expressed how through focusing on the establishment of an effective choice architecture, traditional habits could be steered away from a reliance solely on the TV schedule towards constructing their own viewing menu. This is realized slowly Waldman, argues, through 'nudging the business on a day-to-day basis ... getting consumers to change their behaviour and naturalise it'. In this case, and indeed in relation to its competitors such as Netflix, behavioural changes are informed to a large degree through prosumerism. 'If you know what people like you tend to like, you might well be comfortable in selecting products you didn't know, because people like you tend to like them' (Thaler and Sunstein 2009: 105).

From consumer to prosumer

The concept of the 'prosumer' was brought to public attention by Alvin Toffler (1980). In *The Third Wave* he argued that in terms of producer/consumer relations, pre-industrialization was characterized by the figure of the 'prosumer' who, in the context of an agricultural economy, largely consumed what he produced. Industrialization split these functions, with the former 'prosumer' now becoming 'worker' and with the earnings from wage labour becoming the requisite means to enter the marketplace. The title of the book, however, heralds a third stage, the return of the prosumer, but in a new guise, whereby businesses work in closer alignment to their customer base, enabling this relationship to function more effectively, allowing consumer needs to be more successfully met and concomitantly greater profits to be realized. In practice, Toffler takes the concept of the modern prosumer back to the 1950s with the arrival of the drive-through and which then expanded with cash points, self-service petrol stations and supermarket checkouts. While these examples relate specifically to the consumer's 'work' in realizing the transaction, Ritzer and Jurgenson (2010: 19) argue that it is with the introduction of Web 2.0 that the concept of the 'prosumer' really comes to fruition in that it 'facilitates the implosion of production and consumption' and, as a result, is 'the most prevalent location of prosumption and its most important facilitator' (Ritzer and Jurgenson 2010: 20). Prosumption subsequently is absorbed into the literature – for example, in Andrew Kern's *The Cult of the Amateur* (2007) where he is critical of businesses which are drawing more on this unpaid labour to perform a range of duties. One example of prosumerism in this context relates to the practice of viral advertising: 'commercial publicity passed on by users through pre-existing social networks' (McStay 2010: 56). In this context, facilitated by interactive media, consumers become both co-producers and co-promoters. While no media buying strategy is required, and therefore media costs become heavily reduced, viral relies on creative content that taps into the current zeitgeist to make it worthy of circulation by digital mavens across social networks. As a result, Fallon was able to test its radical, in relation to the Cadbury's brand, Gorilla ad prior to its mainstream launch on TV. Its follow-up, Eyebrows, demonstrates another dimension of prosumerism as viewers began to recreate their own versions for circulation. As a result, we may begin to witness a rupture in the discourse of advertising in terms of asking not what advertising does to people, but rather, what are people doing with advertising, especially in the context of the youth audience. It is important to recognize that creativity can continue outside of the agency in the more localized and personalized spaces of audiences' domestic settings.

Social media, therefore, has significant potential to change the existing relationships between the producer and the consumer in a variety of ways. It opens up channels for communication in real time and with global reach that can influence consumer behaviour in a number of ways: raising awareness about a product or offer; the sharing of information, opinions and reviews about what to buy in any product category; and, finally, post-purchasing evaluations. The 'value' of this kind of information was made manifest at the beginning of June 2012 when personal finance journalist and expert money-saving adviser Martin Lewis sold his website for £87 million. Established in 2003, the site, which offers tips and advice at point of sale, 'has around 5 million subscribers to its weekly email. According to Google Analytics, it attracted around 39 million unique visitors and 277m page impressions in the year ending 31 October 2011. It reported revenues of £15.7m for the same period' (Osbourne and Insley 2012). However, this is not to consider that all such opinions are galvanized around one individual; rather, 'social media is magnifying the impact consumer-to-consumer conversations have in the marketplace' (Mangold and Faulds 2009: 358). As Part II will testify, markets are now conversations and while consumers are talking to each other, companies also have a more direct means to influence and intervene in what is being said. Allowing for a much more rapid response than any advertising campaign can generate, brand managers are using a variety of resources to shape these online conversations to their benefit. Proctor and Gamble, for example, have established a site for new mums as a means of controlling the conversations and anxieties around parenting while at the same time leveraging the value of the brand in an appropriate but not necessarily overt promotional context. Coupled with this is an emerging sense of trust in the brand as consumers feel that they are getting something back through the knowledge provided, opinions shared, experiences exchanged and recommendations made online. In concert, Gabriel and Lang (2008: 327) term this 'narrative knowledge' that feeds, in essence, into the 'image' of the brand and allows for competitive advantage to be accrued. The concept of prosumerism, in summary, therefore affects the promotional industries by challenging traditional communication models. The linearity of the sender sending the message to the receiver becomes deconstructed in recognition that real world communication is, in fact, constituted out of dialogue – in this context, largely online.

Regarding the impact of the closer alignment of producers and consumers in the marketplace, opinion oscillates between two poles. On the one hand, it further challenges the consumer as 'dupe' model and introduces, instead, a sense of agency in relation to our understanding of consumer motivations. Alternatively, one might wish to place this 'agency' in context, a tokenistic gift offered by the major corporations in return for greater free market research, as noted previously. The latter position is exercised by Murdock (2010: 230) who draws attention to how 'prosumer' culture can lead to exploitation, often by the most profitable companies. He, too, cities Proctor and Gamble and their launch of Tremor:

> … a network of carefully selected young people who are involved in product development and are encouraged to publicize new brands on their own websites and in everyday conversation. They are not paid for their

participation. They are rewarded with exclusive previews and samples of new products and the sense of being 'insiders' and 'in the know'.

(Murdock 2010: 230)

McAllister (2011: 159) argues in this vein that the digital consumer can adopt at least four different 'producerly roles' as unpaid labour. 'These four roles are consumers as unpaid focus group members, consumers as unpaid publicity and distribution channels, consumers as unpaid ad creators and consumers as a referent system in the commodity sign.' Jenkins and Deuze (2008: 6) also address the complex debate that unfolds, where the encouraging of user-generated content might either be seen as enabling 'a more diverse and responsive' media culture or as harnessing unpaid creative labour for the brand's benefit when all other creative avenues have been explored and fallen short. Furthermore, as Schor (2007: 25) argues, to return to the subject of the generation of agency, 'it is the companies who figure out how to successfully sell agency to consumers that thrive', whether that is 'You Can Do It, When You B&Q It'; Nike's 'Just Do IT' or L'Oreal's 'Because you're worth it'. Ritzer and Jurgenson (2010: 26) go as far as positing the prosumer as a new but somewhat 'ambiguous' form of exploitation for a new phase of capitalism. Rather than working for low pay, people are, indeed, working for 'no pay at all', with the ambiguity stemming from the fact that we use, for example, Facebook to connect with our friends, while Facebook makes money through advertising out of those activities and friendship ties and specifically through the valuable information that we plough into the site (Beer and Burrows 2010: 10). This latter point is expanded upon by Van Dijck and Nieborg (2009) as they assess who actually is benefiting from this new online prosumerist culture. Online communities, they argue, function to 'inadvertently form attractive profiling communities for advertisers who used to spend a lot of money finding out what demographic group covets similar tastes and products. Life has never been easier for marketers' (Van Dijck and Nieborg 2009: 865). When taken further, it has been argued, we can begin to realize a new form of capitalism for the digital age, 'prosumer capitalism' based on a system where 'content is abundant and created by those not on the payroll' (Ritzer and Jurgenson 2010: 30). In this context, abundance is realized at three levels: the number of people involved; the time now spent online; the output that is produced for free.

Yet the notion of consumer sovereignty remains strong as 'the concept legitimises capitalist market order, which forever pretends that it only serves up what the consumer wants' (Schwarzkopf 2011: 122). For some the integration of the prosumer into marketing activity is deemed to make the message more authentic, and yet it is difficult to actually map the degree of empowerment in practice. Despite the positive elements of convergence culture, in all its facets, it is important to recognize the various sets of interests of those who participate. In terms of those actually producing content online, for example, it has been argued that in relation to Wikipedia, new contributions are made by only 0.5 percent of its total users and edited by only 2.5 per cent (Pierson cited in Cardoso 2011: 128). It is interesting to ask, therefore, what makes it so widely used but reliant on the efforts of such a small minority for its success?

In essence, in the context of the 'free market', one might argue that the consumer has become empowered. Ultimately, however, 'information asymmetries, the existence of monopolies in many markets, the needs of producers to create demand for their goods, and the inability of many consumers to actually express their needs to producers in ways other than the act of buying' (Schwarzkopf 2011:119) make it improbable that there is any true sense of parity in terms of the existent players in market relations. This is so despite the potential move away from the duality of the producer/consumer relationship to the introduction of the 'prosumer' as a more meaningful term to reflect current business practice.

Markets and marketplaces

Markets in the digital age

Markets function to bring buyers and sellers together and to set the quality and price of goods and services bought and sold. A 'market economy' is one in which rival producers compete with the aim of maximizing profits, with success coming to those who can meet the needs, wants and desires of consumers, underpinned by market research. Consumers are free to choose between the range of providers and with differentiation in the product offered allowing for competition to ensue and appropriate marketing strategies to be adopted. If producers fail to attract enough business, then the offer must be reconsidered; if that fails, as recent evidence has shown under the challenging current economic climate, then businesses can fold. In this context, 'the brand emerged historically as a market device ... a device for the organization or management of markets' (Lury 2011: 151). The promotional industries, therefore, function to provide the consumer with knowledge and information to make choices that direct them towards a particular brand or service with the aim of increasing its market share. Customers are marketed to as 'targets' based on their lifestyle preferences in relation to a product category. It is lifestyle today, rather than class, that is predominantly used in market research in targeting potential markets for products. A further function of contemporary markets is that they can be seen to inform consumer culture where 'the relation between lived culture and social resources, between meaningful ways of life and the symbolic and material resources on which they depend, is mediated through markets' (Slater 1997: 8). In the context of neoliberal politics of the late 1980s onwards, the market becomes the hub around which notions of individuality, consumer sovereignty and freedom of choice, coupled with social coordination, can be exercised in parallel. As a result, economic growth is predicated on the expansion of choice into every market and within markets.

This chapter now turns to examine more specifically the characteristics of markets in the digital age and takes as its starting point *The Cluetrain Manifesto* (Levine et al 2000), which adopted the premise that all markets are conversations. As noted above, markets are constructed on the basis that consumer choice and neoliberal politics brings about their introduction into an ever-increasing number of facets of our lives. Categories start off as simple entities and then expand 'like an amoeba dividing in a petri dish' (Trout 2008: 5). This accounts for the rise and operation of the *Long Tail* model, discussed further on in the chapter.

The Cluetrain Manifesto

As the Introduction firmly established, 'convergence' has become a critical element of the discourses surrounding the emergence and development of Web 2.0. As a result, a number of possible new models for doing business have arisen as a consequence and, commensurate with this, new mechanisms by which promotion might take place (Leadbeater 2007; Tapscott and Williams 2008). A forerunner of such models was produced in 2000 – namely, *The Cluetrain Manifesto*, which tapped into both the potential of the web ahead of its commercial development through Web 2.0 and the paradigm shift towards prosumerism that would inform the future changing relationships between businesses and their customers.

The book was not written by or for academics, but rather was the product of four individuals who were heavily involved in the development of the Internet economy either from a business or marketing perspective. *Cluetrain* takes us back 5000 years when 'the marketplace was the hub of civilisation' (Levine et al 2000: xviii): a place where people went to meet and trade but where stories, gossip and news were also exchanged. Following the Industrial Revolution, it is argued, the way in which business operated changed, separating the parties involved and introducing a culture of anonymity. As a result, 'market became a verb: something you do *to* customers' (Levine et al 2000: 76, their emphasis). The chatter between buyers and sellers is replaced by market research, functioning via media in finding out about demand. Knowledge is abstracted and the consumer remains at a distance. Marketing messages are produced for which there is no demand: 'It's an interruption. It's the Anti-Conversation' (Levine et al 2000: 77). Yet, the Internet now allows for the conversations of history to return; but for businesses to successfully take part, the authors propose, they must think carefully how to converse across this new marketing terrain. They must reconsider how to market. In the future, *Cluetrain* argues, it will be as much about listening as talking.

At the point of its publication, Bonello (2001), argued, *Cluetrain* had two key implications for the promotional industries. 'First, it examines the effects that the discourse enabled by the web is having on marketing strategy, and, second, it highlights the importance of the web itself as a communications tool that companies can and should use to build relationships with their customers' (Bonello 2001: 21). These ideas are then made manifest several years later when it emerges that a paradigm shift is evident in terms of how marketers perceive new media consumers – no longer is a top-down communication model prevalent, but rather one that is informed by 'conversational media' (Spurgeon 2008: 2). Enlightened by the fusion of participation and interaction, Spurgeon argues (2008: 7), this allows for 'direct involvement in the selection and distribution of media content, the appropriation and transformation of media content to create new content and the generation and circulation of original content'. The authors of *The Cluetrain Manifesto*, therefore, 'were in the first wave of new media marketers to grasp the significance of Internet-enabled conversation' (Spurgeon 2008: 13). This potential has been capitalized upon more recently with the popularity of Twitter, which trades on the immediacy of the comment. As a result, brands now listen to social media in order to hear what people are saying about them in real time. What started off as eavesdropping has now developed into participation and is tipping over into stimulating the conversations in order to engender both brand communities and useful data for brand development.

The dynamics of the 'conversation' are multiple and stretch across organizations incorporating its owners, its employees and its customers, who, through the Internet, then continue that conversation with others, exchanging experiences, good and bad. In other words, *Cluetrain* challenges traditional business communications models by replacing monologue with dialogue.

The Long Tail

While *Cluetrain* explores how markets are informed by digital technology, *The Long Tail* offers a model regarding how markets are structured in these new times. As digital natives spend more of their leisure time online, so 'the main effect of all this connectivity is unlimited and unfiltered access to culture and content of all sorts, from the mainstream to the farthest fringe of the underground' (Anderson 2007: 3). As a result, the mass market of entertainment is evolving into a market made up of a 'mass of niches' (Anderson 2007: 5).When considered in commercial terms, the new economy of online commerce makes it possible to invert the traditional model of the market from selling large amounts of a few things, to selling small amounts of a large number of things. As a result, the creation of niche, micro-markets is evidence of this fragmentation in taste cultures, all accessible through online search. That which was once 'uneconomic to offer' (Anderson 2007: 6) can now be reviewed in the context of a global marketplace, and in relation to products capable of digital storage, rather than physical, the margins are now considerable revenue earners when considered cumulatively. Thus, when thinking about markets, *The Long Tail* maps 'the true shape of demand in our culture, unfiltered by the economics of scarcity' (Anderson 2007: 9). The Internet has allowed for buyers and sellers to establish a market where supply and demand are evident, and no longer reliant on the economics of the traditional marketplace and traditional trading conditions. 'Who has the stuff we like? Who makes the stuff we need? Interest, curiosity, craft and voice combine to create powerful self-organising marketplaces on the web' (Levine et al 2000: 174).

The Long Tail extrapolates how the application of the Internet to the world of commerce has significant repercussions in relation to traditional media economics. Within this book, which started out as an article in *Wired* magazine (October

2004), Anderson explores an evolving marketplace informed by the dynamics of the global economy and digital technologies that changed the nature of how goods could be both stored and distributed via the concept of virtual shelf space. Taking as its starting point the development of the digital download, it traces the evolution of a retail model based on the value of the niche, thereby inverting the more familiar Pareto rule, where that which is popular functions to sustain the shelf life of the less popular, which is soon reviewed and discarded. Furthermore, by taking into consideration the possibilities of a global online shop window facilitated by the marketing potential of online networking communities, no retailer is tied to sell on the basis of local preferences and taste cultures. As the 'first distribution system in history that is as well suited for the niche as for the mass, for the obscure as well as the mainstream' (Anderson 2010: 3), 'the long tail' model is supported by the development of search technologies that take the consumer further down the tail and into the world of highly specialized, but globally highly profitable, merchandise. The micro-market, therefore, can co-exist with mass markets, and cumulatively their sales have the potential to outperform the latter. Any sense of risk (Beck 1992) is mediated through the peer reviews and recommendations of fellow 'long tailers' either on the site of consumption or on the number of other self-contained review sites that this new economic model has spawned. This is not to deny, however, the existence of the mainstream bestsellers: there will always be a 'Short Head'. Therefore, 'the importance of offering the stuff at both the Head and the Tail is that you can start in the world that customers already know' (Anderson 2007: 148). As a result, this has a significant impact upon the shape of consumer demand. One example of 'the long tail' in practice is the business model utilized by Netflix, where consumer choice is driven by past choices informing future recommendations. In relation to mining a particular genre (e.g., sci-fi), consumers can be taken way down the tail in contrast to failing competitors, such as Blockbuster, which rely heavily on buying more and more of that which is in the bestsellers' list.

Of course, as Anderson (2007: 53) indicates, the mechanisms to promote niches are very different from those used in the context of a mass market product. Recommendations, rankings, bestseller lists and other 'filters' are used to allow the consumer to examine the tail, either in terms of responding to a specific need or simply to explore what is out there. Interestingly, this allows for 'new tastemakers' (Anderson 2007: 98) to emerge. Anyone who wants to comment or critique on a service, direct others towards a product or divulge a supplier can do so via a variety of channels until all niches can now be researched and choices managed accordingly.

However, critiques are manifest, particularly in relation to Amazon's cultivation of the 'long tail'. Amazon has been accused of 'robo-pricing' (Jopson 2012a: 19), impacting directly upon the potential future success of niche sellers on the site. In essence, the online behemoth is drawing on high-speed trading tools used on stock markets to undercut the prices of its competitors. To date, the long tail model has seen many small businesses being opened up to global trading through utilizing

Amazon as their marketplace, but this has now been described as a 'double-edged sword' (Jopson 2012b: 11). The price to pay, it seems, for embedding a business within the Amazon ecosystem is that any retailer loses their autonomy and the recognition that, in fact, Amazon can tap into both their sales and inventories. In essence, Amazon can use the data of businesses on the site to turn into its competitor, identifying where there is demand and then offering these products directly, at a cheaper price. How consumers will react as this practice continues and as the range of distributors once offered is slowly eroded and those who cannot compete slide away remains to be seen.

Marketplaces: The quest for authenticity

The diversity of consumer spaces, both physical and virtual, such as Amazon, speaks to the 'complexity' of consumer behaviour and what consumers want out of retail culture. The key period in the development of consumer culture was from around 1860 to 1914 when a number of features (e.g., railway networks, national markets, development of branding, proliferation of advertising in the mass media) changed products' availability, their aesthetics and how they were marketed. Of these, department stores are the point at which we first begin to think about the design of space as a means of informing the shopping experience: indeed, one critic has even conceptualized them as 'female leisure centres' (Nava 1996). We can locate the department store within the era of Victorian modernization, where mass production requires mass consumption. In this way, the spaces themselves developed as brands and competed for the consumer's attention. Stores such as Selfridges drew the consumer in through newspaper advertising, window displays and regular sales. The development of consumer spaces allows for the expansion of markets, but this is not to suggest a model based on linearity with one form replacing what has gone before. Rather, it is the co-existence, re-emergence and re-imagining of forms that makes the study of contemporary consumer spaces so highly engaging.

The physical marketplace

The shift from a traditional to a post-traditional society informs consumer practices. In traditional society we experienced a containment of the marketplace; it does not affect all aspects of our lives. Trading takes place at a particular time in a pre-determined and regularly attended space, predominantly the market square. In contrast, post-traditional society, precipitated by the Industrial Revolution, leads to the dispersal of the marketplace across space and time as geographical mobility allows for new forms of integration, and the development of abstract systems (Giddens 1991) begins to replace personalized, localized contacts. One of the fore-runners in the changing landscape of consumer practice was the above-mentioned department store, which became a fundamental engine of modernity not only in terms of the range of products it stocked, and the behavioural patterns it introduced in turning shopping into a leisure activity, but in how (through the tropes of spectacle and the experiential) it was to inform the future development of retail spaces both physically and virtually. However, while the history of retail space is generally told in a somewhat linear narrative (markets, shops, arcades, department stores, supermarkets, malls, etc.), the actual post-modern shopping experience is one denoted by the co-existence of different retail forms. This co-existence, it could be argued, stems from a quest for authenticity: of the identity under construction; the products utilized to signify the intended sense of self; and the places where this consumption takes place. Even when we seem to be rejecting consumerism as it is manifested in glossy magazines, we instead revisit old forms of consumption (e.g., farmers' markets) in the quest to be different, or rework old themes, as in the case of the markets in Brick Lane, London, where consumers fill bags with vintage clothes for fixed sums of £10 or £20 depending on the size. As Soper (2008: 32) observes, 'dissatisfactions may find expression in nostalgia for certain kinds of material or for objects and practices that no longer figure in everyday life'. Such activities tend to be highly sociable gatherings and can only become successful if like-minded people will participate.

Case study: Westfield II, Stratford, London

The alignment of free time and consumption came together in the opening of Westfield II, Stratford, in September 2011, established to cater for the 'down time'

FIGURE 1.1 Westfield Shopping Centre, London
Source: Helen Powell

around the Olympic and Paralympic events of London 2012. Over 200,000 customers came through the doors on the first day spending £4 million (Butler 2011/ 2012: 22). In essence, Westfield is the embodiment of the conceptualization of space as spectacle, constructed through its engagement with both the dynamics of the entertainment and experience economies and in which the consumer's imagination and desires are allowed free rein, distanced from the East End world outside. Once inside, 'the shopping-mall mix is calculated to organize the disorienting flux of attributes and needs into a recognizable hierarchy of shops defined by cost, status and lifestyle images', while at the same time managing to strike a balance in each consumer's mind between the 'limited' number of goods available to each consumer and the 'unlimited desires' each will have (Crawford 1992: 13). In this way, champagne bars and Topshop can co-exist, as can casinos and cinemas.

Spectacle is generated via a sensorial overload on all levels throughout the mall, for 'in a world where people's attention spans are shorter and shorter, shopping has to compete in an increasingly visual context' (Miles 2010: 99). At large, the mall is at the heart of the regeneration of East London and part of the legacy of the 2012 Games. Enhanced by its close proximity to the Olympic Stadium and Anish Kapoor and Cecil Balmond's tangled 900 tonne 'The ArcelorMittal Orbit', a commemorative sculpture and observation tower, Westfield II promotes itself directly through the huge plasma screens that enshroud it. To what degree the mall benefits its own local residents is problematic; the majority of residents lack the

FIGURE 1.2 Westfield Shopping Centre (interior)
Source: Helen Powell

necessary economic and cultural capital to fully participate in what Westfield has to offer. This is acknowledged directly through unemployment rates of 8.5 per cent of working-aged adults in the borough (London's Poverty Profile 2012) and indirectly through the maintenance of a smaller shopping centre in close proximity with its own competing Poundland and 99p Store. Encasing the poor relation and functioning to disguise is an abstract, colourful and child-like metallic screening erected just ahead of the opening of the Games.

Yet, these two worlds have the potential never to co-exist: the management of perceptions of Westfield as the archetype of retail splendour is carefully contained via a series of entrance and exit points buried deeply underground and delivering the consumer right into the heart of the mall.

When Victor Gruen, the architect most responsible for the concept of the mall, originally perceived their function, it was as providing 'a vital hub for the local community' (Miles 2010: 104). Instead, the mall functions here as a space in which the market economy is practised and whose own brand value is enhanced when competing with other malls in London, the South East and nationally by the resonance of the Olympic competition and its associations with being 'the best in your field'. If Westfield II exemplifies how the mall might be perceived as 'living testament to the physical domination of consumption upon the urban fabric' (Miles 2010: 98), then when considering the agglomeration of the shops and services that make up its interior it becomes evident how 'image, including its employees' looks, the buildings, clothes, logos and atmosphere ... totally saturates consumption'

FIGURE 1.3 Stratford Shopping Centre (street view)
Source: Helen Powell

(Gabriel and Lang 2008: 331). One example of a brand at Westfield that imbibes all of these elements in constructing its identity is that of global clothing brand Hollister, of parent brand Abercrombie & Fitch. One journalist described the experience of shopping in Hollister, with specific reference to the dark labyrinthine layout of the store, as 'foolish or fabulous, depending on your age' (Craik 2011: 41). The brand addresses its target teens, 'dudes' or 'bettys', through fantasies of laid-back surf imagery of southern California, embodied through the beautiful model-esque staff in-store and who populate the website and its carrier bags. Eric Cerny, head of investor relations at Hollister, recognizes the importance of creating a unique experience that is the fusion of the image of the staff, the store's architecture and the mood generated once inside. 'If we have been doing our job properly, you should feel positive energy and optimism when you walk in, even if it might be something you're not used to feeling every day in your own life' (Cerny cited in Craik 2011: 41). Hollister speaks to the concept of the 'multi-vidual' (Van den Bergh and Behrer 2011: 157), young people who use fashion to both explore a sense of self but also anchor a sense of belonging within a wider community. While the brand remains current, and that in itself remains a challenge when targeting this particular market, it will be seen as a facilitator in the life of its followers rather than directly and overtly as a business profiteering out of the insecurities of youth.

Following the neoliberal agenda, shopping has now taken on a role beyond the functional one of provisioning. It becomes part of the experience economy, with retailers having to constantly reinvent themselves to prevent becoming tired and dated. The extension of the availability of time to shop, with the introduction of Sunday trading in the UK on 28 August 1994, and its rebuttal for the time of the Olympic Games (2012) is testament to the extent to which it has become embedded within our diurnal cycle. After much opposition from religious groups, at The MetroCentre in Gateshead, Tyne and Wear, on the first Sunday of trading 'a special church service went on as 90,000 shoppers flooded through the doors to spend an average £57 per head' (Harnden 1994: 1). The headlines here are not so much about the experience *per se*, but rather the impact of the extension to the amount of time available 'to experience'. More recent examples of the extending of the temporal framework around consumption have included the 'student lock in' whereby Land Securities, the largest shopping centre owners in the UK, have sought to encourage young shoppers, with National Union of Students (NUS) cards, to discounts and entertainment during late night shopping, promoted in advance via social media sites.

The Portas Report

If the mall, as noted above, has digressed from its original function of providing a community hub, it is the regeneration of a sense of community spirit through retail that this chapter now considers. In the spring of 2011 the Coalition government tasked Mary Portas, businesswoman, retail expert and TV personality, with reinvigorating the British High Street. To put this in context, in February 2012, one in seven shops was boarded up, rising to one in four in Blackpool, Rotherham, Grimsby and Hull (Senior 2012: 15). Back in the 1990s and during the dot.com boom it was predicted that the web would bring an end to shopping as we know it, and it appears that these figures reveal this fate. In Europe, according to an Ofcom survey published in December 2011, 79 per cent of Britons with Internet access use the web to buy retail goods. Holland came next with 74 per cent and then Germany with 73 per cent (Smith 2011: 39). Furthermore, according to the consultancy Verdict Research, online sales in the UK have more than doubled to £26.3 billion in the past five years to 2012 and will rise to £40 billion by 2015, with the possibility of a 'quarter of non-food stores vacant by 2020' according to retail analyst Javelin (Butler 2011/2012: 24). However, recent research by Saatchi & Saatchi perhaps hints at better times to come and it is Generation Y who may be the saviours of the High Street's fate. On the one hand, Saatchi's research showed 'extremely high levels of both affection and expectation' for the High Street; but young people also found it lacking in terms of generating any sense of 'sociability' (Senior 2012: 15). This is supported by the Confederation of British Industry (CBI) who argue that 'If the UK high street is to stay alive it shouldn't be afraid of the Internet, but instead find new ways of harnessing its power to make local shopping as entertaining and relevant as ever' (Butler 2011/2012: 27).

Portas published her own findings on the state of the British High Street in December 2011, and it is worth detailing in full the causal factors that she identified as having produced this current 'crisis':

> The phenomenal growth of online retailing, the rise of mobile retailing, the speed and sophistication of the major national and international retailers, the epic and immersive experiences offered by today's new breed of shopping mall, combined with a crippling recession, have all conspired to change today's retail landscape. New benchmarks have been forged against which our high streets are now being judged. New expectations have been created in terms of value, service, entertainment and experience against which the average high street has in many cases failed to deliver. These reasons alone conspire to create a new shopper mindset which cannot and should not be reversed.
>
> *(Portas 2011)*

As a result of such observations, she puts forward a series of proposals to be actioned through pilot towns in an attempt to breathe life back into High Street retail culture. Interestingly, her recommendations include the 'need to start a conversation about what we need and what we want our high street to be' (Portas 2011). To stimulate such dialogue her vision of the High Street is one comprising a fusion of indoor and outdoor markets; extending the number of people trading; and turning them into a social and civic occasion, including 'National Market Day'. In essence, she posits a return to the original conception of the 'market' that the authors of *Cluetrain* identified as the starting point of their own analysis.

The digital marketplace: e-Bay

e-Bay is a marketplace created by users with e-Bay as the facilitator bringing buyers and sellers together over the Internet via auction or 'Buy It Now' trading options. Starting off as person-to-person transactions, it has now extended to become a virtual global shop front for small and niche businesses. Many larger brands also use e-Bay as an outlet store. For the majority of consumers it is a means of identifying the availability of a specific, often niche, product that in the past would have taken a considerable time to track down on foot or via the telephone. Social utility is also increased as items that one seller no longer requires find a home elsewhere. Data from May 2012 indicate that visitors to the site spend an average of 34 seconds on each page view and a total of 17 minutes during each visit (www.alexa.com).

One of the interesting sets of dynamics in establishing virtual relationships between buyers and sellers is the increased awareness of sellers of the role of self-promotion in making the object attractive to prospective purchasers. Informative descriptions, photographs and any additional, often autobiographical, details relating to its original purchase or past history both authenticate the sale and set it apart from similar items. Even 'defects' can be turned into patina that, when articulated, actually enhances the value of the object due to its originality. In this way 'consumption through e-Bay is not just about the goods purchased but about the consumption of the narratives and imagery that inform and support these acts of consumption' (Beer and Burrows 2010: 8). As with all e-commerce, its success both in transactional and experiential terms relies heavily on information provided in lieu of the actual physicality of the product. To help counter this position, e-Bay has also used pop-up stores to draw consumers to the brand and mediate issues around its sensorial limitations.

In addressing the appeal of e-Bay, on the one hand, it speaks to austere times with notions of recycling and up-cycling built into it, but it also simultaneously speaks to a key trait of the new consumer – namely, the quest for authenticity (Lewis and Bridger 2001). Even on the BBC TV series *The Apprentice* (2012), the notion of creating authentic items was tapped into when pop-up stores were opened in fashionable parts of London trading in recycled and up-cycled items that the contestants had to source, stage and sell. In a highly engaging paper, Denegri-Knott and Molesworth (2010) explore the unique experiential dynamics of e-Bay, positing the experiences encountered as quite different from other physical and virtual settings. The starting point for their paper is the infinite possibilities that e-Bay has to offer in terms of the number and range of products for sale. The television ad in the UK (May 2012) interestingly tries to represent in 2D the experience of searching online and the vast array of objects one might find: some 30 million products, the ad suggests. Once on the site 'it sets up a cycle of revelation and discovery, always unclear and ill-defined; full of surprises, dangers, opportunities and promises' (Denegri-Knott and Molesworth 2010: 59).

The introduction of PayPal was critical not only for the success of e-commerce, in general, and embedding a layer of trust into the payment process, but also for the development of peer-to-peer trading more widely. As a result, sites such as Preloved and Gumtree have subsequently sprung up which bypass more centralized markets allowing consumers to sell items directly to others. Furthermore, this online model has spawned and rejuvenated physical replicas, including 'the garage sale', 'and created a whole new market for second-hand and recycled goods which has a positive impact from an environmental perspective' (Fortin and Uncles 2011: 473).

Conclusion

Ultimately, when considering shopping both as a leisure activity and as a functional necessity, consumers are seeking a choice in terms of how potentially fulfilling any experience can be and how it ties in with their own limitations of time and concentration when faced with decision-making. In view of this many retailers have recognized the value of adopting a multi-channel model, the convergence of the physical and virtual rather than the domination of one over the other. Today the most successful retailers operate across multiple platforms, keeping the marketing message and the customer experience consistent, whether that is in-store, via a website or on a mobile shopping app. How this will then develop has been proposed by Maureen Hinton of Verdict Research:

> In the future, the most successful retailers will have flagship stores in high-density locations where large numbers of shoppers congregate, plus satellite stores carrying a much smaller range, with click and collect and online ordering facilities. Retailers will use online and mobile commerce to fill any gaps.
>
> *(Hinton, cited in Barrett 2012: 17)*

Bibliography

Anderson, C. (2007) *The Long Tail: How Endless Choice is Creating Unlimited Demand*, London: Random House.

——(2010) *Free: How Today's Smartest Businesses Profit by Giving Something for Nothing*, London: Random House.

Barrett, C. (2012) 'High Street Bows to Super Highway', *Financial Times*, 18 January, p17.

Beck, U. (1992) *Risk Society: Towards a New Modernity*, London: Sage.

Beer, D. and Burrows, R. (2010) 'Consumption, Prosumption and Participatory Web Cultures: An Introduction', *Journal of Consumer Culture*, vol 10, no 1, pp3–12.

Bonello, D. (2001) 'The Cluetrain Consumers', *Campaign*, 10 August, pp20–22.

Butler, S. (2011/12) 'Retail Therapy?', *Business Voice: The CBI Magazine*, December/January, vol 13, no 2, pp22–27.

Cardoso, G. (2011) 'From Mass to Networked Communication', in S. Papathanassopoulos (ed) *Media Perspectives for the 21st Century*, Abingdon, UK: Routledge.

Craik, L. (2011) 'Hunting for Teen Cool in the Dark', *The Times*, 10 December, p41.

Crawford, M. (1992) 'The World in a Shopping Mall', in M. Sorkin (ed) *Variations on a Theme Park*, New York, NY: The Noonday Press.

Denegri-Knott, J. and Molesworth, M. (2010) 'Love It. Buy It. Sell It: Consumer Desire and the Social Drama of eBay', *Journal of Consumer Culture*, vol 10, no 1, pp56–79.

Dittmar, H. (2008) *Consumer Culture, Identity and Well-Being: The Search for the 'Good-Life' and the 'Body Perfect'*, Hove: Psychology Press.

Elliott, A. (2008) *Concepts of the Self*, Cambridge: Polity Press.

Elliott, R. and Davies, A. (2005) 'Symbolic Brands and Authenticity of Identity Performance', in J. E. Schroeder and M. Salzer-Mörling (eds) *Brand Culture*, London: Routledge.

Ewen, S. (2001) *Captains of Consciousness: Advertising and the Social Roots of the Consumer Culture*, 25th anniversary edition, New York, NY: Basic Books.

Forrest, C. (2009) 'Is Research Failing to Enlighten the Ad Industry?', *Campaign*, 1 May, p7.

Fortin, D. and Uncles, M. (2011) 'The First Decade: Emerging Issues of the Twenty-First Century in Consumer Marketing', *Journal of Consumer Marketing*, vol 28, no 7, pp472–475.

Gabriel, Y. and Lang, T. (1995) *The Unmanageable Consumer*, London: Sage.

——(2006) *The Unmanageable Consumer*, 2nd edition, London: Sage.

——(2008) 'New Faces and New Masks of Today's Consumer', *Journal of Consumer Culture*, vol 8, no 3, pp321–340.

Giddens, A. (1991) *Modernity and Self-Identity: Self and Society in the Late Modern Age*, Stanford, CA: Stanford University Press.

Gottschalk, S. (2009) '"Hypermodern Consumption and Megalomania": Superlatives in Commercials', *Journal of Consumer Culture*, vol 9, no 3, pp307–327.

Harnden, T. (1994) 'Sunday "Tops for Shopping" as Big Stores Make History', *Daily Telegraph*, 29 August, pp1–2.

Havas Worldwide (2010) 'The New Consumer in the Era of Mindful Spending', *Prosumer Report*, summer, vol 8, http://www.thenewconsumer.com/study-highlights/, accessed 20 January 2013.

Jenkins, H. (2008) *Convergence Culture: Where Old and New Media Collide*, New York, NY: New York University Press.

Jenkins, H. and Deuze, M. (2008) 'Editorial: Convergence Culture', *Convergence*, vol 14, no 1, pp5–12.

Jopson, B. (2012a) 'Algorithms on Amazon Raise Fears on Pricing', *Financial Times*, 9 July, p19.

——(2012b) 'From Warehouse to Powerhouse: The Amazon Economy', *Financial Times*, 9 July, p11.

Keat, R., Whiteley, N. and Abercrombie, N. (1994) *The Authority of the Consumer*, London: Routledge.

Kern, A. (2007) *The Cult of the Amateur: How Today's Internet is Killing Our Culture and Assaulting Our Economy*, London: Nicholas Brealey Publishing.

Leadbeater, C. (2007) *We-Think*, London: Profile Books.

Levine, R., Locke, C., Searles, D. and Weinberger, D. (2000) *The Cluetrain Manifesto: The End of Business as Usual*, Harlow, UK: Pearson Education Ltd.

Lewis, D. and Bridger, D. (2001) *The Soul of the New Consumer*, London: Nicholas Brealey Publishing.

Lister, M., Dovey, J., Giddings, S., Grant, I. and Kelly, K. (2009) *New Media: A Critical Introduction*, Abingdon, UK: Routledge.

London's Poverty Profile (2012) 'Unemployment by Borough', 27 January, http://www.londonspovertyprofile.org.uk/indicators/topics/work-and-worklessness/unemployment-by-borough, accessed 29 June 2012.

Lury, C. (2011) *Consumer Culture*, 2nd edition, Cambridge: Polity Press.

McAllister, M. P. (2011) 'Consumer Culture and New Media: Commodity Fetishism in the Digital Era', in S. Papathanassopoulos (ed) *Media Perspectives for the 21st Century*, London: Routledge.

McStay, A. (2010) *Digital Advertising*, Basingstoke, UK: Palgrave Macmillan.

Mangold, W. G. and Faulds, D. J. (2009) 'Social Media: The New Hybrid Element of the Promotion Mix', *Business Horizons*, vol 52, pp357–365.

Miles, S. (2010) *Spaces for Consumption*, London: Sage.

Morning, S. (2010) 'Hey, What's the Long Idea?', in *Campaign: Supplement: I Believe …* , 22 October, pp12–18.

Moshe, M. (2012) 'Media Time Squeezing: The Privatization of the Media Time Sphere', *Television and New Media*, vol 13, no 1, pp68–88.

Murdock, G. (2010) 'Networking the Commons: Convergence Culture and the Public Interest', in J. Gripsrud (ed) *Relocating Television: Television in the Digital Context*, Abingdon, UK: Routledge.

Nava, M. (1996) *Modernity's Disavowal: Women, the City and the Department Store*, London: Routledge.

Osbourne, H. and Insley, J. (2012) 'Martin Lewis Sells MoneySavingExpert for £87m', *The Guardian* online, 1 June, www.guardian.co.uk/money/2012/jun/01/martin-lewis-sells-moneysavingexpert, accessed 0 June 2012.

Packard, V. (1962) *The Hidden Persuaders*, London: Pelican.

Portas, M. (2011) *The Portas Review: An Independent Review into the Future of Our High Streets*, December, http://www.maryportas.com/news/2011/12/12/the-portas-review, accessed 4 April 2012.

Powell, H. (2009) 'Time, Television and the Decline of DIY', *Home Cultures*, vol 6, no 1, pp89–108.

——(2012) *Stop the Clocks! Time and Narrative in Cinema*, London: I. B. Tauris.

Ritzer, G. and Jurgenson, N. (2010) 'Production, Consumption, Prosumption: The Nature of Capitalism in the Age of the Digital "Prosumer"', *Journal of Consumer Culture*, vol 10, no 1, pp13–36.

Schor, J. B. (2007) 'In Defense of Consumer Critique: Revisiting the Consumption Debates of the Twentieth Century', *The ANNALS of the American Academy of Political and Social Science*, vol 611, no 16, pp16–30.

Schudson, M. (1981) 'Criticizing the Critics of Advertising: Towards a Sociological View of Marketing', *Media, Culture and Society*, vol 3, pp3–12.

Schwarz, B. (2004) *The Paradox of Choice: Why More Is Less*, New York, NY: HarperCollins.

Schwarzkopf, S. (2007) 'Culture and the Limits of Innovation in Marketing: Ernest Dichter, Motivation Studies and Psychoanalytic Consumer Research in Great Britain, 1950s–1970s', *Management and Organisational History*, vol 2, no 3, pp219–236.

——(2011) 'The Political Theology of Consumer Sovereignty: Towards an Ontology of Consumer Society', *Theory, Culture & Society*, vol 28, no 3, pp106–129.

Senior, R. (2012) 'Generation Y Can Answer the High Street's Woes', *Campaign*, 10 February, p15.

Shaw, F. (2002) 'Uncertainty and the New Consumer', *Foresight*, vol 4, no 6, pp4–13.

Simmel, G. (1904/1957) 'Fashion', *American Journal of Sociology*, vol 62, no 2, pp541–558.

Simms, J. (2010) 'Brands Feel the "Nudge"', *Marketing*, 10 November, p18.

Slater, D. (1997) *Consumer Culture and Modernity*, Cambridge: Polity Press.

Smith, H. (2011) 'Nation of Online Shoppers', *Metro*, 15 December, p39.

Soper, K. (2007) 'The Other Pleasures of Post-Consumerism', *Soundings*, no 35, March, pp31–40.

Spurgeon, C. (2008) *Advertising and New Media*, London: Routledge.

Sutherland, R. (2012) 'IPA Website: Behavioural Economics Channel', http://www.ipa.co.uk/page/behavioural-economics-channel, accessed 2 April 2012.

Tapscott, D. and Williams, A. (2008) *Wikinomics*, London: Atlantic Books.

Thaler, R. H. and Sunstein, C. R. (2009) *Nudge: Improving Decisions about Health, Wealth and Happiness*, London: Penguin.

The Apprentice (2012), BBC 1, 11 April.

Toffler, A. (1980) *The Third Wave*, London: Collins.

Trentmann, F. (2009) 'Crossing Divides: Consumption and Globalisation in History', *Journal of Consumer Culture*, vol 9, no 2, pp187–220.

Trout, J. (2008) *Differentiate or Die: Survival in Our Era of Killer Competition*, 2nd edition, New Jersey: John Wiley & Sons.

Tungate, M. (2007) *Adland: A Global History of Advertising*, London: Kogan Page.

Universal McCann (2011) 'Wave.5: The Socialisation of Brands', *Social Media Tracker, 2010*, www.slideshare.net/Olivier.mermat/universal-mccann-wave-5-the-socialisation-of-brands, accessed 5 February 2012.

Van den Bergh, J. and Behrer, M. (2011) *How Cool Brands Stay Hot: Branding to Generation Y*, London: Kogan Page.

Van Dijck, J. and Nieborg, D. (2009) 'Wikinomics and Its Discontents: A Critical Analysis of Web 2.0 Business Manifestos', *New Media & Society*, vol 11, no 5, pp855–874.

Waldman, S. (2011) 'Digital Disruption: The Next Twenty Years', 31 November, www.iabuk.net/video/simon-walman-digital-disruption-the-next-20-years, accessed 8 March 2012.

Wernick, A. (1991) *Promotional Culture*, London: Sage.

Williams, R. (1980) 'Advertising: The Magic System', in *Problems in Materialism and Culture*, London: Verso.

2

THE PROMOTIONAL INDUSTRIES

Helen Powell

The promotional industries that comprise Part I of this text, advertising, marketing, branding and public relations (PR), emerged in the context of industrialization and the expansion of markets to a national and global scale. As a result, local knowledge of both producers and sellers was supplanted by the utilization of a mass media to communicate information that promoted a client and its wares to a burgeoning urban mass that could also, through access to applicable media, be assembled into audiences through which different product ranges and taste cultures could be marketed. As this relationship between the various promotional methods and the media developed in more sophisticated formats throughout the twentieth century, so it has sought to take account of, and respond to, how society itself is changing, informed by the dynamics of market systems and new technologies. As a result, mapping the changes to promotional methods throughout the twentieth century and into the twenty-first has to take on board and recognize, as an integral part of its transformation, the social, economic and cultural changes that inform and shape the way in which its industries carry out their business. In considering these changes and their impact, this chapter will start by focusing on three specific trends that have had a significant bearing on promotional culture: 'free' media, the 'attention economy' and the 'experience economy'. This will then be followed by an overview of the promotional industries under consideration, providing a platform for the more detailed interrogations that will ensue in the chapters on integrated marketing communications (IMC), branding and PR.

As Anderson (2010) documents, the concept of 'free media' is not new and dates back to early models of commercial radio, free to listen to on the basis of content subsidized by advertising. The model has extended to a much wider range of media consumed today and provides a very potent argument for the need for advertising in that it allows for affordability and choice across media markets. Anderson (2010: 24) articulates that in the traditional media model, newspaper and magazine publishers, for example, 'don't charge readers anything close to the actual cost of creating, printing, and distributing their products. They're not selling papers and magazines to readers, they're selling readers to advertisers.' This latter model, however, is under threat, he argues, from the ubiquity of free online content where 'pretty much everything is given away for free in some version with the hopes of selling something else – or, even more frequently, with no expectation of pay at all' (Anderson, 2010: 2). This is demonstrated via the buoyant commuter-targeted free press such as the newspapers *Metro* and the *Evening Standard* and the magazines *Stylist* and *Sport*, and the recently launched for free *Time Out*. As a result, money is made not from media content but from a new relationship with advertising.

According to Anderson, Google, for example, offers a whole range of free products but derives its profits through advertising, mainly search. In this context he juxtaposes old and new ways of revenue accumulation where in relation to traditional broadcast media, the model was, in essence, 'annoy the 90 percent of your audience that is not interested in your product to reach the 10 percent who might be … The Google model is just the opposite: Use software to show the ad only to the people for whom it's most relevant' (Anderson 2010: 139). Anderson puts forward a series of reasons for this shift in behaviour, fundamentally comprising a fusion of change in 'generational taste but also by technological trends' (Anderson 2010: 140). He draws our attention to a generation who have grown up not expecting to pay and this will then filter on down to those who follow them. With so much content available, but only ever a limited time available to view, 'free' becomes a fundamental motivation to choose: note the success of both YouTube and Facebook in this context. As a result, consumers begin to question why content that is available free online shouldn't also be free in a broader context.

However, for this model to be successful the content itself must be highly engaging – that is to say, worthy of attention. Whereas for Cardoso (2011:119), as noted in the Introduction, the major challenges for news industries comprise the on-going quest by the consumer for information, for the advertising and marketing businesses an alternative set of problems circulate. In 1997 Goldhaber articulated a new set of economic laws for the age of the Internet – namely, that while it still stands that 'what is scarce commands value', in this context that which is now most highly valued is 'attention'. This is a particularly important insight in relation to the promotional industries subject to investigation in this book, for it recommends the adoption of a revised perspective in relation to how commercial messages are framed. With an abundance of information online, what is scarce is attention, and the promotional industries need therefore to consider what consumers are prepared to pay attention to and what value it can bring to their lives. For example, how can brands earn attention through forging a connection with consumers so that they can sell to them? How can they make an impression in order to lead to behavioural change? For brands that understand this and embed it back within their brand communication, a distinct point of competitive advantage can be forged. For Goldhaber (1997), the emphasis on creativity here is paramount: 'Since it is hard to get new attention by repeating exactly what you or someone else has done before, the new economy is based on endless originality, or at least attempts at originality' mined increasingly, I would argue, through the potential of participatory culture. Furthermore, through a model of networked individualism, in contrast with traditional mass marketing, once seeded effectively, brand messages can be distributed virally on the basis that they carry content worthy of attention. Virals also allow hegemonic positions to be challenged as they permit small companies to compete in a promotional landscape that is all too frequently dominated by those who can afford the cost of mainstream planning. In contrast, viral advertising shifts the emphasis away from the traditional Pareto '80/20' rule of media space costs dominating the creative spend.

This emphasis on creativity is inextricably linked to the effect of promotion. In this context, Pine and Gilmore (1999) also debate the changing nature of economic value, recognizing that following industrialization, value oscillated around the ability of goods to deliver intangible qualities, informed by a burgeoning set of promotional industries. However, a second phase saw a turn towards the commodification of services as an integral part of the neoliberal agenda, as discussed in Chapter 1, with businesses creating value beyond their core. The range of products offered by supermarket giant Tesco, including eye-tests and car insurance, is an example of this. Now we are in the third phase of the transformation of economic value, one that centres on the commodification of experiences to produce competitive advantage with the concept of authenticity becoming a critical quality that consumers crave and brands seek to be identified with. By developing the experience, which can be anything from a money-off voucher to the inclusion of a game on a brand's website, it generates qualities of differentiation within the sector and allows for supporting promotion to become informed and enriched by this additional content. The experience economy relies heavily on convergence culture for its success as experiences must somehow be harnessed and prolonged beyond the purchase and consumption of the product. Therefore, through the use of technology, brands can bring the consumer added value. For example, a more prolonged brand engagement was generated by Sure deodorant for men (June 2012) where in their 'beat the elements' online game, participants navigated across their choice of tough terrains to win cash prizes (www.suremen.co.uk). However, for brands to be able to deliver on experiences, they need to understand the types of experience that consumers value and how this might be achievable. Therefore, knowing your consumer, as the previous chapter indicated, remains constant in the development of any promotional strategy.

Advertising in the context of integrated marketing communications

The popular television series *Mad Men* reflects the internal challenges, conflicts and romances of personnel at the fictitious advertising agency Sterling Cooper during the early 1960s. Yet, on a macro scale, advertising at this juncture was fighting a more significant battle, seeking to reposition itself away from its associations with the 'dark arts', as Vance Packard had so damningly painted it in his book *The Hidden Persuaders* (1957). In response, advertising was in the throes of cultivating its own professional standing through the adoption of extensive market research techniques and the appropriation of a new agency role, the account planner, functioning as the voice of the consumer in the agency. A later significant milestone in relation to the changing identity of the advertising agency was embodied by HHCL, described as the 'first postmodern agency' by Nicola Mendelsohn (2011), president of the IPA (Institute of Practitioners in Advertising). HHCL was one of the UK's most admired advertising agencies during the 1990s and is probably best known for Ronseal and Tango commercials, leading to *Campaign*'s prestigious accolade of Agency of the Decade. But on the cusp of the millennium, several significant accounts were lost and after a series of restructurings and takeovers, it finally merged into WPP's Grey London in 2007. Yet, it was not just creative content that in their heyday set them apart from their competitors; rather, their anthropological approach towards consumer research also marked a significant point of difference.

The agency's marketing strategy was presented in a manifesto which stated that 'agencies must not only change how and what they do, but that they must also change how they see' (HHCL and Partners 2000: 4). This 'new way of seeing' evolves out of the established history of marketing since World War II, when advertising was based on the discernible differences in the products it promoted and where consumers were passive subjects, reliant on TV for knowledge in terms of what was available and how to use it. In the context of mass production, effectiveness in advertising was measured through monitoring consumer behaviour and calculating outcomes, encapsulated in acronyms such as AIDA (attention, interest, desire, action), which saw consumer behaviour as informed by rational linear processes. HHCL believed in 2000 that this approach had continued to seep into the veins of every advertising agency, producing campaigns that had very little discernible difference between them. In contrast, the anthropological approach of HHCL recognized that consumers were no longer passive but were very much in tune with product life-cycles, pricing strategies and even media planning. '"You're buying a lot of off-peak airtime" a 24 year old observes in a focus group discussion' (HHCL and Partners 2000: 13) As a result, and in tune with one of the key themes running throughout this book, HHCL (2000: 17) suggested that it was important to 'know' the consumer and to achieve this to 'look on every new medium as a conversation opener'. At the start of a new millennium, HHCL recognized that the discourses that informed marketing strategies were subject to revision and that, in practice, advertising agencies would themselves need to restructure to deliver effective promotion for the 'new times' ahead. Ultimately, assisted and accelerated by new media, success would come from recognizing that the point of difference of the product is no longer enough, but rather point of difference is achieved through involving and interacting with consumers and building your marketing around them.

As the previous chapter documented, one of the fundamental consequences of media convergence is the amount of information now available to the consumer. It is estimated that individuals in Europe and North America see as many as 3000 ads per day (Clarke 2010: 102). In response, brands can no longer rely on promotional strategies that are unidirectional but must engage in dialogue with consumers in this socially networked marketplace. The forms through which this engagement might take place are consistently characterized by the qualities of interaction and participation. Nestlé, for example, as Walkers crisps had done before them, allowed consumers to vote via Facebook on the survival of new flavours of its Kit Kat chocolate bar. The camera manufacturer, Canon, on the other hand, focused on the experience of taking photographs through its 'Take Stories' online campaign. Here it offered professional advice and the opportunity to share practices, while simultaneously seeking to enhance the emotional connection the brand has with its consumers through positioning itself at the hub of this collective engagement in photographic practice. In this way 'brands have an opportunity to be valuable facilitators in return for consumers' attention' (Bashford 2010: 16) yet must recognize that consumers will only engage if there are tangible benefits and experiences to be gained. Another example in this setting is Intel's 'Museum of Me' where intangible benefits are injected into a somewhat anonymous product – namely, a micro-processer, through the unpacking of how we shape and store our digital memories online, replacing the physicality of the museum and album with personalized virtual digital spaces. However, to actually qualify the nature of the specificity of these benefits from the consumers' perspective and how one might constitute them in the generation of additional brand value is a key objective of the promotional industries. At its starting point is the gaining of an understanding of the nuances of digital interaction in relation to everyday life and the extent to which each digital device provides a specific environment for the delivery of the brand message. The message and the device must complement each other effectively, and media planning must take on board the delivery potential of the variety of small screens on offer – for example, smartphone versus tablet.

One of the significant changes in terms of the dynamic nature of promotional culture in the first decades of the twenty-first century has been the embedding of digital mobile devices within everyday life. This has led, for example, to the introduction of the app, which allows consumers access to new services and information and the means to purchase beyond traditional retail spaces – indeed, in distinctively 'non-places' (Augé 2009). Smartphone technology is seeing the acceleration of personalized offers, both in relation to previous purchases made and in real time, via global positioning systems (GPS), dependent on their current location in a store or a mall (Knights 2012: 4). As a result, e-commerce is now being supplemented by m-commerce, the smartphone functioning as a portal through which retailers can engage visually with a mobile consumer. At home, as we multitask, we use mobile devices in conjunction with other larger permanent screens. Digital agency Razorfish found that in a survey they conducted in conjunction with Yahoo! '80% of respondents are mobile multitasking while watching

TV' (Lockhorn 2012). Indeed, as Caroline Clancy, digital strategy director of Vizeum UK notes, '60 percent of Tweets in the evening [are] based on TV shows' (Campaign 2012). Furthermore, as Jeremy Lockhorn (2012) of Razorfish delves deeper into this top line data, he reveals that communication and content are the main drivers for multitasking:

> … 94% of multitaskers engage in some kind of mobile communication. In order-text, talking, email, social networking and IM (instant messaging) … On the content side of things, 60% of multitaskers are accessing additional content of some type … 36% of multitaskers use their connected devices for looking up information on a commercial they just saw.

This has important implications for marketers, and Lockhorn (2012) therefore makes the following recommendation for those spending heavily on TV advertising:

> Content and experiences that move seamlessly from one screen to another are an absolute must. This is bigger than simply having a mobile- or tablet-optimized web site. It means a cohesive communications strategy where the spots and the experience on mobile devices work together and build toward a greater whole.

In this respect, Sheehan and Morrison (2009) introduce the concept of 'confluence culture' to capture the changes advertising as an industry is undergoing in the digital age, where 'confluence culture' 'encourages the blending of new and traditional media outlets and blurs the boundaries of professional and amateur'. In particular, the concept engages with the notion of multitasking as outlined by Lockhorn above. As a result, a portfolio of media options remains a given, especially in relation to the hard-to-reach 18 to 30 target group, and integrated marketing communications shifts from being optional to a requirement, with social media as an integral facet. IMC looks to coordinate and control the various promotional elements that are utilized by brands and services to target an increasingly fragmented target audience through a series of touch points that map onto their daily activities. The increasing amount of time people are spending online, recognized in the appeal of the Facebook IPO, outlined below, has seen a number of online strategies being applied to IMC. These include brands being 'liked' and users demonstrating their willingness to be associated with these brands on, for example, company-sponsored websites, where additional information and opportunities to interact with the brand complement and reinforce their above-the-line activities. However, in an increasingly 'confluent' culture, informed by both convergence and remediation, IMC becomes largely reconfigured: less 'top-down in how it controls communication' and instead needing to adapt in order to 'embrace the new reality of interactive content' (Sheehan and Morrison 2009). As a consequence, the concept of 'conversation' once again rears its head with the agency no longer the bastion of ideas creation, but instead becoming more outward-facing, positively encouraging open discussions with a range of digital specialists, clients and consumers as to how the brand can be most effectively promoted.

In terms of advertising online, Springer (2009) charts what he sees as five distinct phases in the development of digital technology since the beginning of the 1990s that have enabled advertisers to get closer to consumers. In the first phase, traditional push media was applied online by below-the-line agencies in the form of banners and pop-ups. Following public annoyance at this form of interruption and the development of blocking software, the shift towards the engagement of the consumer through dialogue commenced via more interactive formats that included highly entertaining viral ads. With the development of social networking sites and higher percentages of leisure time spent online, so the third phase embraced the possibilities of Web 2.0 with promotion and entertainment becoming inextricably linked. In the fourth phase, the elision between media producers and consumers was positively encouraged: through sites such as YouTube, brands recognized the value of participation as a means not only for greater immersion in the brand but through widespread circulation of user-generated content, the brands' activities became conversation pieces too. In the current phase, phase five, Springer (2009: 274) sees brands positioning themselves through social networking sites as facilitators or 'enablers' in the lives of consumers and cites the example of the collaboration between Nike and Apple as evidence of how brands can bring something unique to the lives of runners who engage. 'By mashing up existing digital search technology and melding the sports expertise of Nike with the digital music management expertise of Apple, consumers were able to utilize a purpose-designed enabler by moulding it to suit their own musical tastes and fitness regimes' (Springer 2009: 285). In this way, he argues, within the context of convergence culture, 'it could therefore be said that designed processes, rather than messages, have become powerful promotional tools in an advertising saturated era' (Springer 2009: 286). Furthermore, what characterizes this fifth phase is its range of approaches in contrast to the banners and pop-ups of earlier online incarnations. In total, argues Anderson (2010: 144), 'today there are at least fifty different models online, and each one is changing by the day'. As a result, UK Internet adspend for 2011 was £5 billion (Woods 2012: 13) with potential for future growth and clients 'prepared to pay more for that which they know less about' (Spanier 2012: 41).

Therefore, an important consideration in relation to online media development is its emergence as a reliable and cost-effective advertising market. This stands in contrast to traditional mass media platforms as generators of advertising revenue that relied on the assemblage of large audiences to see the advertisement in question, and where effectiveness was measured on the basis of how this then affected sales over the period of time the ad was on air. Now with so much free content online, as documented above, this affects the means by which media providers make money through advertising. There are a number of different models as to how online advertising operates. Take Google, for example. Here the ads that run are dependent on the search term entered and advertisers only pay when a reader clicks on that ad (cost-per-click model). Search advertising is a growth area as the desire for the product is already there, with technology allowing for those desires and providers of possible solutions to come together. This is a significant leap from early models of display advertising (e.g., banners), which ultimately adopted the old model of 'push' advertising but within the context of a new media environment. The outcome was on-screen clutter, and strategies were subsequently employed to block such advertising.

The rise of Facebook and YouTube, sites formulated with the specific directive of sharing content, offer an interesting and seemingly more agreeable media space for advertisers who work to 'blend' promotion with everyday exchanges. In this way, over a longer period of time, brands have the potential to build up a relationship with consumers as it becomes an integral part of online life; consequentially, the quality of the 'experience' (Pine and Gilmore 1999) one has with the brand becomes more valuable to advertisers and their clients than simply measuring the quantity of people seeing an ad or the ability to recall it. From the client perspective, 'click-through' produces a new effectiveness model from which it is easy to chart results: if an ad is attractive then consumers will literally act on it. 'Such measurements increase the incentives for non-commercial sites to create an ad-friendly environment and ensure visitors notice the ads' that are placed there (McAllister 2011: 153).

Case study: The Facebook IPO

A number of the themes and issues discussed to date can be reframed when considered through the lens of the activities that led up to the IPO (initial public offering) of Facebook. In the week leading up to its floatation, the BBC documentary series *The Money Programme* featured an in-depth interview between Facebook's founder, Mark Zuckerberg, and BBC journalist Emily Maitlis (*The Money Programme* 2012). At the opening of the programme, Facebook was contextualized largely through numbers: 900 million of the world's population were now signed up; on average, each user has 140 friends and this reach encapsulates the potential for Facebook to become a major revenue-generating business, with the appointment of Sheryl Sandberg from Google presented as a significant turning point in the development of Facebook as a business model. To date, Google had made money from search, where the ad appears based on what you are already looking for – that is to say, in a facilitating context rather than an invasive one. In contrast, Sandberg, as Facebook's chief operating officer, argued that advertising on Facebook does not operate on this basis but rather through the scientific utilization of sophisticated software that taps into information already provided by users. So, for example, if you are a beauty salon that wishes to offer discounts on makeovers for brides-to-be, ads can be placed on the basis of algorithms utilizing 12 targeting criteria – in this case, including 'women' who reveal their status as 'engaged'. Using this model Facebook generated '£3.2 billion' in ad revenue in 2011 (*The Money Programme*, 2012). A second revenue stream emerged out of inviting businesses themselves onto Facebook and setting up their own pages. Pages then act as people: you 'like' a business and allow it to send you messages as you would a friend, encouraging conversations about the brand to ensue; between the brand and the 'friend'; and between 'friends' who might recommend a brand to one another. The Levi's 'friends' store allows its visitors to 'like' what's in-store but at the same time show them which products their network of friends also 'like'. As a result, the future of Facebook lies in its ability to keep users engaged for longer and longer periods on a daily basis in an attempt to draw other software developers to the site, embedding their own games and apps within what Maitlis terms 'a technology eco-system with Facebook right at the core' (*The Money Programme*, 2012).

An example of this expanding ecosystem, in practice, is reflected in the acquisition by Facebook of Instagram, a photo-sharing company, for $1 billion just ahead of its floatation in an attempt to enhance its advertising offer on smartphones. 'As people increasingly migrate to app experiences while on the move, advertisers and marketers need to adjust their approach commensurately; providing richer, more engaging and highly targeted mobile advertising experiences is key to monetising the space' (Tansey 2012: 16). Through its app the brand allows for visual engagement or, rather, a visual dialogue between brands and consumers. At the point of the takeover, Instagram had already been successfully used in a promotional capacity by Audi, Banana Republic and Burberry. 'Using the killer combination of Facebook and Instagram, brands can now leverage a more connected social and mobile multiplatform audience pool and tap into their interests' (Tansey 2012: 16).

Facebook became a listed company on the NASDAQ Stock Market on 18 May 2012, making its founder a multibillionaire. In the first five minutes, '100 million shares were traded as the frenzy for Facebook stock began' and technical difficulties were evident as the exchange struggled to cope with burgeoning demand (Ahmed 2012: 3). However, at the close, analysts attributed the stock's disappointing first-day performance on 'a weak market, as well as very aggressive pricing of the offering and concerns about the site's potential to gain advertising revenue' (Ahmed 2012: 3). News followed that Zuckerberg, 'the billionaire, along with the banks and big investors, faced a huge backlash after it was revealed how they profited at the expense of small buyers' unloading shares before their price plummeted (Gardner 2012: 8). As questions were raised over the early days of trading, a major issue arose – namely, the belief that Zuckerberg and his closest allies were party to information that the majority of potential investors were not: that Facebook's revenues were not as healthy as expected as they had not revealed the limits posed on revenue generation by Facebook gravitating to mobiles and therefore limiting the advertising potential. A new verb, 'to be Zucked', quickly followed to sum up the debacle (Gardner 2012: 8). At the point of writing, Zuckerberg and the other directors of Facebook have been issued with a lawsuit filed on behalf of three investors, but the law firm behind the complaint expects it to become a class action on behalf of every other investor who signed up to the float. The complaint states:

> The true facts at the time of the IPO were that Facebook was then experiencing a severe reduction in revenue growth due to an increase of users of its Facebook app or website through mobile devices rather than a traditional PC, such that the company told the underwriter to materially lower their revenue forecasts for 2012.
>
> *(Foley 2012: 43)*

The floatation of Facebook in May 2012 was a widely anticipated event, not only in the context of the global expansion of this social networking site over a relatively short period of time, but also in terms of what it signified as a platform for income generation. Universal McCann (2012: 18) predicted that for the IPO to be deemed a success 'Investors will expect a return on their investment and the growth of the platform will be a key performance indicator. Facebook will need to find ways to get consumers to spend more time with them and further commercialise their services.' Sir Martin Sorrell, chief executive officer of WPP Group, is not convinced that the latter is possible and raises concerns regarding the commercialization of Facebook and the potential impact that this has on the privacy of its users, pointing instead to a future of 'closed networks that are more private' (Sorrell on *The Money Programme* 2012). These concerns were echoed by Jon Woods, president of the ISBA, who has argued that advertising needs to work to strike a balance between 'valid concerns on privacy … and enhancing the consumer experience' (Woods 2012: 13). So while, on the one hand, the value of Facebook as a marketing tool is that it, for example, knows the age, likes, relationships status of its users and can therefore embed itself into these networks accordingly, it also can be seen as both invasive and intrusive.

In the context of Facebook's IPO, the seismic shift towards portable devices has therefore been received to date as both a blessing (numbers on the site) and a curse (impact upon advertising revenue generation). On average, a consumer aged between 16 and 54 owns four digital devices, the majority of which are used to access the Internet (Universal McCann 2011: 57). While smartphones, for example, function best in terms of an organizational tool, tablets, through their larger screens, enhance the user's creative potential and capacity to access entertainment on the go. The size of the screen is important in a promotional context. The build-up to and floatation of Facebook was, as noted above, marred soon after with reports that many shareholders had not received full information regarding future profit forecasts, which recognized that long-term revenue generation from advertising could be limited due to the high percentage of Facebook users gravitating to mobile devices. The seriousness of this disclosure draws attention to the embeddedness of mobile devices in our lives, both as an emotional investment and professional tool, and the challenges this draws for advertisers to reach consumers effectively via their phones. Their portability generates an interesting paradox. On the one hand, they engender a sense of liberation; yet, from a promotional perspective, it means that consumers can be reached anytime, anywhere. Creatively, however, the size of the screen limits the opportunities available.

The rise of the app, an online application that can be downloaded onto a mobile platform such as an iPhone, is testament to responses to this marketing conundrum as touch screen phones allow for both high-end media content and interactivity along with the customization of content that speaks to a specific user. Apps have become increasingly successful based not only on their entertainment value but also on their 'branded utility' – namely, using the technology and creativity available for the brand to create a 'promotional service' (Clarke 2010: 105). For example, Barclaycard's Waterslide Extreme game, produced by Dare, has amassed a stagger-ing 12 million plus downloads, while in 2011 AKQA won a gold Cyber Lion for its Heineken Star Player app, which allowed Union of European Football Asso-ciations (UEFA) Champions League fans to interact in real time and predict when goals would be scored, thus returning to the app, and the brand, again and again (Levy 2011a: 17). A more utility-driven example is that of O2's Priority Moments app, which flagged up offers for the brand's 22 million customers from nearby retailers participating in the scheme. Created by R/GA London, the app detected money-off opportunities based on a user's location and then prompted them to download vouchers corresponding to a particular offer. The users then redeemed the virtual voucher in a participating outlet (*Campaign: The Annual* 2011: 41).

Finally, concluding this analysis of the immersion of social media into IMC, it is worth mentioning the advertising potential of Twitter. Twitter is based on the premise that the international capacity for text messages is 160 characters, so it was created to fit a 140-character plus a username in the space of a text so that people could Tweet via SMS. Tony Wang, the general manager of Twitter UK, distin-guishes Twitter from Facebook, where Twitter is 'an information network that goes beyond social since, unlike a traditional social network, it does not depend on mutual relationships' (Levy 2011b: 12). In terms of how advertising might benefit from this, he adds: 'Brands are not intruding on social conversations, because it is natural for them to exist in a space where people are there primarily to stay informed' (Levy 2011b: 12). In this context, Twitter advertises via Promoted Tweets, Promoted Trends and Promoted Accounts, allowing a brand to be more visible to a consumer by ensuring that it is at the top of their timeline, the trend feed or recommendations regarding whom one should follow. So, for example, the Promoted Tweets ensure that someone who follows Starbucks will know that they have a particular 'happy hour' offer on their Frappuccino's in June. Paid-for Tweets are positioned at the top of search pages and labelled as 'promoted'. In contrast, Promoted Trends enable advertisers to tap into trending topics, whilst Promoted Accounts suggest who else to follow based on current preferences.

Brands and branding

'If identity is the idea that marks the twenty-first century, then branding operates at its point of delivery' (Olins 2008: 18). For Olins, branding is about design; it is a marketing communications and human resources tool and, he argues, it should inform and influence every part of an organization or company. In practice, brands take up consciousness space, allowing us to encode things in the memory, facilitating and functioning as shortcuts to meaning-making and, indeed, decision-making when choice is required. For branding to function effectively, the brand message must be decoded consistently in relation to every consumer touch point through which it is accessed: on a t-shirt, billboard, at a festival or in a store. But brands will only become successful if based on a good product; brands do not succeed based on image alone. Branding is now an intrinsic part of promotional culture and can be employed effectively if the goal is to engender brand loyalty through the development of long-term emotional connections affiliated to lifestyle construction, documented in the previous chapter, via the mental associations triggered when coming into contact with the brand in question. Brand value, therefore, comes from the success of these intangible qualities that function as an aura around the product, offering an experience that the consumer is prepared to pay more for in order to become a part of something that extends beyond the point of sale. Consequently, Arvidsson (2006: 7) argues, brands must strive to develop the alchemy to turn the affect generated by brand involvement into maximum financial value – namely to enhance opportunities to generate 'immaterial capital'. This can be achieved through a brand management strategy that seeks to build relationships with consumers where brand managers study what consumers do with the brand and, in particular, how it makes them feel, and then embed that back within their communication about the brand (Arvidsson 2006: 68).

Therefore, when it is so incredibly difficult to gain competitive advantage on the basis of a superior product alone, point of difference must rely on the intangible dimensions of any brand that sets it apart from its competitors. Over the years, one brand that has achieved this successfully through advertising is MasterCard and its 'Priceless' campaign. The advertising to support this credit card refuses to allow the consumer to drown in the detail and instead focuses on softer values, painting identifiable lifestyle snapshots all framed in the context of MasterCard allowing you to engage in enriching experiences with strong emotional attachments which are 'Priceless'. Such an approach is also conducive to MasterCard as a global brand: 'Priceless' experiences can be tweaked for each indigenous target market where the ad is screened. Therefore, in tapping into a central theme of this book, as technology and communication become integrated within people's everyday lives, so brands must take advantage of new ways to access consumers that bring discerning advantages to those who choose to engage through experiences which are authentic, valuable and tailored to the consumers' needs. The brands with the most compelling content will gain competitive advantage.

Therefore, in order to leverage brand value and provide a benchmark of sustainable growth to shareholders, brands must seek to develop a loyal customer base. This is nothing new and was a fundamental goal in advertising's contribution to brand development. However, convergence culture allows for more dynamic sets of relationships to flourish online, with the brand providing a locus for conversations to be carried out between consumers and the brands, and between consumers around the brand online. Furthermore, from a research perspective, the conversations people have about brands will enhance focus group findings, allow for problems to be stymied early on and creativity to flourish out of the stories being told. However, it is critical that these conversations are followed in real time. In terms of the specific nature of these online relationships, they are engendered by the brand with the aim of bringing consumers together who will then talk directly to the brand and/or with each other about the brand. The constitution of these groups can be 'very formal and structured' or they can be 'informal and loose' (Veloutsou 2009: 128). In the same vein that Bauman (1990, 1992), Maffesoli (1996) and Thompson (1998) identified social groupings based around the premise of neo-tribes 'marked by their fluidity: they are locally condensed and dispersed, periodically assembled and scattered' (Lury 2011: 202), so by extension the brand must work hard to retain the interest of these online equivalents. It is worth the brand investing its efforts here, for while such relationships might be 'fragile, ephemeral and unstable', when actually bought into 'they command intense emotional or affective involvement from their fickle members' (Lury 2011: 202). Indeed, if successfully managed, allegiances are maintained for as long as the brand remains both interesting and relevant.

As Veloutsou (2009: 129) documents, the relationships people have with brands 'depend on certain characteristics of both market segments and product features, and that relationships are more likely to exist with high involvement products characterised by inelastic demand, with which customers have regular interaction'. The success that Harley Davidson have had in generating a highly durable brand community which in itself has reinforced a particular identity for both the consumer and the brand is testament to the potential achievement of this strategy. However, interestingly, this then returns us to the issue of empowerment, for in gaining a more participative brand community we witness a shift in the brand sphere from that of 'brand manager' to that of 'brand host' (Christodoulides 2009: 141). Christodoulides (2009) effectively documents this change in positioning *vis-à-vis* the brand and its users in the context of the evolving nature of online promotion since the introduction of Web 2.0. Early online marketing in essence replicated the 'push' strategies employed in traditional above-the-line mass media. The turn towards greater degrees of participation and interaction online now enables the facilitation of conversations around the brand. This has the potential to reach the point where the constructed networked market knows more about a company's products than the company itself as people come together to exchange their 'consumption related experiences' (Christodoulides 2009: 143). While this can facilitate the brand, it can also make transparent any defect in the product (www.ipodsdirtysecrect.com) or highlight poor aspects of customer service. This peer-to-peer communication (P2P) therefore enhances the reach and speed at which good and bad information can travel.

The role of the promotional industries, therefore, is to create and maintain an image for the brand and the connotations embedded should not only enable immediate identification but, through its sign-value, the brand should also generate affect as we recognize, or not, the ability of that brand to affect our lives in some way. As Hegarty (2011: 42) argues: 'in reality a brand only ever exists in the minds of consumers', for in a media-saturated economy, the signifier floats free and becomes loaded with possibilities which the consumer identifies with in accordance with the particular lifestyle templates that they have adopted. As brand communication embraces social media, so there will emerge a discernible shift in our understanding of creativity, one that focuses on social creativity and the quest to produce inspiring social content that sets conversations in motion. Instead of positioning the 'big idea' at the heart of campaign planning, social media as promotion requires a revised approach, one that is driven by what is happening in real time and, as a consequence, produces a very different dynamic and temporal register to traditional above-the-line campaigns, informed by both a heightened sensitivity to the zeitgeist and how to capitalize on this before the brand's currency wanes.

Public relations

The impact of social media on promotional culture is epitomized by the changing nature of the PR industry. Public relations centres on the exchange of information via a communications strategy: management wishing to send out a message about an organization and to receive information from stakeholders in terms of how they perceive that organization. Such communications 'seek to enhance or consolidate reputation, which can be seen as the basis of trust. Indeed, some regard "reputation management" as a useful explanation of PR' (Phillips and Young 2011: 4). However, Phillips and Young (2011) suggest that this is perhaps too simplistic a definition and propose 'relationship optimisation' as an alternative in that it suggests a more organic approach to what PR does, where the next step taken is always 'predicated on responses and reactions'. In the digital age, it is critical for practitioners to be able to understand how information is circulated and exchanged and then to influence these circuits accordingly. As noted throughout this chapter, this allows for a more mature response in understanding the changing relationships between businesses and their customers: no longer is the company the 'gatekeepers of information' (Phillips and Young 2011: 6). Rather, social media allows conversations to take place over which the company has no control; indeed, the company can be left out in the cold. PR enables the company to reposition itself at the heart of such online conversations and at the same time add value through the provision of additional branded content factoring in the platforms used, the channels employed to access information and the context in which all of this is happening, temporally and spatially. That is to say, depending upon the device used at the point of consumption, the receiver will interpret the message accordingly, taking into consideration that attention levels are never consistent. In this context 'what convergence means to PR people is that it affects the way people use the internet. It means that more information is available on a wider range of devices and platforms and that messages are no longer constrained by the media they were designed for' (Phillips and Young 2011: 113). A press release can be published by a newspaper; go on the client website; be viewed on a tablet. How, when and where people access information is critical information for PR to embrace.

PR differs from the other promotional methods considered here in that it functions to set agendas, address perceptions and drive conversation. Unlike advertising, PR does not pay traditional above-the-line media for the media exposure that it secures. Public relations professionals use many techniques to achieve these aims, from media relations and lobbying to sponsorship and viral campaigns. In this context, depending upon the client's needs, a campaign might be short lived in the context of perhaps a product launch, or may have longer-term strategic aims, such as raising a brand's profile within a particular product category. For example, in 2010 PR agency Threepipe was appointed by Rachel's, the leading brand of organic yogurt and chilled dairy products in the UK, to 'create an on-going, proactive campaign to deliver brand and product coverage in consumer lifestyle, national and "foodie" media to reach an ABC1 35–55 year old, primarily, audience' (www.prca.org.uk.). In line with the brief, the agency established the following objectives:

- Create quality editorial coverage within consumer lifestyle, food and national media.
- Maximize consumer awareness of new product development and limited edition flavours.
- Communicate the brand's messages of superior taste and quality.
- Improve the brand's presence within the trade media to support the sales process.
- Support Rachel's in achieving overall growth of 10 per cent in 2010.

Threepipe put in place an integrated PR and social media campaign to achieve these objectives that included:

- *Product PR:* a programme of desk visits to over 50 key media contacts was established to present new Rachel's products as they were released. This face-to-face contact was crucial in building relationships, communicating the key messages and, most importantly, encouraging journalists to try each new flavour.
- *Facebook:* in collaboration with the client, a Rachel's Facebook page was created. By focusing the content on foodie topics and by offering recipes and rewards as well as product and brand news, a highly engaged and growing fan community was created.
- *Bloggers:* 'Foodie' bloggers were identified and kept informed of brand developments to generate buzz about the new launches.

In terms of editorial coverage, 400 separate pieces were delivered in 2010, including:

- 172 in consumer/lifestyle media;
- 14 in national media;

- 69 in specialist and trade media;
- 107 in regional media;
- 38 blogs.

Finally, in terms of rolling out a campaign that did not use any advertising:

- In 2010, Rachel's became the fastest growing established supplier in their category, with 23.8 per cent year-on-year growth.
- Its share of the market increased from 21.9 per cent in 2009 to 30 per cent in early 2011.
- A total of £6.25 million of value added to the brand was generated in 2010.
- The media coverage achieved a cumulative reach of over 240 million at a cost per thousand of just £0.25.

If PR is to function effectively as a brand advocate, then the nature of the industry needs to change as consumers forge different opinions about brands and respond to them in different ways. Francis Ingham, chief executive of the Public Relations Consultants Association (PRCA), argues that:

> PR is all about reputation. It is the result of what you do, what you say and what others say about you. It is used to gain trust and understanding between an organisation and its various publics – whether employees, customers, investors, or the local community – or a combination of those stakeholder groups.
>
> *(Ingham 2009: 7)*

In essence, he continues, it is about relationship-building and therefore has the key words of 'engagement' and 'conversation' at the heart of its strategy (Ingham 2009: 7). And this remains constant within the context of media convergence; what has changed is 'the mass-adoption of the internet. The number of people saying things about you has changed, as has the ease with which they can say it and the number of people to whom they can say it' (Ingham 2009: 7).

While it was earlier noted how difficult it is for PR agencies to control what is being said about their clients in the digital era, this can also enhance PR activity, providing agencies with a real-time steer regarding key themes and issues as they arise. In this context, the Internet delivers two positive functions for PR: it allows PR to map and evaluate its effectiveness more easily due to the increase in transparency of conversations, coupled with the way in which such transparency leads to the more effective building of trust – for example, between a consumer and a brand. This element of trust can be critical in terms of consumer decision-making, as argued in the previous chapter by Lewis and Bridger (2001). To build such a relationship, Lewis and Bridger argue, brands must be honest, truthful and add value to the consumer's life. PR can facilitate in the execution of all three elements by tapping into what consumers actually want from brands and how they feel and think about them, via the conversations they are already having about them. PR is therefore effectively positioned to manage these relationships through new media by developing a dialogue on a one-to-one basis through the creation of stories and the building of narratives. Indeed, the story, rather than the medium, must come first, as articulated by James Warren who believes in 'inline communications' – that is to say, 'those planned and executed in such a way that an organisation's story is told simultaneously and seamlessly through digital and traditional channels. The story, not the communications channel, must always remain at the heart of every campaign' (Warren 2009: 17).

Digital offers up the potential for these stories to be passed on virally. One example of a story to be told is PR agency Porter Novelli and their work for Boris Bikes, sponsored by Barclays. This was more than simply generating column inches about access to hire bicycles across the capital: rather, it was about turning Londoners into brand advocates for the scheme. Another US example was generated by Weber Shandwick as part of the publicity campaign behind the refurbishment of KFC's 14,000 restaurants in 80 countries. The task was how to get young people talking about the rebrand. The agency worked with technical experts to build a massive logo featuring the Colonel's face in the Nevada desert, making KFC the first brand logo visible from space. As a result, 'amazing images of the Face from space were picked up by media and reached billions as thousands of

FIGURE 2.1 Boris Bikes sponsored by Barclays
Source: Helen Powell

bloggers asked "have you seen this?" The result: on launch day KFC's sales increased globally' (http://weber shandwick.co.uk/#!/work/j_r/kfc_face+from_-space).

In conclusion, Stuart Wilson, writing as CEO of MS&L in 2008, argued that 'much of the challenge for today's PR practitioner lies in the convergence of many marketing disciplines. Only people with a strong marketing knowledge, and more importantly, collaborative skills will make a difference' (Wilson 2008: 21). In this statement he firmly positions PR activity at the heart of IMC. Yet, while this is a noted strength, being at the heart of the communication strategy, it can also be its potential Achilles heel as PR needs to prove its point of difference from other promotional industries, especially advertising. These points of difference come through in the ways in which people relate to the output of PR differently from that of advertising. As the director of PR agency Shine argues: 'studies have shown that consumers see editorial coverage as far more credible than advertising and it achieves higher recall, thereby deepening relationships' (Brett 2010: 17).

Bibliography

Ahmed, A. (2012) 'Status Update: I Am Very Rich (But Not Quite as Rich as I Was a Few Hours Ago)', *The Times*, Saturday 19 May, p3.

Anderson, C. (2010) *Free: How Today's Smartest Businesses Profit by Giving Something for Nothing*, London: Random House.

Arvidsson, A. (2006) *Brands: Meaning and Value in Media Culture*, London: Routledge.

Augé, M. (2009) *Non-Places: Introduction to an Anthropology of Supermodernity*, London: Verso.

Bashford, S. (2010) *Fluid: PHD on Harnessing the Rising Speed of Influence*, 'Foreword: Mike Cooper', London: PHD.

Bauman, Z. (1990) *Thinking Sociologically*, Oxford: Blackwell.

——(1992) *Intimations of Postmodernity*, London: Routledge.

Brett, R. (2010) 'At the Heart of the Action', PR Essays, *Marketing*, 13 October, p17.

Campaign: The Annual (2011) 'Top 10 Apps', 16 December, p41.

Campaign (2012) 'Is Advertising on Mobile Social Media Effective?', 13 July, p25.

Cardoso, G. (2011) 'From Mass to Networked Communication', in S. Papathanassopoulos (ed) *Media Perspectives for the 21st Century*, Abingdon, UK: Routledge.

Christodoulides, G. (2009) 'Branding in the Post-Internet Era', *Marketing Theory*, vol 9, no 1, pp141–144.

Clarke, C. (2010) 'Your Brand Is an Ape', in D. Fiandaca and P. Burgoyne (eds) *Digital Advertising: Past, Present, Future*, London: Creative Social.

Foley, S. (2012) 'Facebook Investors Sued for "Defrauding Investors"', *i*, 24 May, p43.

Gardner, D. (2012) 'Facebook's Zuckerberg Saved £111m Cashing in Shares Early', *Evening Standard*, 24 May, p8.

Goldhaber, M. (1997) 'The Attention Economy and the Net', *First Monday*, vol 2, no 4, 7 April, http://firstmonday.org/article/view/519/440.

Hegarty, J. (2011) *Hegarty on Advertising*, London: Thames & Hudson.

HHCL and Partners (2000) *Marketing at a Point of Change*, 4th edition, London: HHCL and Partners.

Ingham, F. (2009) 'The Future's Bright', PR Essays, *Marketing*, 14 October, p7.

Knights, M. (2012) 'Bricks and Mortar, Bits and Bytes', in *The Future of Retail*, Raconteur Media, 28 February, p4 (distributed by *The Times*).

Levy, K. (2011a) 'Should Brands Be Investing in Apps?', *Campaign*, 19 August, p17.

——(2011b) 'Twitter Ready To Step Up the Courtship of Advertisers', *Campaign*, 28 October, p12.

Lewis, D. and Bridger, D. (2001) *The Soul of the New Consumer*, London: Nicholas Brealey Publishing.

Lockhorn, J. (2012) 'Forget Mobile: Think Multiscreen', *Razorfish Outlook Report*, vol 10, http://razorfish.com/articles/forgetmobile.aspx, accessed 10 May 2012.

Lury, C. (2011) *Consumer Culture*, 2nd edition, Cambridge: Polity Press.

Maffesoli, M. (1996) *The Time of the Tribes*, London: Sage.

McAllister, M. P. (2011) 'Consumer Culture and New Media: Commodity Fetishism in the Digital Era', in S. Papathanassopoulos (ed) *Media Perspectives for the 21st century*, London: Routledge.

Mendelsohn, N. (2011) 'The Mad Men We Love To Hate: Our Changing Relationship with Advertising', *RSA Lecture*, 8 July, accessed via iTunes podcast.

Olins, W. (2008) *The Brand Handbook*, London: Thames & Hudson.

Packard, V. (1957/1962) *The Hidden Persuaders*, London: Pelican.

Phillips, D. and Young, P. (2011) *Online Public Relations: A Practical Guide To Developing an Online Strategy in the World of Social Media*, 2nd edition, London: Kogan Page.

Pine, B. J. and Gilmore, J. H. (1999) *The Experience Economy: Work Is Theatre & Every Business a Stage*, Boston, MA: Harvard Business School Press.

Sheehan, K. B. and Morrison, D. K. (2009) 'Beyond Convergence: Confluence Culture and the Role of the Advertising Agency in a Changing World', *First Monday*, vol 14, no 3, 2 March, http://firstmonday.org/htbin/cgiwrap/bin/ojs/index.php/fm/article/view/2239/2121.

Spanier, G. (2012) 'Mobile app clients help Saatchi profits double', i, 21 March, p. 41.

Springer, P. (2009) *Ads to Icons: How Advertising Succeeds in a Multimedia Age*, London: Kogan Page.

Tansey, B. (2012) 'Facebook's Deal with Instagram Is a Gift to Marketers', *Campaign*, 27 April, p16.

The Money Programme (2012) 'Inside Facebook: Zuckerberg's $10 Billion Gamble', BBC 2, 14 May.

Thompson, C. (1998) 'Living the Texts of Everyday Life', in B. B. Stern (ed) *Representing Consumers: Voices, Views and Visions*, London: Routledge.

Universal McCann (2011) 'Wave.5: The Socialisation of Brands', *Social Media Tracker, 2010*, http:www.slideshare.net/Olivier.mermat/universal-mccann-wave-5-the-socialisation-of-brands, accessed 25 July 2012.

Veloutsou, C. (2009) 'Brands as Relationship Facilitators in Consumer Markets', *Marketing Theory*, vol 9, no 1, pp127–130.

Warren, J. (2009) 'Advocacy Comes First', in PR Essays, *Marketing*, 14 October, p17.

Wilson, S. (2008) 'Leading Integrated Teams', in *PR Week* supplement: 'The Future of the PR Agency', October, p21.

Woods, J. (2012) 'Adland Must Police Itself as the Digital Revolution Rolls On', *Campaign*, 4 May, p13.

3

FROM INTEGRATION TO CONVERGENCE

The Management of Marketing Communications in Promotional Culture

Chris Hackley and Rungpaka Amy Hackley née Tiwsakul

Introduction

This chapter will explore the implications of convergence for the management of marketing communications. Marketing communications is a catch-all term common in managerial literature, embracing the entire scope of mediated promotional communication. The term suits our purpose here since we are looking at the implications for managers, consumers and society of convergence between media channels, which, driven by technology, constitutes not only an increase in the reach of marketing as a sales tool, but also an increase in its scope as a form of social communication (Leiss et al 2005). As social communication, advertising and promotion are far from neutral and have promotional intent encoded within them (Kelly et al 2005) at many levels. In addition, the genres, grammar and syntax of promotional culture have become embedded in many wider discourses as carriers of market ideology into many domains of public and private life (Hackley 2001a, 2003a, 2009a; Mautner 2010). In a convergent media era, this broadening influence of the language and genres of the market amounts to a consolidation and extension of Wernick's (1991) 'promotional culture'. The chapter will review research issues in the management of integrated marketing communications before concluding with a focus on the practical aspects of two key domains which lie at the heart of promotional culture: advertising and product placement.

The social communication of marketing and media convergence

The focus in this chapter on the management of marketing communications is not only important for understanding the effect of convergence on work processes, but also for understanding its cultural implications. Many cultural analyses of advertising have paid no attention to the material practices of the field; but these are important (Cronin 2004; McFall 2004). Theorists have made various claims about the cultural meaning and import of particular advertising campaigns, creative executions and branding strategies, without necessarily taking account of how these evolved and in what ways technological, managerial, regulatory and other influences framed and shaped the creative content that was eventually produced and consumed. Marketing communications are often conceived of as causes of social events, such as identity crises, greed, consumerism, eating disorders, racial stereotyping, or sales increases, and so on. When one understands how marketing communication campaigns evolve, it becomes clear that they too must be understood as complex cultural constructions, and not simply as autonomous causal influences. It may be tempting to blame the Mad Men for the social ills of rampant consumerism, but it isn't entirely fair. For example, John Webster, renowned creative at London agency Boase Massimi Pollitt, was the first to sell alcohol using imagery previously only seen in pre-school children's TV (Hackley 2010a). His Hofmeister Bear character[1] took the UK by storm in the mid-1980s, decimating sales of traditional dark British beer in favour of continental lager beer. The ads also pioneered a change in the tone of alcohol marketing as it became far more youth oriented, colourful and frivolous. Today, those who were toddlers when they first saw Webster's ads are contributing to an unprecedented spike in early onset alcoholic liver disease. Consideration of the causes of this cultural and epidemiological phenomenon must include, but cannot be confined to, alcohol advertising and marketing (Szmigin et al 2011; Hackley et al 2012a).

Marketing is invariably inflected by communication (Hackley 2010a) and, in many respects, is inseparable from it. The operations of supply chain management, production and distribution may be fundamental aspects of the marketing process but they are largely unseen by end consumers. Communication may be the tip of the marketing iceberg in a sense, but its role in branding cannot be underestimated. Self-evidently, for consumers, the brand is little more than the sum of its communications. Not only is communication central to brand marketing, but marketing language and values have crossed into the communication and media industries, to the extent that media channels (such as Channel 4, or BBC 1) and media vehicles (*Dr Who*, *X Factor*) are now treated as brands, to be marketed in their own right (Hackley et al 2012b). This reflects another aspect of media convergence. It isn't simply about the creation of new software platforms and hardware for transmitting multiple channels of content on mobile media. It also reflects a political economy in which lateral mergers in the media industry, changing media business models, and the domination of a neoliberal ideology are infusing mediated communication with the values and norms of the market. Marketing and media have a symbiotic relationship, so that much mediated communication assumes a promotional character, constituting an ideologically integrated promotional culture (Wernick 1991; MacRury 2008). Technological convergence acts to reflect and amplify this effect.

The following sections describe marketing communication's evolution as a discipline straddling academic and practitioner worlds by outlining some of the main streams of research in the field, while also discussing the role of advertising in marketing. The relationship between marketing and communication is elaborated upon in the context of a shift from a largely theoretical ideal of strategic integrated marketing communications (IMC) (Schultz et al 1993; Shimp 2010) towards a reactive and pragmatic managerial approach to technology-driven media convergence. In other words, media convergence, along with changes in media production and consumption patterns, may have overtaken IMC to make the use of multiple media channels in promotional campaign planning a default position, rather than a special case for marketing communications management. The chapter then goes on to discuss the implications of the new media landscape for campaign planning and content creation. Finally, the chapter discusses advertising management and product placement, the latter as a prime example of the way in which convergence is playing out in the entertainment economy (Wolf 1999).

The development of marketing and advertising studies

Marketing has a 100-year history of university teaching and research, and yet there remain sharp disagreements in the academic literature about its rightful empirical scope and theoretical orientation (Morgan 1992; Marion 2006; Tadajewski 2008; Tadajewski and Brownlie 2008). Research and thinking in marketing management is often divided along arts versus science lines (see, for example, Belk 1986; Brown 1996, 1997, 1999). Advertising, conceived as a sub-discipline of marketing communication in the managerial literature,[2] is divided along similar lines. Within advertising agencies there is a persistent tension between the creative and the scientific ways of conceiving advertising and its effects (Hackley 2000, 2001b; Hackley and Kover 2007). There have been attempts to manage this tension, for example, by instituting the account planning discipline during the 1960s (e.g., Hackley 2003b), but it has never been resolved.

Marketing studies began as an outgrowth of microeconomics and were concerned with the analysis of market efficiency, with the goal of creating and refining demand management interventions for organizations (Hackley 2009b). The discipline challenged the central assumption of microeconomics – namely, that consumers are uniformly motivated by product utility. Instead, it examined the scope of heterogeneous consumer motivation (Alderson 1957) and choice, and its role in driving demand. Although marketing studies rejected the key assumption that still holds in economics about consumer rationality being driven by what economists call utility (the evaluation of consumer goods in terms of practical value), the nascent discipline initially had a leaning towards positive and historical analysis. Marketing studies did not take on until the 1960s the normative ideological tone with which it is widely associated today. Under the influence of the boom in management studies and the growth of the university business school, managerial marketing studies started to become the commodified product it is today, its stylized genre of how-to texts (originally, Kotler 1967) fuelling a vast industry of mass-selling vocational management books, consulting contracts and lucrative university courses (Hackley 2003b).

Marketing studies and communication

Communication (broadly, advertising of one form or another) has an uneasy role in the evolution of marketing studies (Hackley 2010b). As one element of marketing's most ubiquitous acronym, the notorious 4 Ps of price, product, promotion and physical distribution (McCarthy 1981), communication was relegated to a minor role in the managerial marketing scheme. It was conceived as an afterthought, serving the strategy by communicating the offer. The model of communication dominating marketing studies was, and remains, the engineering transmission model (Larzarsfeld 1941; Lasswell 1948; Schramm 1948; Shannon 1948). It dovetailed superficially (Hackley 2010b) with a group of theories known as 'hierarchy of effects' (Barry and Howard 1990), of which the best known is the Attention, Interest, Desire, Action (A-I-D-A) model of persuasive communication (Kitson 1921; Strong 1929). A-I-D-A began life as a theory of personal selling before it was seamlessly mapped on to mediated advertising without anyone apparently commenting on the lack of fit. The simplistic notion that advertising 'works' by gradually eroding the resistance of a passive consumer by the force and quantity of a univocal message with a rational appeal still implicitly and explicitly underpins much research and practice in the area.

Communication is conceived as the final step in the marketing process, communicating the offer to consumers to cause a sales response. Typical marketing text books have little to say about the constitutive role of creative marketing communication in the cultural construction of brand values and choice, taste and identity (Hackley 2003a). In spite of the history of marketing studies as a dissenting tradition of thought, the rational, literal and utility-driven consumer of microeconomics still hovers like a phantom over the field (Cook and Kover 1998) in spite of penetrating critiques of the inadequacy of communication theory in advertising (e.g., Stern 1993a; Heath and Feldwick 2008).

The dominance of the machine model of communication in managerially oriented marketing texts notwithstanding, there are pockets of research falling outside the mainstream which reflect the complexity of marketing communication as a form of discourse (Cook 2002). Advertisements refer to discourse forms beyond the commercial world (O'Donohoe 1997), drawing on imagery, narrative styles, genres and techniques from art, aesthetics, movies, television and pop culture, literature, sport, politics and street subcultures and so on. Advertising agencies play a role of 'cultural intermediary' (Hackley 2002; Cronin 2004) tacking between the cultural and commercial worlds to invest marketed brands with symbolic values (Levy 1959). These symbolic values reflecting social status and group membership drive brands by offering consumers a means of symbolically pursuing identity projects. This hybrid character of promotional communication as a combination of the commercial and the cultural has stimulated cross- and multidisciplinary research drawing on, for example, semiotics, linguistics, mass communications, cognitive science and social psychology, information processing and artificial intelligence, cultural anthropology and ethnography, sociology and literary theory, among others (see, for example, Sherry 1987; Scott 1990, 1994; Mick and Buhl 1992; Stern 1993b; Tanaka 1994; Blake et al 1996; Ritson and Elliott 1999; deWaal Malefyt and Moeran 2003). Such a wide conceptual scope is necessary because advertising has implications which are hugely significant for the economy but which also impact upon the personal, cultural, ethical, legal and regulatory areas.

Advertising and its origins

It can be helpful to understand something of the evolution of marketing communications in order to place today's issues in some historical context. Advertising began with classified announcements in the press in the early days of printing, in the UK, during the 1600s. Street advertising was also common at this time, and all manner of bizarre promotional posters and sandwich boards would be paraded through London's streets, to the displeasure of many citizens. Advertising agencies began as space brokers, selling the classified advertising space to business clients. Over time, the agencies developed a good understanding of the media available and the needs of consumers and clients, and began to make use of this unique cross-industry vantage point to offer strategic advice. They tried to match clients with publications and soon established skills in artwork, typography and printing to enable the quality of the advertisements to match that of the publications. In the early years of the industry all tasks in the agency were performed by the same person: the division of labour between account planning, market and consumer research, media buying, creative/copywriting and art production came much later (Hackley 2010a).

Printing and communications technology developed over time to allow more flexibility in creative executions. As early as the 1800s, Victorian entrepreneurs in the UK such as Thomas Holloway were placing billboards in China. Holloway and his contemporaries in the pottery industry, such as William Boulton, were also pioneers in product placement since they were acutely aware of the prestigious effect of having their products placed in royal portraits, books and London stage plays (Hackley 2005; Quickenden and Kover 2007). By the twentieth century, advertising was beginning to develop into a profession, and attempts were made to draw on early psychological theory to institute methods of advertising practice. American copywriter John E. Kennedy (1904) is credited with one of the earliest attempts to formalize advertising craft with his frequently repeated assertion that advertising is 'salesmanship in print'. Kennedy later conceived of 'reason why' advertising, which advocated persuasive logic in copywriting. The copywriter's art, according to Kennedy, was to give concrete reasons for the consumer to buy, in easy-to-understand terms, which made sense for the consumer (Fox 1984). Several decades later 'reason why' was reborn as the *Unique Selling Proposition* by Rosser Reeves (McDonald and Scott 2007).

By the 1960s, the era of the Mad Men had arrived and, with it, the 'creative revolution'. American advertising man Bill Bernbach is often credited with pioneering the new creativity, especially with his iconic use of ironic self-deprecation in campaigns for Volkswagen. Ideas such as Bernbach's creativity, David Ogilvy's 'brand personality' and Leo Burnett's use of dramatic realism revolutionized advertising creativity by linking it graphically with lifestyle, identity and social status, and transformed advertising into a glamorous and lucrative creative industry aligned with movies and TV, rather than simply a business service. The creative revolution, though, failed to change the way in which advertising was conceived theoretically as a management practice. Most marketing and marketing communication textbooks today still repeat the mathematical transmission model of communication alongside the A-I-D-A model of persuasive advertising communication as the gold standard of advertising theory, some 80 years after the latter was first published.

The management of advertising

Advertising management embraces not only the management of advertising, but also the management of advertising agencies. It is difficult to delineate the styles of management of advertising agencies since what occurs in them can look like organized chaos. Suffice to say that most advertising agencies around the world use similar role titles, but the internal climate and working culture of different agencies can differ. Most agencies organize client work into account teams consisting of three main roles (Hackley 2000): account manager, account planner and creative. The account manager (also called account executive) has overall responsibility for keeping the client happy and coordinating the work. Then there is the account planner, a role not all agencies use, and those that do conceive of it differently. The account planner ensures that evidence-based facts, deriving from research, guide the development of advertising. This individual needs to have excellent research, communication and presentation skills (Hackley 2003b).

The account manager and, if the agency has one, account planner will write the creative brief. The creative brief is the key document of the advertising development process. It distils the information about the client marketing objectives, the research about the brand, the market and the target consumers into a form of words which are designed to motivate, inspire and also guide the third main role: the creatives. This role is described in the plural because, by common agreement, there are usually two creatives working as a team: often, but not necessarily, a words specialist and a visualization specialist. Copywriter is the term for an advertising professional who writes copy, but this was broadened as the development of print technology pushed images into the forefront of advertising. Today, many creative teams operate with interchangeable skills and can take charge of the visual or verbal aspects of an idea. Between them, these people create the advertising we all know and love.

In many respects, the work of ad agencies is more like that in other cultural industries, such as theatre production companies, orchestras or media companies, than it is like management in manufacturing, production or customer service delivery settings. Perhaps there is an analogy with professional services, though unlike universities or legal or medical practices, the raw materials that advertising agencies work with are not commonly shared laws or generally agreed bodies of knowledge: their raw material is culture, and their output is ideas. While many agencies look superficially similar in the way that they organize their work, they each carry their tasks out with differences of emphasis. Some might have a reputation for daring creativity, others for effectiveness in delivering communication solutions that sell product, others for specialist expertise in a particular sector such as retail advertising or TV. Most large advertising agencies work across international borders, raising complex issues of cross-cultural communication (Hackley and Tiwsakul 2008).

Given the managerial and social significance of advertising agencies, there is surprisingly little research which details exactly how campaigns emerge from what can often appear to be a serendipitous process (Cornellisen and Lock 2002). Agencies suffer from stereotyping, with the domineering account executive, the histrionic creative and the exasperated client featuring in many jokes. But in spite of their quirkiness, advertising agencies' contribution to the world of marketing is often understated. It is hard to conceive of the world's most powerful and well-known brands without advertising. Advertising has been central in the formation of what is sometimes known as consumer culture (Marchand 1985, 1998). In addition to advertising's contribution to economic growth, national competitiveness and brand marketing business, many advertisements have become iconic representations of particular cultural trends or social movements, talked about and even enjoyed as popular entertainment in TV shows and websites.

Yet, as McFall (2004) has pointed out, and we noted earlier in the chapter, much of the sociocultural research on advertising completely ignores the crucial but little-known practices of advertising, the things people in ad agencies do to create a campaign. Advertising campaigns are a collective achievement, and research such as Hackley (2000), Kelly et al (2005), Svensson (2007) and, more recently, McLeod et al (2009, 2011) are among relatively few empirical studies which have looked at the detail and interpersonal dynamics behind the advertising development process. A small number of others have taken a critical ethnographic approach to study the production of gender in ad agencies, examples being Alvesson (1998) and Cronin (2008).

Advertising agencies manage one thing above all else: creativity. Hackley and Kover (2007) note that creatives operate in a quite different *milieu* than the other roles. Their cultural reference points are drawn from art, aesthetics and popular culture (McLeod et al 2009, 2011), in contrast to those of the account managers and client marketing directors, who often have a quantitative research background from an MBA training. Creatives tend to feel politically disadvantaged in the power relations of ad agencies, even though it is they above all others who create the stuff the agencies sell, and they sometimes have to resort to devious strategies just to get their work respected and produced (Kover and Goldberg 1995). Both Hackley (2003c) and Kover (1995) note that many of the misunderstandings and conflicts in agency account teams arise because the respective account team personnel have fundamentally different ways of looking at the advertising world, but these differing mental models are invariably implicit rather than explicit. This can lead to fundamental conflicts and oppositions. The discipline of account planning was created during the 1960s with the aim of reducing internal conflict by mediating between creative and account management roles (Feldwick 2007).

So, advertising agencies sit at the hub of promotional culture, operating in the margin between business and art, translating symbols from prosaic culture into commerce in order to valorize brands and normalize consumption as a symbol of identity, group membership and social status. Much of the tradition and mythology of advertising agencies arose from a time when TV grew into the dominant medium and the big agencies were able to manoeuvre themselves into the position of gatekeepers to TV advertising. But the age of the Mad Men is long gone. The big ad agencies lost much of their power when their biggest assets, the media buying function and the market research function, both became so strong that they were hived off to become separate businesses in their own right, while other functions such as art production and TV production which were sometimes dealt with in-house were being sub-contracted to outside operators for reasons of cost. Just as the agencies were losing their genuine capability to deliver truly 'full service' solutions for clients, management academics came up with the idea of integrated marketing communications as a supposedly radical new approach in marketing communications management.

Integrated marketing communications and convergence

'Integrated marketing communications (IMC), referring broadly to the use by brands of multiple communication channels in coordinated campaigns, has been a presence in the managerial marketing communications research literature for two decades now (Schultz et al 1993). But what it means exactly and what it implies about management methods remains unclear. Practitioners have found it difficult to implement IMC for organizational, conceptual and practical reasons. The marketing communications disciplines, including advertising, public relations, sales promotion, direct marketing, media planning, direct sales, digital and out of home (OOH) still, by and large, maintain their separate professional associations and career structures. Some of the larger global advertising agencies have tried to bring more channel expertise in-house; but integrating the different worldviews into a single strategic plan is difficult. Conceptually, there is no viable theory for planning integrated campaigns. Even some of the most well-known exponents answer the question 'Why use IMC?' by listing reasons why organizations have not implemented it, rather than offering any theoretical reasons why they should (e.g., Shimp 2010: 8–9). The assumption, asserted without empirical or theoretical support, is that using more channels should improve the sales effect. On this basis the idea of IMC has generated a stream of largely pointless research publications in the managerial literature (e.g., Hackley and Kitchen 1998).

It would be inaccurate to represent IMC as a naive 'more is better' argument, although the ability to reach more target consumers with lots of channels rather than just one is certainly one aspect of its appeal. Intuitively, IMC might be conceived as an attempt to answer, or at least to ask the question, 'In what ways might the brand story be told so that the messages from different channels dovetail in a persuasive way?' However, this question concerns the design of creative content and therefore falls beyond the scope of managerial text books and research. Even psychological studies in advertising research have little substantive to say about the reinforcement effects of multiple channel exposure. There is simply no viable research that can measure the cross-media exposure effect with confidence. Intuitively, multiple channel communication might enhance reinforcement in a behavioural sense through repetition, and in so doing increase the possibility of consumer engagement. Obviously, media with instant response capability are more suited to generating consumer engagement, although a communication on any medium can reference a website. Conversely, using multiple media channels may lead to duplication and consumer attention fatigue, also known as boredom. A more practical issue is how can professionals get a creative execution that works well on TV to work as well on digital or outdoor? The technical problems, particularly with digital, can often be insurmountable.

Drivers of IMC

The impetus for IMC was partly driven by trends in media consumption and technological developments. Media audiences worldwide have fragmented, while the number of media vehicles has multiplied. It has become essential for brand marketing communication campaigns to use several media channels simply to reach an aggregate number of target consumers that makes the business model viable because a single above-the-line medium can no longer guarantee the necessary number of 'eyeballs'. For example, the top UK television shows reached audiences of 30 million during the 1970s. Today, the very top shows barely achieve 12 million. In the US, 100 million people still watch the Super Bowl, and its spot advertising slots are the most expensive in the world; but in all other genres the viewing audience has slumped. UK newspaper circulation similarly has fallen, as it has all over the world. Media audience fragmentation is easy to explain, given the rise in popularity of the Internet as an alternative source of information and entertainment. As a result, many major print publications, including long-established national newspapers, are struggling to cover their costs as spot advertising revenue falls, along with circulations. On the other hand, there has been rapid growth in the number of specialist print publications serving small readerships.

These publications get by on small circulations because digital printing has brought production costs down, so operations that can subsist with a tiny number of staff can be viable. Traditional national newspapers have huge overheads and massive staffing costs. Of the remaining national newspapers in the UK, for example, most run at a considerable loss (*The Sun*, *The Daily Mail* and *The Telegraph* are exceptions). Internet and mobile have been the fastest growing advertising markets for several years (Sharma et al 2008) and this trend is continuing, drawing an increasing proportion of advertising revenue away from mass media. The proliferation of research papers espousing the value of IMC in marketing communications journals may simply have been making a virtue out of a necessity.

'Media-neutral' planning

In the event, as IMC was becoming a cliché in the management literature, digital technology and audience fragmentation were already pushing marketing communications planning towards a multi-channel outlook. By the early 2000s, advertising agencies had started to claim a 'media-neutral' planning approach which sought to deliver solutions for clients that were not driven by preconceived ideas about a hierarchical communications mix with mass media advertising at the top. Instead, they claimed, their planning was based on pragmatic creativity which served the strategic needs of the brand client and treated media choice as a strategic decision and not a default resort to mass media advertising. Several notable campaigns had, sometime before, shown that mass media advertising need not sit at the apex of every major brand communications campaign, but out of home (OOH) campaigns, direct (mail or electronic) marketing, viral and even public relations were used successfully in leading campaigns which eschewed mass media advertising. The launch of the upmarket American ice cream brand Häagen-Dazs in the UK, for example, was famously led by public relations, with print advertising deployed eventually in a supporting role.

The fashion for media neutrality was part of a general blurring between the marketing communications disciplines. Agencies began to redefine their scope. Below-the-line specialists moved into above-the-line advertising from their direct mail and business-to-business roots. Media agencies have also encroached on the advertising agencies' turf, emboldened by the movement of media strategy into the centre of brand planning. The media agencies claim they know exactly who is reading/viewing/listening to what, and when. They also claim to understand how particular consumers engage with and consume specific media. Why shouldn't they hire a few creatives and make the ads too? For their part, more traditional advertising agencies are buying in specialist expertise in digital, print, viral, mobile and other disciplines to broaden their planning scope and make good their claim to be 'full service', whatever that may mean in today's confusingly demarcated media landscape. Media production is also normally bought in, even though some big agencies still house their own print and TV production facilities.

Blurring of the promotional mix hierarchy

With all this traffic moving between disciplinary boundaries, there is now greater career mobility between the channels for media and marketing communication professionals, but the traditional barriers are still not entirely eroded. Progress is slow because the different disciplines often speak a different language. The most obvious example is digital, and the digital planners now being hired by top advertising agencies often speak of their problems in educating other account team colleagues about what is or is not possible on digital media. They have an even more difficult problem in educating clients about the value of digital creativity. Traditionally, creative teams could be as adept in writing a radio or TV script as in designing a 16 sheet billboard, but the specialisms themselves are demanding increased technical knowledge – for example, with the increase in digital billboards, mobile applications or web page animations. A great idea is still a great idea, but difficulties with the translation of the creative idea across media channels have become a major problem with integration.

So, integrated marketing communications is far from being a new idea, although it has never quite gained the credibility with practitioners that it had with some academics. In contemporary marketing communications, technological forces and the changes in media consumption have changed the hierarchical order of the promotional mix. That is, the notion that mass media advertising must be the mainstay of a campaign with sales promotion, OOH, cinema, public relations and direct marketing in support has been upturned by the rise of digital communication and the shift in emphasis towards branded entertainment and away from interruptive advertising spots. Technological convergence is highlighting, heightening and facilitating the interdependence of marketing and media, ushered along by economic and behavioural changes. As software developers work towards platforms that will deliver mobile, television and Internet content on the same hardware, the marketing communications industry is struggling to keep up. Content and context need to develop in tandem.

Convergence in practice: Advertising and product placement

This chapter will conclude with two short case examples of how integration is being managed in the engine room of promotional culture.

The creative advertising development process in the digital era

The first example draws on a week (January 2012) that the author spent in a top five UK advertising agency, interviewing people from every discipline. The aim of the week was to update work begun a decade before (Hackley 2000) into the advertising development process. One aspect had not changed: in top agencies the development of advertising takes place through many hours of meetings, so the most valued skills are interpersonal and social skills. People working in the top agencies tend to come across as highly poised, with the emotional intelligence to easily create instant rapport. They could all talk very articulately and insightfully about their craft.

As expected, the way in which account teams are organized had changed to reflect the increased emphasis on media neutral planning and integration. Most importantly, a new role of digital planner had been created and this person was present in meetings throughout the creative development process, right from the initial client meeting. This is a clear attempt to bring digital thinking into the core of the creative advertising development process. But there remain problems. The digital planners complained that a big part of their job was internal education. They found it difficult to explain to other creative people how ideas might work, or not, on digital platforms. Nonetheless, the agency felt that it is important to bring digital in to the process rather than relying on external digital agencies to supply the digital creativity that many clients now expect to be provided as a part of the package. Many of the specialist digital agencies were now struggling, as they were employed to do mundane things such as maintain websites, instead of being asked to provide ground-breaking creative ideas. Digital technology is moving so quickly that several digital planners admitted that even they were finding it difficult to keep up with new developments.

This particular agency had its own print shop and TV production house; nevertheless, integrating cross-media campaigns was a far from simple task. The creatives could be asked to write radio scripts, design visuals and write TV scripts; indeed, they might have to turn their skills to any kind of advertising creativity. Their experience often helped in understanding what ideas might work on different media, but digital always presented a problem given the complexities of different digital platforms. The issues were not merely technical but also creative: what works in digital is not simply a technical question but also a matter of functionality, aesthetics and consumer engagement.

While integration had become the default position in advertising planning, it also seemed as if technology had changed the balance of power in account teams. The creative role seems to have lost some of its charisma, status and prestige. It remains the key role, since nothing can happen without creative input; but there is an oft-repeated claim that 'good ideas can come from anywhere', which inhibits any instinct creatives might have to act like prima donnas. Indeed, much of the discussion around ideas is concerned with practical or technical issues of how they might work through different platforms, rather than being concerned with the creation itself. The creativity in advertising can often be less original than it might appear given the number of times even major campaigns are seen to use ideas which first gained fame on YouTube. The growth of social media and video networking has democratized advertising creativity, perhaps making it more of a craft than an art. Integration, as we note, is the default position, and the task of the agency is to try to make sense of creativity across different media platforms. The idea of the advertising agency as a hub of cultural influence was, perhaps, somewhat exaggerated by some theorists. Advertising has always acted in tandem with other media in popular culture, synthesizing, amplifying and glamourizing images and behaviours that were already present in culture. Their role seems all the more derivative in the age of convergence. The key elements are technology and content, and advertising agencies are not in the lead in either area.

Product placement

Product placement might well be the key site of convergence for marketing communications, practically and conceptually. The practice of putting brands in entertainment vehicles is far from new, as we note above, and has been mentioned in modern broadcast media since silent movies (Hackley 2010a). Product placement can be broadly conceived as the presence of brands in any entertainment vehicle (Hackley 2003d; Tiwsakul et al 2005), including movies, TV shows, radio broadcasts, novels, stage plays and computer and video games. Product placement is a hybrid form of promotion (sometimes called entertainment marketing, brand placement or branded entertainment) since it combines elements of advertising, promotion, sponsorship and celebrity endorsement. For example, TV sports viewers are used to seeing sports stars wearing prominent branded clothing during post-match TV interviews. There is no payment made to the broadcaster: the star receives a fee for being sponsored by the brand and for wearing the item while competing.

In addition, the convergence of media is increasingly expanding the scope of product placement. For example, a TV show containing a sight or mention of a brand might be broadcast on many different channels worldwide, sold on DVDs or downloaded from video streaming websites, and clips of the show might well appear on video-sharing websites with potential audiences of many millions. The entertainment economy (Wolf 1999) is mobilized and articulated through media convergence, and the goal of product placement, to insert brands seamlessly into consumers' experience of mediated entertainment (Hackley and Tiwsakul 2006), is fully realized. What is more, viewers who want to find out more about a branded item they see in their entertainment can now purchase it almost instantly, either by using one of the many retail websites specializing in stocking products that have appeared on TV or in movies, or by viewing content on click-through enabled technology so they can click a cursor on the item to instantly go to a retail interface.

The latter development could be seen as a direct threat to the future of traditional, 'interruptive' spot advertising (Hackley 2010a). However, traditional advertising spots on TV have proved a robust form of promotion: they remain a powerful platform for gaining attention and generating engagement, provided they resonate with consumers. Younger entertainment consumers, in particular, though tend to be well disposed towards brands in entertainment because they add verisimilitude to the scene and also because viewers resent their entertainment being interrupted for commercial breaks, in spite of concerns about the ethics of product placement (Hackley et al 2008). Ethical concerns around marketing in general tend to focus on the apparently hidden or deceitful aspects of marketing techniques (Hackley 2007).

The interesting thing about product placement for our purpose in this chapter is that although it can be seen as an even more insidious and subtle form of ideological control than conventional advertising, the way in which it is organized lacks the planned, directed and unified character one might expect. For example, in the UK, about 12 product placement agencies handle the majority of brands seen in TV shows (Hackley and Hackley née Tiwsakul 2012). These agencies supply branded goods as scene props free of charge to the TV companies. The agencies take a retainer fee from the brand clients. The advantage for brand clients is that not only is the exposure very inexpensive, it is not publicized: the TV shows do not have to declare any branded content that is not paid for. Neither the clients nor the agencies have any direct control over how, when or where branded goods appear in a scene: the exposure they gain is completely serendipitous. However, the agencies can show that their clients' brands gain far more aggregate seconds of broadcast exposure than brands that have no agency representation. Many of these agencies also negotiate paid-for placements for their clients in movies.

Advertising agencies play no part in this: traditionally, product placement had been regarded as outside their remit. But the TV channels have recently (since 2011) been allowed by the media regulator Ofcom to sell paid-for brand exposure under strictly controlled conditions. Major channels, working closely with media agencies, have tried hard to build business in direct product placement sales to brand clients. However, this paid-for product placement market has not taken off in the UK in anything like the volume that was expected, partly because the regulations are so tight that the free prop supply system is easier, cheaper and more convenient for brand clients. Even in the US, which has a mature paid-for TV product placement market, some four out of five brands seen on TV are not contracted and paid for. They are there serendipitously because TV producers and directors need brands to make scenes realistic, and they need scene props. The huge volume of TV programming made each year means that there simply isn't the time to organize contracted placements for every brand in a scene. Most brand clients are quite happy for their brand to gain TV exposure, often regardless of the context.

So, the convergence era is enabling the subtle commercialization of mediated news, information and entertainment to an unprecedented degree. The controls and regulations over this are piecemeal and often contradictory. Yet, while it is hard to deny that Wernick's (1991) notion of a promotional culture is more salient than ever before in the convergence era, it is also important to note that analyses which posit consumers or media as passive tools of an ideological sphere of influence are one sided. Promotional culture in the convergence era has an amorphous and dialectical character: it influences and magnifies but also reflects. A close and frank examination of how advertising and other promotional domains are organized reveals conflicted and conflated interests, serendipity and accident. Any sensible analysis of media influence would also have to account for attempts to use media to shape public opinion and support certain (often hidden) interests, most obviously through news organizations. But, at the same time, cultural analyses which propose promotional culture as a unified influence *upon* non-commercial culture can benefit from a nuanced approach which acknowledges the chaos, accident and pragmatism of marketing organization.

Notes

1 A clip of one of Webster's famous Hofmeister Bear ads is here on YouTube, accessed 30 March 2012: http://www.youtube.com/watch?v=LkR0krOm9M4.
2 By 'managerial literature' I mean to refer to texts, courses and research which ostensibly support the aims, values and ends of organizational managers, in contrast to intellectual work which is pursued for its own sake as sociology, literary research, etc.

Bibliography

Alderson, W. (1957) *Marketing Behavior and Executive Action: A Functionalist Approach to Marketing*, Homewood, IL: Richard D. Irwin.
Alvesson, M. (1998) 'Gender Relations and Identity at Work: A Case Study of Masculinities and Femininities in an Advertising Agency', *Human Relations*, vol 51, no 8, pp969–1005.
Barry, T. E. and Howard, D. J. (1990) 'A Review and Critique of the Hierarchy of Effects in Advertising', *International Journal of Advertising*, vol 9, pp121–135.
Belk, R. (1986) 'Art Versus Science as Ways of Generating Knowledge About Materialism', in D. Brinberg and R. J. Lutz (eds) *Perspectives on Methodology in Consumer Research*, New York, NY: Springer-Verlag.
Blake, A., MacRury, I., Nava, M. and Richards, B. (eds) (1996) *Buy This Book: Studies in Advertising and Consumption*, London: Routledge.
Brown, S. (1996) 'Art or Science? Fifty Years of Marketing Debate', *Journal of Marketing Management*, vol 12, no 4, pp243–267.
——(1997) 'Marketing Science in a Postmodern World: Introduction to the Special Issue', *European Journal of Marketing*, vol 31, no 3–4, pp167–182.
——(1999) 'Marketing and Literature – the Anxiety of Academic Influence', *Journal of Marketing*, vol 63, no 1, pp1–15.
Cornelissen, J. P. and Lock, A. R. (2002) 'Advertising Research and Its Influence upon Managerial Practice: A Review of Perspectives and Approaches', *Journal of Advertising Research*, vol 42, no 3, pp50–55.
Cronin, A. (2004) 'Regimes of Mediation: Advertising Practitioners as Cultural Intermediaries?', *Consumption, Markets and Culture*, vol 7, no 4, pp349–369.
Cronin, A. M. (2008) 'Gender in the Making of Commercial Worlds: Creativity, Vitalism and the Practices of Marketing', *Feminist Theory*, vol 9, no 3, pp293–312.
Cook, G. (2002) *The Discourse of Advertising*, London: Routledge.
Cook, W. A. and Kover, A. J. (1998) 'Research and the Meaning of Advertising Effectiveness: Mutual Misunderstandings', in W. D. Wells (ed) *Measuring Advertising Effectiveness*, Hillsdale, NJ: Lawrence Erlbaum Associates.
Danesi, M. (2006) *Brands*, London and New York: Taylor and Francis/Routledge.
deWaal Malefyt, T. and Moeran, B. (2003) *Advertising Cultures*, London: Berg.
Feldwick, P. (2007) 'Account Planning: Its History and Significance for Ad Agencies', in G. Tellis and T. Ambler (eds) *The Sage Handbook of Advertising*, London: Sage.
Fox, S. (1984) *The Mirror Makers: A History of American Advertising and Its Creators*, New York, NY: William Morrow.
Hackley, C. (2000) 'Silent Running: Tacit, Discursive and Psychological Aspects of Management in a Top UK Advertising Agency', *British Journal of Management*, vol 11, no 3, pp239–254.

——(2001a) *Marketing and Social Construction: Exploring the Rhetorics of Managed Consumption*, London: Routledge.

——(2001b) 'Looking at Me, Looking at You: Qualitative Research and the Politics of Knowledge Representations in Advertising and Academia', *Qualitative Market Research: An International Journal*, vol 4, no 1, pp42–51.

——(2002) 'The Panoptic Role of Advertising Agencies in the Production of Consumer Culture', *Consumption, Markets and Culture*, vol 5, no 3, pp211–229.

——(2003a) '"We Are All Customers Now": Rhetorical Strategy and Ideological Control in Marketing Management Texts', *Journal of Management Studies*, vol 40, no 5, pp1325–1352.

——(2003b) 'Account Planning: Current Agency Perspectives on an Advertising Enigma', *Journal of Advertising Research*, vol 43, no 2, pp235–246.

——(2003c) 'How Divergent Beliefs Cause Account Team Conflict', *International Journal of Advertising*, vol 22, no 3, pp313–332.

——(2003d) 'IMC and Hollywood – What Brand Managers Need to Know', *Admap*, November, 44–47.

——(2005) *Advertising and Promotion: Communicating Brands*, London: Sage.

——(2007) 'Marketing Psychology and the Hidden Persuaders', *Psychologist*, vol 20, no 8, August, pp488–490, http://www.thepsychologist.org.uk/archive/archive_home.cfm/volumeID_20-editionID_150-ArticleID_1228-getfile_getPDF/thepsychologist%5C0807hack.pdf.

——(2009a) 'Parallel Universes and Disciplinary Space: The Bifurcation of Managerialism and Social Science in Marketing Studies', *Journal of Marketing Management*, vol 25, no 7–8, pp643–659.

——(2009b) *Marketing: A Critical Introduction*, London, Sage.

——(2010a) *Advertising and Promotion: An Integrated Marketing Communications Approach*, 2nd edition, London: Sage.

——(2010b) 'Theorizing Advertising: Managerial, Scientific and Cultural Approaches', in P. MacLaran, M. Saren, B. Stern and M. Tadajewski (eds) *The Sage Handbook of Marketing Theory*, London: Sage.

Hackley, C. and Hackley née Tiwsakul, R. A. (2012) 'Unpaid Product Placement: the Elephant in the Room in the UK's New Paid-for Product Placement Market', *International Journal of Advertising*, vol 31, no 4, pp703–18.

Hackley, C. and Kitchen, P. (1998) 'Integrated Marketing Communications (IMC): A Consumer Psychological Perspective', *Marketing Intelligence and Planning*, vol 16, no 3, pp229–235.

Hackley, C. and Kover, A. (2007) 'The Trouble with Creatives: Negotiating Creative Identity in Advertising Agencies', *International Journal of Advertising*, vol 26, no 1, pp63–78.

Hackley, C. and Tiwsakul, R. A. (2006) 'Entertainment Marketing and Experiential Consumption', *Journal of Marketing Communications*, vol 12, no 1, pp63–75.

——(2008) 'Comparative Management Practices in International Advertising Agencies in the UK, Thailand and the US', in C. Smith, B. McSweeney and R. Fitzgerland (eds) *Remaking Management: Between Global and Local*, Cambridge: Cambridge University Press.

Hackley, C., Bengry-Howell, A., Griffin, C., Mistral, W., Szmigin, I. and Hackley née Tiwsakul, R. A. (2012a) 'Young Adults and "Binge" Drinking: A Bakhtinian Analysis', *Journal of Marketing Management*, DOI: 10.1080/0267257X.2012.729074.

Hackley, C., Brown, S. and Hackley née Tiwsakul, R. (2012b) 'The *X Factor* Enigma: Simon Cowell and the Marketization of Existential Liminality', *Marketing Theory*, vol 12, no 4, pp451–69.

Heath, R. and Feldwick, P. (2008) '50 Years Using the Wrong Model of Advertising', *International Journal of Advertising*, vol 50, no 1, pp29–59.

Kelly, A., Lawlor, K. and O'Donohoe, S. (2005) 'Encoding Advertisements – the Creative Perspective', *Journal of Marketing Management*, vol 21, pp505–528.

Kennedy, J. E. (1924) *Reason Why Advertising Plus Intensive Advertising*, Indiana: TWI Press, Inc.

Kitson, H. D. (1921) *The Mind of the Buyer*, New York, NY: MacMillan.
Kover, A. J. (1995) 'Copywriters' Implicit Theories of Communication: An Exploration', *Journal of Consumer Research*, vol 21, no 4, pp596–611.
——(1996) '*Why* Copywriters Don't Like Advertising Research – *and What* Kind of Research Might They Accept?', *Journal of Advertising Research*, vol 36, no 2, pp8–12.
Kover, A. J. and Goldberg, S. M. (1995) 'The Games Copywriters Play – Conflict, Quasi-Control – a New Proposal', *Journal of Advertising Research*, vol 35, no 4, pp52–68.
Kotler, P. (1967) *Marketing Management: Analysis, Planning, Implementation and Control*, Englewood Cliffs, NJ: Prentice-Hall.
Larzarsfeld, P. F. (1941) 'Remarks on Administrative and Critical Communications Research', *Studies in Philosophy and Science*, vol 9, pp3–16.
Lasswell, H. D. (1948) 'The Structure and Function of Communication in Society', in L. Bryson (ed) *The Communication of Ideas*, New York, NY: Harper.
Leiss, W., Kline, S., Jhally, S. and Botterill, J. (2005) *Social Communication in Advertising: Consumption in the Mediated Marketplace*, London: Routledge.
Levy, S. (1959) 'Symbols for Sale', *Harvard Business Review*, vol 37, July, pp117–124.
MacRury, I. (2008) *Advertising*, London: Routledge.
Marchand, R. (1985) *Advertising the American Dream: Making Way for Modernity, 1920–1940*, Berkeley, CA: University of California Press.
——(1998) *Creating the Corporate Soul: The Rise of Public Relations and Corporate Imagery in American Big Business*, Berkeley, CA: University of California Press.
Marion, G. (2006) 'Marketing Ideology and Criticism', *Marketing Theory*, vol 6, no 2, pp245–262.
Mautner, G. (2010) *Language and the Market Society: Critical Reflections on Discourse and Dominance*, London: Routledge.
McCarthy, E. J. (1981) *Basic Marketing: A Managerial Approach*, Homewood, IL: Irwin.
McFall, L. (2004) *Advertising: A Cultural Economy*, London: Sage.
McDonald, C. and Scott, J. (2007) 'A Brief History of Advertising', in G. Tellis and T. Ambler (eds) *The Sage Handbook of Advertising*, London, Sage.
McLeod, C., O'Donohoe, S. and Townley, B. (2011) 'Pot Noodles, Placement and Peer Regard: Creative Career Trajectories and Communities of Practice in the British Advertising Industry', *British Journal of Management*, vol 22, no 1, pp114–131.
——(2009) 'Elephant in the Room? Class and Creative Careers in British Advertising Agencies', *Human Relations*, vol 62, pp1011–1039.
Mick, D. and Buhl, G. (1992) 'A Meaning-Based Model of Advertising Experiences', *Journal of Consumer Research*, vol 19, no 3, pp317–338.
Morgan, G. (1992) 'Marketing Discourse and Practice: Towards a Critical Analysis', in M. Alvesson and H. Willmott (eds) *Critical Management Studies*, London: Sage.
O'Donohoe, S. (1997) 'Raiding the Postmodern Pantry – Advertising Intertextuality and the Young Adult Audience', *European Journal of Marketing*, vol 31, no 3–4, pp234–253.
Quickenden, K. and Kover, A. J. (2007) 'Did Boulton Sell Silver Plate to the Middle Class? A Quantitative Study of Luxury Marketing in Late Eighteenth-Century Britain', *Journal of Macromarketing*, vol 27, March, pp51–64.
Ritson, M. and Elliott, R. (1999) 'The Social Uses of Advertising – an Ethnographic Study of Adolescent Advertising Audiences', *Journal of Consumer Research*, vol 26, no 3, pp260–277.
Schramm, W. (1948) *Mass Communication*, Urbana, IL: University of Illinois Press.
Schultz, D. E. and Kitchen, P. J. (1997) 'IMC in US Ad Agencies: An Exploratory Study', *Journal of Advertising Research*, vol 37, no 5, pp7–18.
Schultz, D. E., Tannenbaum, S. I. and Lauterborn, R. F. (1993) *Integrated Marketing Communications*, Lincolnwood, IL: NTC Publishing Group.
Scott, L. M. (1990) 'Understanding Jingles and Needledrop: A Rhetorical Approach to Music in Advertising', *Journal of Consumer Research*, vol 17, pp223–236.
——(1994) 'The Bridge from Text to Mind: Adapting Reader-Response Theory for Consumer Research', *Journal of Consumer Research*, December, pp461–490.

Shannon, C. E. (1948) 'A Mathematical Theory of Communication', *Bell System Technical Journal*, vol 27, July and October, pp379–423, 623–656, http://plan9.bell-labs.com/cm/ms/what/shannonday/shannon1948.pdf.

Sherry J. F. (1987) 'Advertising as Cultural System', in J. Umiker-Sebeok (ed) *Marketing and Semiotics*, Berlin: Mouton.

Stern, B. B. (1993a) 'A Revised Communication Model for Advertising: Multiple Dimensions of the Source, the Message, and the Recipient', *Journal of Advertising*, vol 23, no 2, pp5–16.

——(1993b) 'Feminist Literary Criticism and the Deconstruction of Ads: A Postmodern View of Advertising', *Journal of Consumer Research*, vol 19, pp556–566.

Sharma, C., Herzog, J. and Melfi, V. (2008) *Mobile Advertising – Supercharge your Brand in the Exploding Wireless Market*, Hoboken, NJ: Wiley.

Shimp, T. (2010) *Integrated Marketing Communication in Advertising and Promotion*, 8th edition, Mason, OH: South Western College.

Strong, E. K. (1929) *The Psychology of Selling and Advertising*, Chicago, IL: American Library Association.

Svensson, S. (2007) 'Producing Marketing: Towards a Social-Phenomenology of Marketing Work', *Marketing Theory*, vol 7, pp271–290.

Szmigin, I., Bengry-Howell, A., Griffin, C., Hackley, C. and Mistral, W. (2011) 'Social Marketing, Individual Responsibility and the "Culture of Intoxication"', *European Journal of Marketing*, vol 45, no 5, pp759–779.

Tadajewski, M. (2008) 'Incommensurable Paradigms, Cognitive Bias and the Politics of Marketing Theory', *Marketing Theory*, vol 8, no 3, pp273–297.

Tadajewski, M. and Brownlie, D. (2008) (eds) *Critical Marketing Issues in Contemporary Marketing*, London: Wiley.

Tanaka, K. (1994) *Advertising Language: A Pragmatic Approach to Advertisements in Britain and Japan*, London: Routledge.

Tiwsakul, R., Hackley, C. and Szmigin, I. (2005) 'Explicit, Non-Integrated Product Placement in British Television Programmes', *International Journal of Advertising*, vol 24, no 1, pp95–111.

Wernick, A. (1991) *Promotional Culture – Advertising, Ideology and Symbolic Expression*, London: Sage.

Wolf, M. (1999) *The Entertainment Economy: How Mega-Media Forces Are Shaping Our Lives*, New York, NY: Crown Business Books.

4

CONNECTING WITH CONSUMERS

Branding and Convergence

Cheryl Martens

Introduction

Within the marketing communications literature, brands are considered an important means of differentiating an organization's offer and communicating with consumers. Through the systematic coordination of multiple messages and across a wide range of media platforms via brand narratives and brand conversations (Dahlen et al 2010), branding is now understood to be a key promotional method of relevance to private as well as public organization culture. Deeply embedded in everyday life through a wide array of tactics, from product placement in television, movies, video games, mobile and other platforms, to corporate sponsorship of every realm of community life, brands' presence in our daily practices has been facilitated by ubiquitous interactivity. An 'always on culture' of mobile technology now makes it possible to reach consumers at any time of day.

Social and cultural theorists draw attention to brands' symbolic and ideological impact upon contemporary culture. Some authors argue that brands culturally constitute meanings, where images and reality are blurred, through convergence, making for a type of 'hyper-reality', particularly influenced by the cultural context where the brand may be produced. In Baudrillard's (1998) view, consumers actively engage with and manipulate signs. In relation to the processes of branding, even corporate logos can become fashion accessories in the hyper-reality of consumer culture. Brand names such as Nike, Dunkin' Donuts and Harley Davidson, through the practice of permanently tattooing corporate logos, for example, make it possible for the body to become a multidimensional billboard. Corporate logo tattoo consumers may not necessarily be interested in the product, but by expressing various simulations of reality and possibilities for their identities, they are fetishizing both the social meanings of the brand and the commodity-sign logo (Orend-Cunningham 2003). Authors from media studies traditions, in contrast, focus on the role of brands in articulating and reproducing certain ideologies and views of the world and mediating various subject positions where notions of communities and identities are continuously being built and rebuilt (Kellner 1995; Morley and Robins 1995). Social theorists such as Urry (2000) argue that brands also play a role in producing models of global citizenship and certain modes of being.

In the context of promotional culture and convergence, the brand can also be understood as a sign in relation to an increasingly aestheticized everyday life (Featherstone 1991; Lash and Urry 1994). The brand, however, acts as a medium for exchange, as well as a referent (elaborated upon by Lash 2002), involving not solely the production of the sign, but also how consumers interact with it. From this perspective, the meaning of brands is not only interpreted but also *constituted* by consumers, a position further developed by Lash (2002) and Lury (2004).

Of particular interest for the purpose of this chapter is the role of the brand as a new media object, implicating social relations (Lury 2004). According to Celia Lury (2004), a brand embodies a new media logic, as it is both an object of information and objectifies information, which involves images, processes and products and multidimensional relations between products *in time*. Lury argues that while a brand may be considered incorporeal or intangible, it is 'not immaterial ... while not fixed in time or space, it is a platform for the patterning of activity, a mode of organizing activities in time and space ... not a closed object, but open, extending into or implicating social relations ... not a matter of certainty, but object of possibility' (Lury 2004: 2). Expanding on Lury's work, Arvidsson (2006) argues that brands work as a platform that anticipates and pre-structures certain kinds of actions or feelings. Arvidsson suggests that 'brands today do not so much stand for products, as much as they provide a part of the context in which products are used ... . With a particular brand I can act, feel and be in a particular way' (Arvidsson 2006: 8). The brand understood from this perspective is a 'propertied frame of action', empowering consumers to orientate themselves in a particular direction, while recouping the effects of such activity as its own (Arvidsson 2006: 8). Implicated in brand design and performance, consumers emotionally engage and interact with brands as users, or even creators, rather than audiences or readers, in processes that are often ephemeral and emotional, rather than cognitive processes of reflection (Lash 2002).

This chapter will examine some of the processes of the relations between the products and services that constitute branding in the context of convergence and promotional culture. Through a case study of the promotion of HIV/AIDS prevention, it will consider how branding has become part of even the most intimate corners of our lives, including what was once considered the domain of governmental and non-governmental actors. The chapter will begin with a discussion of brand value and brand positioning as distinguishing features of brands within contemporary promotional culture and will consider the impact of convergence culture upon the branding process. The chapter will then provide an analysis of the branding of MTV's *Staying Alive* and Viacom's HIV/AIDS campaigns.

Brand value

The valuation of a brand in the marketing and communications and business fields is commonly presented as a complex process, involving the analysis of present profits and projected benefits (Interbrand 2012). Intimately related to what customers do or are projected to do with the brand, brand equity has become as important an asset as factories, inventory and cash because strong brands strengthen a company's relations with consumers, as well as investors and other stakeholders. In the context of convergence, brands act as an interface (Lury 2004) where virtual meanings and associations made by consumers play a key role in constituting brand value.

Brand value in convergence culture is centrally related to meaning-making. Arvidsson (2006: 7) argues that it is 'what consumers do with the brand in mind' that affects a brand's value. Although brands may be thought to be intangible or incorporeal objects, they are not immaterial, but significant in terms of contemporary forms of exchange (Lury 2004). For some authors, brands are akin to 'virtual real estate' (Schiller 1999) or 'virtual goods' (Shields 2003). Arvidsson (2006) suggests that brands become valuable in so far as they manage and programme human interaction and communication processes to produce shared understandings of meaning.

Brand value is closely associated with brand reputation. Corporate brand strategy plays an instrumental role in the managing of brand equity in the minds of consumers, employees, stakeholders, investors and communities. This process often begins with internal branding, as the values of the brand are communicated within the company and employees are encouraged to 'live the brand' and become 'brand champions', with the aim of earning understanding and influencing public opinion and behaviour (Dahlen et al 2010). It is associated with a reconfiguration of work which is perceived by employees as 'a means of adding value to themselves' (Lury 2004: 35; see also du Gay 1996).

With a growing emphasis on corporate social responsibility (CSR) and social partnerships as constituting an important aspect of companies' philosophies, 'living the brand' increasingly means engaging in ethical performances that reflect socially responsible principles. These opportunities are increasingly organized through partnerships with non-profit agencies addressing particular social issues. Social responsibility is offered to employees and consumers as a means of cultivating cultural skills and capital, as well as socially responsible identities, while promoting the brand's philosophy and image. Convergence of a wide range of media facilitates these interactions and fosters a certain type of brand image through involvement in social networking sites such as Facebook, YouTube and Twitter.

The valuation of a brand, according to the widely cited brand consultancy and brand rankings generator Interbrand, is a process involving the analysis of present profits and the projected benefits of future ownership (Interbrand 2012). Increasingly, however, valuation is associated with its reputation and approached through the development of corporate social responsibility strategies which also impact upon the brand's position and associations concerning the brand. As Sir Michael Perry, chairman of Centrica Plc and Dunlop Slazenger Group, argues: 'The brands that will be big in the future will be those that tap into the social changes that are taking place' (cited in Grayson 2004).

Brand positioning: Differentiation and association

Key to building a brand's value is its position in the marketplace. Techniques of differentiation and association work to consolidate the brand within certain categories in consumers' minds, while differentiating them from the competition. Association, according to Keller (2000), works as 'points of parity' and make it possible to occupy certain niches in customers' minds, while 'points of difference' serve brands in differentiating them from competitors through unique category attributes.

Considering the brand as a new media object, positioning works as a vertical axis of signification which, according to Lury (2004: 86), enables the position and activities of the consumer to be internalized in the processes and products of production and distribution. Functioning similarly to computer programming, information about consumers can be traced through a range of data-gathering techniques such as consumer profiling, lifestyle clustering and data mining. Brands can thus make use of such techniques by reincorporating this information within the brand, orienting both brand strategy and brand communication. Lury likens this process to the concept of 'looping' (Manovich 2001), which involves the compulsory reincorporation of consumer tastes, styles and actions in brand-making into the branding process, which can, on the one hand, help to distinguish the brand from competitors and also serves to ensure their continued growth and relevance. Another axis of signification is that of association, where the logo becomes meaningful 'in relation to a *sequence or series* of products, images and events' (Lury 2004: 88). Here, information about the audience is used to multiply qualities or attributes of the brand (i.e., design, style and image).

Connecting with consumer aspirations: Emotional branding and branding online

Successful brands in convergence culture are those that engage consumers to meet their aspirations through interactivity (McWilliam 2000; Arvidsson 2006). Marc Gobé (2001), in his bestselling book *Emotional Branding*, emphasizes the significance of engaging the senses and emotions of consumers. Gobé argues that focusing on people's desire to transcend material satisfaction and experience fulfilment enables marketers to tap into people's aspirational drives, thus motivating their actions. Rather than facilitating transactions, it is interaction that is key to successful branded campaigns: 'what fascinates consumers is the quality of dialogue he or she can engage in' (Ind and Rodino, cited in Arvidsson 2006: 101).

A key aspect of interactivity in relation to the brand is that it permits the inclusion of information about consumers' everyday lives while simultaneously allowing for a natural integration of brands within the diurnal. Implicated in brand design and performance, consumers interact with brands as users and even creators, rather than audiences or readers. Consumers thus engage in processes of distraction, such as social networking groups, and can be found regularly Tweeting about brands in relation to their lives, engaging in what Lash (2002) terms embodied 'play' rather than reflection.

The integration of internet and mobile culture within everyday life has meant new possibilities for sociality, with consumers becoming directly involved in branded communities through a range of social networking sites – the relevant branded content produced by consumers themselves. Brand communities on social networking sites such as Facebook, for example, are often based on information posted by consumers rather than brand promoters. Consumers are thus 'put to work' (Zvick et al 2008) for brands, becoming brand ambassadors and also shaping the types of references and values associated with the brand.

Partnerships, alliances and co-branding

The main benefits of alliances between companies are the lessening of risks and costs involved in managing certain projects. This is particularly relevant to media industries which are reliant on high technology, requiring expensive research and development costs, making interdependence an attractive option (Hesmondhalgh 2002; see also Castells 1996). Convergence also makes co-branding strategies particularly feasible in guaranteeing the production of quality content. By teaming up with other major brands to offer products and services, brands are able to produce engaging and quality services. Brands such as Orange, for example, team up with MasterCard for payments on their e-commerce promotions, while Vodafone regularly works with Manchester United to provide football information and gossip (Arvidsson 2006).

There are, however, a number of other reasons corporations choose partnerships, networks and co-branding strategies. These benefits include lobbying power and avoidance of competition through bypassing foreign government involvement, thus providing access to wider markets via partnerships. However, given the increasingly important role of the media in the symbolic economy, maintaining corporate image is also compelling media corporations into forming partnerships, networks and alliances to carry out programmes of social responsibility.

Case study: The branding of HIV/AIDS prevention – Viacom and MTV's HIV/AIDS campaigns

The discussion here will situate the approaches of Viacom, MTV and its partners in relation to HIV/AIDS education in terms of how it is being branded and distributed across a range of platforms. Increased market reach via cross-platform programming and alliances with governmental and non-governmental agencies and competing companies are techniques which increase audience numbers, thus influencing the global reach of the messages. How these techniques coincide with Viacom's corporate brand strategy is of particular relevance to understanding how HIV/AIDS awareness campaigns are being promoted. This networking and diversity marketing approach to HIV/AIDS education is part and parcel of its branding and aestheticization. The communication of sensorial experiences and values, for example, is increasingly a point of focus, with emotions and aspirations addressed as points through which not only to connect, but also to develop relationships with audiences.

The distribution of HIV/AIDS communication has been facilitated by the process of the conglomeration and vertical integration of large corporations. A global campaign of the scale produced by Viacom, valued at $600 million over three years (Henry J. Kaiser Family Foundation 2007), could not be conducted other than as cross-platform (i.e., television, outdoor advertisements and radio) or reach as many audiences. Programming across various corporations and platforms and the pursuit of partnerships and alliances are the main approaches used to extend the reach of MTV and Viacom's HIV/AIDS education campaigns. The following discussion will look at how these approaches build on corporate brand strategies used to foster brand awareness. On the one hand, these approaches integrate HIV education within an unprecedented spectrum of media, providing new spaces for HIV/AIDS information. On the other hand, Viacom and MTV products increase their exposure to audiences via new partnerships and alliances made possible through the corporations' HIV/AIDS education initiatives. As a result, information processes can be seen as increasingly synergistic, with corporate identities becoming entwined in processes that have hitherto been the domain of multilateral organizations and non-governmental organizations (NGOs).

Cross-promotion: New spaces for HIV/AIDS education

Following major mergers and acquisitions during the 1990s,[1] Viacom implemented cross-company, cross-platform promotions to improve sales. This vertical integration has proven invaluable to increase the reach of their products (Herman and McChesney 1997: 53). This cross-promotion branded entertainment approach has included MTV's promotion of Paramount films, Simon & Schuster's Nickelodeon book imprint, and a *Beavis and Butthead* book series based on the MTV show characters. These strategies are significant in that the vertical integration of Viacom's various brands maximizes both audience reach and company profits.

Viacom used these same strategies to launch the KNOW HIV/AIDS campaign, running public service messages across Viacom's TV, radio and outdoor properties. This initiative encompassed AIDS-related themes woven into various Viacom-produced entertainment series (i.e., *Star Trek, Queer as Folk, Jag, Open Mic, The Parkers, Soul Food*) and also includes an educational guide and website. In addition, CBS, UPN, Spike TV and Infinity have aired public service announcements and programmes on HIV/AIDS and sexual health, and Showtime, Paramount, the N and VH1 have produced original programming and movies.

In the UK and Europe, Viacom's HIV/AIDS awareness campaigns have been incorporated within the MTV *Staying Alive* brand and work across several platforms. The brand, for example, launched the Brighton Paramount Comedy festival. Viacom Outdoor provided access to the transport system, while Blockbuster put sexual health messages in movie and games magazines and Simon & Schuster put sexual health messages in their books. Viacom's various properties work together in a process that makes collaborative use of the information produced by the *Staying Alive* Campaign. Cross-platform programming provided at 'no cost' to MTV thus increases the reach of HIV/AIDS campaigns. Dollar estimates of the value of the campaigns, however, may be somewhat misleading, as the spaces being assigned to the campaign depend upon market conditions. In other words, the use of these spaces relies on their availability on a particular day at a particular time.

Partnerships and alliances

Partnerships and alliances with other companies are increasingly central to the pursuit of brand growth and these are facilitated by the possibility of working across a range of platforms. The key changes are unprecedented collaboration between competing corporations and the growing leadership role of media corporations in multilateral processes. First of all, these alliances are often facilitated by working in conjunction with a range of multilateral institutions such as the United Nations Population Fund (UNFPA) and the Joint United Nations Programme on HIV/AIDS (UNAIDS), as well as international NGOs such as the Gates Foundation, the Kaiser Family Foundation and Family Health International. The executive producer of the *Staying Alive* Campaign explains:

> And the other thing that we've done increasingly … is enlarge our partnership, so now we have UNAIDS and the World Bank, Family Health International, USAID, DIFID, Kaiser Family Foundation, the Gates Foundation … Gates funded us on a specific project, but the rest of that group come in and fund us year on year, which is fantastic, because they believe that the work we do is significant … I mean, this is the longest-running and the largest and unfortunately only youth global HIV/AIDS-prevention programme out there.
>
> *(MTV* Staying Alive *executive producer, 2007)*

With regard to the Viacom and MTV HIV/AIDS campaigns, partnerships and alliances with multilateral institutions, particularly as they are funded year on year, lend credibility to the content produced. Partnerships also facilitate working relationships with other corporations, such is the case of the Global Media AIDS Initiative, founded in 2004 by Kaiser and UNAIDS, with Viacom as its first signatory.

Partnering with other media corporations means that costs can be significantly reduced and the distribution of Viacom and MTV products increased beyond their distribution areas. An example of this kind of partnership arrangement is that of Viacom's KNOW HIV/AIDS and the BBC World Service Trust alliance, which broadcast HIV/AIDS awareness messages in seven languages to 60 million people in Africa and the Caribbean. Like the *Staying Alive* Campaign, this media partnership was supported by the Kaiser Family Foundation, the Bill & Melinda Gates Foundation and UNAIDS, both financially and practically, in terms of the content of HIV/AIDS information.

While media corporations devise the messages, stakeholder collaboration takes place in order to arrive at messages in which all stakeholders are in agreement. In the case of MTV's *Staying Alive* 'Sex Drive' public service announcements, for example, some adverts interpreted as 'culturally offensive'[2] by key stakeholders from international organizations were omitted from the campaign (MTV production assistant). Although the messages are produced by corporations such as MTV, interaction through censorship by stakeholders can and does occur, thus influencing the nature of information presented.

The production of HIV/AIDS communication is thus best understood as a synergistic process within the context of partnerships, alliances and vertical integration, where HIV information production is negotiated with various stakeholders and increasingly globally distributed as part of the company's brand strategy.

The aestheticization and emotional branding of HIV/AIDS prevention

The involvement of private corporations in marketing HIV/AIDS education[3] is not a new phenomenon; yet marketing strategies in HIV/AIDS prevention have only recently made a concerted effort to brand HIV education in relation to aesthetic information and values. In the context of global brand initiatives, HIV/AIDS prevention is increasingly packaged in the context of branding, as brands that need to connect with consumers on emotional levels. The idea is that if the prevention efforts are packaged in an attractive enough way in tune with the target audience's consumer values, not only will messages be sold to them on a one-off basis, they will seek out this information as part of their lifestyle.

Actor Richard Gere, founder of the Heroes Project in India which works closely with Viacom and media corporations in India, emphasizes the selling of HIV as an aesthetic object that needs to be 'sexy' and 'alive':

> [Journalists] said look we've done the articles, we've talked about it what else do you want us to do? And then my response is look, think about HIV/AIDS like it's a product. How would you sell the product and keep it alive? How do you sell HIV and make it sexy and alive and interesting over and over and over again? You've got to be creative about it. And that was one of the reasons we had our creative summit. It was talking about exactly that issue, on keeping it alive for the journalists and for the writer so they're still interested, they're still open to this and they're creative, but to feed more

stories, more possibilities, more angles, more humor, more life, more human interests, not just facts. Facts are dead, can't tell that story anymore.

(Gere 2005)

Gere's perspective with regard to selling and bringing HIV 'to life' as a product follows branding work in the area of emotional branding, as discussed above. Gere's approach to HIV/AIDS education therefore concurs with Gobé's perspective on emotional branding, conceptualizing HIV/AIDS as a product incorporating an aestheticized vision of how this information should be packaged to reach the senses and aspirations of the audience.

Seeking to move beyond 'facts' towards aspirations, the advertising agency for Viacom's Knowing is Beautiful campaign, Crispin Porter + Bogusky, embraces this view. Using gap-like multicultural models, the campaign connects the promotion of HIV testing with the marketing techniques involved in branding:

> What if we made HIV testing seem cool? What if we treated it like a fashion brand? Instead of trying to scare people into getting tested, what if we made it something they actually aspire to?

(www.cpbgroup.com)

This view of HIV testing and prevention – as a product to be branded and an object to be related to – is central to Viacom's conception of HIV/AIDS health promotion. The HIV antibody test, for example, was promoted as potentially 'enhancing human intimacy'.

In addition, HIV/AIDS information campaigns increasingly integrate audiences in the production process through blog and Twitter contributions, as promoted on the *Staying Alive* website (http://www.staying-alive.org). Young people participate in the posting of a range of sexual health issues of importance to them and receive answers to their various questions from sexual health experts who collaborate with MTV's *Staying Alive* Foundation. Reports 'in the field' by *Staying Alive* grantees also increase the visibility of MTV's funding of a range of HIV/AIDS education programmes throughout the world. Videos, stories and news are shared among grantees and not only consolidate the image of the *Staying Alive* Foundation but also reflect on the MTV brand as a sponsor.

This discussion of Viacom and MTV in the wider context of global marketing and aestheticization has served to demonstrate how the corporations are conducting HIV/AIDS campaigns within their current strategies for global growth and having a profound influence on the global reach of the message being produced. Furthermore, it is important to consider how the corporations themselves increasingly constitute their brands through pro-social activities.

Beyond logos: Corporate social responsibility and brand valuation

Considered one of the world's fastest growing media brands, based on the widely cited brand consultancy Interbrand's ratings system, the assessment of projected earnings, for example, of the MTV brand was valued in 2011 at $6.3 billion (Interbrand 2011). In addition, the branded HIV/AIDS campaigns are new media objects conditioning not just meanings, but the practical outcomes and experiences produced, further enhancing the value of the brand.

With regard to reputation, 'reaching other broadcasters' and taking a leadership role in relation to HIV/AIDS education in the media has been an often discussed theme for MTV and Viacom since 2004. In the launching of 'Creative Summits' hosted by MTV, president of MTV Networks International and UNAIDS goodwill ambassador Bill Roedy emphasizes MTV's history and leadership role in responding to HIV/AIDS:

> Because of MTV's long history addressing this issue among our youth audience, we are well suited to call together the first-ever creative meeting on HIV/AIDS, fulfilling a promise made at the UN Global Media AIDS Initiative launch. HIV/AIDS remains a top priority at MTV to continue to raise awareness through the Staying Alive campaign and engage others to form their own response to the epidemic.
>
> *(Roedy 2004)*

Both MTV and Viacom play highly visible roles in the field of HIV/AIDS education media leadership. On 15 January 2004, Viacom was the first of 21 signatories in the Global Media AIDS Declaration, which promises 'to expand public knowledge and understanding about HIV/AIDS through their companies practices' (Arieff 2004). Mel Karmazin, former president and chief operating officer of Viacom, emphasizes Viacom's leadership role in a press release about the Global Media AIDS Initiative by calling for cross-platform and cross-corporate cooperation:

> We hope other media companies around the world will join us in fighting this epidemic with the most powerful communications tools that exist – their television, radio, outdoor, newspaper, magazine and online assets.
>
> *(Viacom 2003)*

This statement by Karmazin demonstrates Viacom's approach to building its reputation within the realm of corporate social responsibility through high-visibility HIV/AIDS education campaigns. In addition, this CSR side of Viacom is regularly stressed across all of its companies, in its employee magazine and on its website. In the initial stages of its CSR efforts, from 2003 to 2005, Viacom centrally positioned corporate social responsibility on its homepage, next to information for investors and press releases. The heading for corporate citizenship linked the words 'corporate social responsibility' not to a summary of Viacom's position on CSR, but the company's HIV/AIDS campaign and the many awards it has won.

For brands, logos often play a central role in relation to brand identification (Klein 2000; Lury 2004). However, in the case of branding HIV/AIDS prevention, the role of logos and intellectual property rights is not straightforward. Sometimes, for example, both the logos are removed and intellectual property rights waived, increasing audience size. MTV's *Staying Alive* executive producer (EP) discusses this process with the interviewer (I):

EP: Last year we distributed to 74 per cent of the world's TV households … . And it's rights-free and free of charge. And in some countries for some broadcasters, it's good to have the MTV logo on it, but for other broadcasters, they don't want to air it with the MTV logo on it. So we had people coming to us and saying, 'Well, we would air it, it's good, but no, it's MTV.' So we'd say, 'Fine, take it off … .' I think I am hated by marketing people at MTV, because the brand here is, well, it's what we're about – we're the leading media brand in the world. But with Bill Roedy's permission and say-so, it's OK for anybody to take off the brand because it's not important. If it works, great, but the most important thing is it gets out there. And we now have a pretty permanent footprint of broadcasters in sub-Saharan Africa where the only AIDS material they're airing is from us.

I: OK. But there do they also take off the MTV logo?

EP: It depends on each broadcaster.

I: Who does it tend to be that is opposed to the showing of the logo?

EP: Probably not so much in sub-Saharan Africa, and quite frankly if they're going to air something, they just chuck the tape on air, they don't want to go to the expense of taking it off. It's more going to be a broadcaster in Western Europe who could be a competitor of ours, for example. But as far as we're concerned, there is no competition when it comes to AIDS.

(MTV executive producer, 2007)

The above exchange concerning branding and the logos of HIV/AIDS education materials is an interesting paradox. On the one hand, the MTV brand is emphasized to be what MTV is all about. However, in relation to HIV/AIDS health promotion, the executive producer states that 'it's not important' because it is more important that the messages get out to as wide an audience as possible. With or without its logo, the MTV and Viacom brands provide certain frames of display and ways of evaluating the brand, which happens not just through logo placement, but through the careful cultivation of brand image.

Signs and spaces, in the case of the campaigns discussed above, are both owned and produced by Viacom brands and play a particularly significant role in the cultivation of brand image. In the case of partnerships with NGOs and community-based organizations, discounts are often provided for joint work and use of outdoor signage. This contributes to brand image, on the one hand, as its outdoor signs bear messages in line with Viacom's CSR objectives. On the other hand, Viacom's reputation within the community is raised through the discounts provided. In addition, as was the case with regard to the creation of film festivals, these AIDS service organizations now serve not only to enhance the cultivation of brand image, but provide a new target market for advertising. This further benefits the corporation in terms of corporate image and in its performance of corporate social responsibility, which is documented as fostering the trust of investors and audience (Seitanidi 2005).

A key marketing technique used by Viacom and MTV in their management of the CSR image is that of differentiation and integration in the positioning of their brands. Properties such as MTV put much effort into internalizing the consumer in their production processes. On a yearly basis it conducts more than 200 focus groups globally and also makes use of online survey data and consumer movement across their websites. The focus groups mainly consider brand awareness, but also look at what young people want out of the brand. Whether the audience would rather support a socially responsible MTV is a central point of investigation, which, according to an MTV production assistant, feeds into the support and development of MTV's *Staying Alive* brand.

This final point, and which the discussion of CSR in relation to brand image has served to emphasize, is that while, on the one hand, HIV/AIDS awareness and information processes are visibly transformed through social marketing techniques, notions of corporate social responsibility and brand identity themselves are transformed by the corporations' involvement in social issues and possibilities for information-gathering about their audiences both online and off-line. Furthermore, the sacred world of intellectual property and logos may be somewhat modified in the branding of HIV/AIDS communication. However, being the top media brand in the world, closely attuned to audience, as the case of MTV demonstrates, logo or no logo, branded health communication has become integral to Viacom and MTV's corporate practice and identity.

Conclusion

This chapter has explored how branding in convergence culture takes place via complex webs, alliances and the integration of messages across a wide range of properties and media. This allows for greater possibilities of distribution and brand awareness. Partnerships and alliances and the opportunity to work simultaneously across a range of platforms permit a greater synergy of information between stake-holders and also provide the opportunity to become more attuned to audience and consumer interests.

In addition, the case study has demonstrated how aestheticized consumer values promoted through global media marketing of customer desire, emotions, aesthetic values and diversity are becoming central rhetorical tools in the branding process. The cultivation of brand image and the internalization of consumer values and consumer participation via a range of media is evident in the design and style of its products and the signs and spaces. Connecting with consumers in this way contributes to the building of brand value and also shapes new directions for the brand in the context of promotional culture.

Notes

1 Viacom's two major acquisitions in the 1990s were Blockbuster and Paramount in 1994.
2 The example given by the production assistant was that of Italian young people saying that they didn't see anything wrong with using condoms if you loved someone, playfully criticizing the stance of the Pope.
3 See, for example, the United Colours of Benetton Condom Campaign, 1991.

Bibliography

Arieff, A. (2004) 'Public Health & Education: U.N. Secretary-General Annan Launches Global Media AIDS Initiative To Educate Public About HIV/AIDS', http://www.kaisernetwork.org/daily_reports/rep_index.cfm?DR_ID=21719.
Arvidsson, A. (2006) *Brands: Meaning and Value in Media Culture*, Oxon, UK: Routledge.
Baudrillard, J. (1998) *The Consumer Society*, London: Sage.
Castells, M. (1996) *The Rise of Network Society*, Oxford: Blackwell.
Dahlen, M., Lange, F. and Smith, T. (2010) *Marketing Communications: A Brand Narrative Approach*, Chichester, UK: Wiley.
du Gay, P. (1996) *Consumption and Identity at Work*, London: Sage.
Featherstone, M. (1991) *Consumer Culture and Postmodernism*, London: Sage.
Gere, R. (2005) 'AIDS and the Media: New Responses from India and Russia', http://www.kaisernetwork.org/health_cast/uploaded_files/102704_eurasia_media.pdf, accessed 2 July 2012.
Gobé, M. (2001) *Emotional Branding: The New Paradigm for Connecting Brands to People*, New York, NY: Allworth Press.
Grayson, D. (2004) *The CSR Brand*, http://www.iqa.org/publication/c4-1-77.shtml, accessed 28 June 2012.
Henry J. Kaiser Family Foundation (2007) *KNOW HIV/AIDS: Learn About the Campaign*, www.know hivaids.org/learn_about.html.
Herman, E. S. and McChesney, R. W. (1997) *The Global Media: The New Missionaries of Corporate Capitalism*, London: Cassell.
Hesmondhalgh, D. (2002) *The Cultural Industries*, London: Sage.
Interbrand (2011) *Best Global Brand 2011: Creating and Managing Brand Value*, http://issuu.com/interbrand/docs/bestglobalbrands2011-interbrand?viewMode=presentation&mode=embed.
——(2012) 'About Us', http://www.interbrand.com/en/about-us/Interbrand-about-us.aspx.
Keller, K. L. (2000) 'The Brand Report Card', *Harvard Business Review*, January–February, pp3–10.
Kellner, D. (1995) *Media Culture: Cultural Studies, Identity and Politics between the Modern and Postmodern*, London: Routledge.
Klein, N. (2000) *No Logo: Taking Aim at the Brand Bullies*, Toronto: Knopf Canada.
Lury, C. (2004) *Brands: The Logos of the Global Economy*, Oxon, UK: Routledge.
Lash, S. (2002) *Critique of Information*, London: Sage.
Lash, S. and Urry, J. (1994) *Economies of Signs and Spaces*, London: Sage.
Manovich, L. (2001) *The Language of New Media*, Cambridge, MA: MIT Press.
McWilliam, G. (2000) 'Building Stronger Brands through Online Communities', *MIT Sloan Management Review*, Spring, http://sloanreview.mit.edu/the-magazine/2000-spring/4133/building-stronger-brands-through-online-communities/.
Morley, D. and K. Robins (1995) *Spaces of Identity: Global Media, Electronic Landscapes, and Cultural Boundaries*, London: Routledge.
MTV executive producer (2007) Interview, London: MTV International.
Orend-Cunningham, A. (2003) 'Corporate Logo Tattoos: Literal Corporate Branding?', *Consumers, Commodities, Consumptions*, vol 5, no 1, https://netfiles.uiuc.edu/dtcook/www/CCCnewsletter/5–1/Orend.htm.

Roedy, B. in *Kaiser Daily Report* (2004) 'First Ever Global HIV/AIDS Creative Meeting at the United Nations Brings Together Creative Experts from 35 Media Companies'. Online. Available: http://www.kff.org/hivaids/phip112304nr.cfm.

Seitanidi, M. M. (2005) 'Corporate Social Responsibility and the Non-Commercial Sector. What Does Corporate Social Responsibility Mean for the Non-Commercial Sector? And Is It Different from the CSR for Businesses?', *New Academy Review*, vol 3, no 4, pp60–72.

Shields, R. (2003) *The Virtual*, London: Routledge.

Schiller, D. (1999) *Digital Capitalism*, Cambridge, MA: MIT Press.

Urry, J. (2000) *Sociology Beyond Societies*, London: Routledge.

Viacom (2003) 'Viacom and Kaiser Family Foundation Launch Comprehensive Initiative to Fight HIV/AIDS', *Press Release*, January, http://www.kff.org/hivaids/upload/Viacom-and-Kaiser-Family-Foundation-Launch-Comprehensive-Initiative-to-Fight-HIV-AIDS-January-6-2003.pdf.

Zwick, D., Bonsu, S. K. and Darmody, A. (2008) 'Putting Consumers to Work: "Co-Creation" and New Marketing Govern-Mentality', *Journal of Consumer Culture*, vol 8, no 2, pp163–196.

Websites

www.cpbgroup.com
www.gbc.com
www.knowhivaids.org
www.interbrand.com
www.staying-alive.org

5

THE PUBLIC RELATIONS PERSPECTIVE OF PROMOTIONAL CULTURE

Heather Yaxley

Public relations as a promotional industry

> Every man, however hopeless his pretensions may appear, has some project by which
> he hopes to rise to reputation; some art by which he imagines that the attention of the
> world will be attracted; some quality, good or bad, which discriminates him from the
> common herd of mortals, and by which others may be persuaded to love, or
> compelled to fear him.
>
> (Samuel Johnson, *The Rambler*, 1751)

Johnson's writing aimed to inform the growing middle-classes of the eighteenth
century how they could be accepted into high society. In itself *The Rambler*
represented a 'booming industry of middle-class monthly magazines' (Camlot
2008: 54) acting as a promotional device that established Johnson's personal fame
(Lynn 1992). This reflects Wernick's (1991: 182) perspective that 'a promotional
message is a complex of significations which at once represents (moves in place of),
advocates (moves on behalf of), and anticipates (moves ahead of) the circulating
entity or entities to which it refers'. A similar web of promotion can be seen in
contemporary pseudo-reality television shows, such as *The Only Way Is Essex*,
where ordinary people are cast as 'characters' who are promoted through the programme and other media, drawing attention to themselves, the show and, ultimately, the businesses and products which individuals launch to capitalize on their
newly found 'fame'. In Johnson's time, the 'rise to reputation' (Johnson 1751: 24)
largely relied on an individual's actions. Today public relations practitioners are
behind such promotional efforts. Although modern public relations has a history
dating back over a century (L'Etang 2004), it was during the 1990s that it became
'a noticeable and widespread activity' (Moloney 2006: 31) in the UK, where, as an
industry, it is estimated currently to be worth £7.2 billion and employ 61,600
people (Gorkana 2011).

This recent history is notable as it coincides with the emergence of a world dominated by a promotional culture (Wernick 1991). Public relations is both a cause and an outcome of the pluralistic society where values, ideas, interests and issues (let alone products and services) are all traded in a public sphere. Moloney (2000: 35) claimed that public relations has prospered as a result of modern society's 'promotional mindset'. Even critics of public relations rely on its techniques to promote their own work and anti-public relations stance. Taking Wernick's view (1991: 182) of promotion as 'not defined by what it says but by what it does' and L'Etang's (2006a: 147) observation that what public relations does is 'a relatively under-researched and unresolved area', it is feasible to describe public relations as a promotional industry.

Defining public relations

Established definitions do not consider public relations to be a promotional industry. The term 'public relations' is traced to the US in 1882 (Goldman 1948) with Bernays (1961: 20) claiming the title of 'public relations counsel' in 1920. His use 'described an activity that concerns itself with the relations between an enterprise and the public it serves and on which it is dependent' (Bernays 1961: 17). The essence of this explanation can be found in formal definitions in public relations literature such as that proposed by Cutlip et al (2000: 1): 'public relations is a management function that identifies, establishes and maintains mutually beneficial relationships between an organization and the various publics on whom its success or failure depends'.

The Chartered Institute of Public Relations provides a UK definition that advocates the discipline as that which 'looks after reputation, with the aim of earning understanding and support and influencing opinion and behaviour' (CIPR 2012). Although influence could be taken to mean a persuasive approach, an emphasis is placed on a need for an organization 'to listen to the opinions of those with whom it deals and not solely provide information'.

Early twentieth-century pioneers such as Bernays (1961: 21) argued that 'public relations is not publicity', the latter identified as a one-way street 'seeking to promote an individual, a group or an organization'. Constance Hope (1941), a publicist running her own agency in New York during the 1930s, observed a hierarchy of roles. At the bottom was the press agent: 'the fellow who believes that there is no such thing as bad publicity. He operates on the theory that even if his client plays the leading role in a murder trial, it's justified by the space he gets in the papers … he reasons that a plug is a plug, even in the obituary column' (Hope 1941: 17). This is evident in modern promotional culture with the attention and resultant commercial activity after the death of a celebrity. For example, sales of music by Michael Jackson, Amy Winehouse and Whitney Houston soared immediately on news of their deaths. Similarly, celebrities and members of the public who attract unwanted public attention (e.g., a court case or rumours of infidelity) immediately employ a press agent, such as Max Clifford, to protect and promote their interests. As Goldman (1948: 1) noted: 'the press agent, at least as old as the medieval fair and certainly as new as tomorrow's prima donna, has slithered along with little change in essential function'. The publicist was placed above the press agent. Hope described the pecking order in economic terms: 'the publicist, as a general rule, makes more money than the press agent, but the Public Relations Counsel is rich like anything' (Hope 1941: 18). Bernays dismissed the publicist; in return, Hope wrote (1941: 19): 'The P.R.C. prepares impressive campaigns, studded with surveys, graphs and excerpts from Freud, to show how he will mold the mass mind, psychoanalytically. (The P.R.C. scorns anything less than eight-cylinder words.)' The insult was clearly directed at Bernays, the nephew of Sigmund Freud.

Marketing literature has generally presented public relations as press agentry: a 'mass-promotion technique' (Kotler et al 1999: 830) primarily concerned with 'planting news ... in the media not paid for by the sponsor' and 'handling or heading off unfavourable rumours, stories and events'. This perspective sees public relations as a 'lower cost' option to advertising and dismissed as involved in 'simply communicating' (Kotler et al 1999: 831). Within public relations literature, publicity is viewed largely as a limited, one-way press agentry model, criticized as propaganda, where truth is not essential (Grunig and Hunt 1984).

This distinction made between the promotional and relationship perspectives of public relations can be found in the 'ambiguous and controversial' (Kitchen 1997: 224) relationship between marketing and public relations. This is best addressed by seeking to understand areas of similarity and overlap, as well as differences and unique competencies, in order to develop a mature and strategic partnership. Indeed, it may be resolved by the emergence of a more hybrid function, which is considered later in this chapter.

An isolationist stance seems at odds with the increasing convergence in communications that has been accelerated by the development of online and mobile technologies. However, subsuming public relations within the marketing mix ignores its strategic value. This means that promotion should be considered within a relationship framework. For example, attempts to build mutually beneficial relationships or to collaborate with publics or stakeholders starts with someone promoting a position, which others can agree with, or counter with their own promotional messages. In this way, public relations can be seen as a promotional industry, albeit with a focus on developing strategically beneficial relationships.

Lehr (2012) argues that where 'marketing is the ability of a company to say they are good and advertising is a platform to deliver that message, then public relations is the process of having others outside of a company, third-parties, say that the company is good'. Such endorsement requires public relations practitioners to build relationships that offer promotional, reputational and, consequentially, economic benefits. Public relations uses communicative actions – including promotional messages – to extract social capital from relationships. Its practitioners act as cultural and economic intermediaries between organizations and their publics. Their role is to engage directly and through influencers, using dialogue (the exchange and convergence of promotional messages) to build strategically valuable relationships.

Promotional trends

One key aspect of public relations is media relations. Davies (2008: 59) identifies what could be considered a promotional trend in the rise of 'churnalism', with journalists relying on ready-to-use materials supplied by public relations practitioners. This blames public relations for contributing towards the commercialization of mainstream media, with promotional messages carried as editorial rather than as advertising. A further promotional aspect is evident in the use of social media by journalists and publications/broadcasters, as well as public relations practitioners, to link to stories that themselves are hyped as much as possible through other mainstream and online media. In this way, mainstream and online media can be seen as promotional channels for organizations and individuals, with public relations as the means by which this opportunity can be exploited.

Likewise, the rise in celebrity – of those without much talent, high-profile individuals and brands as personalities – alongside the mega-spectacle (in politics, sports, entertainment, legal trials, product launches, charity fundraisers, television events, and so on) is pervasive in the media and public relations practice. Public relations practitioners use events and personalities as promotional vehicles to gain attention, using direct and mediated means of communications.

It is not just in the commercial sector where public relations practices are used for promotional purposes. Practitioners working in charities and non-governmental organizations (NGOs) promote causes, while those in the public sector devise campaigns to nudge the public towards adopting certain behaviours. A study undertaken in 2005 by the Chartered Institute of Public Relations (CIPR) and the Centre for Economics and Business Research (CEBR) estimated that one third of the turnover of UK-based public relations consultancies could be accounted for by those focused on the public sector and health and charity sectors. Somerville and Ramsey (2011) report the significant cost of government communications in the UK, noting that the Department of Health, for example, had a budget for communications of £52.2 million in 2007/2008. They outline how government communications have been carefully managed in recent years, particularly to privilege specific views rather than reflect the wider public interest. Techniques used to announce political ideas, policies and initiatives are reminiscent of the launch of new products, indicating the press agentry or publicity model of public relations (Grunig and Hunt 1984).

Public relations is at the centre of recent UK government initiatives such as the Public Health Responsibility Deal, which aims 'to tap into the potential for businesses and other organisations to improve public health and tackle health inequalities through their influence over food, alcohol, physical activity and health in the workplace'. Here, the government believes that working with commercial partners will be faster and more effective than adopting a regulatory strategy. Such moves have been criticized by high-profile organizations, including Diabetes UK and the British Heart Foundation, while the House of Commons Health Committee Twelfth Report stated: 'those with a financial interest must not be allowed to set the agenda for health improvement'. This example highlights resistance to a commercially oriented promotional culture in respect of issues traditionally viewed as outside its influence. This belies the promotional activities of the charity and public sectors in persuading the public through 'pro-healthy lifestyle messages' (Springston and Lariscy 2010: 547).

From a convergence perspective, these developments position public relations within an integrated marketing communications (IMC) framework. Hutton (2001: 205) contends that IMC has been seen as 'marketing imperialism' over public relations, echoing what Kitchen (1997: 226) terms a 'reductionist view' that subsumes, or subordinates, public relations to marketing. Within marketing textbooks, public relations is presented commonly as little more than a tactic within the promotional mix, utilizing media relations to achieve marketing objectives. Hutton (2001) goes further in claiming a reinvention of marketing has seen it moving into traditional public relations territory. This is evident in the rebranding and greater commercialization of community relations as cause-related marketing, internal communications as employee marketing, and public information campaigns as social marketing. Where public relations has always sought to engage a wide range of stakeholders and influencers, marketing has only recently expanded its focus beyond consumers or the retail trade. The focus of public relations on reputation management is countered by brand marketing. Indeed, Hutton (2001: 211) notes: 'virtually the whole of "public relations" has been repositioned outside the field as "relationship marketing"'.

In this regard, the promotional trends affecting public relations practice place greater emphasis on commercial (exchange) relationships rather than ones that reflect any wider communal, socially responsible purpose. This raises practical and ethical concerns relating to the credibility of promotional messages.

Credibility and public relations

On-going commercialization of communications potentially reduces the credibility of relationship development, particularly the value of earning third-party endorsement. Independent appraisal by media and other influencers has traditionally led to organic word of mouth communications. This multi-step flow through informed intermediaries (whether of an expert nature, higher social status or as peer-group referents) has been a core principle of public relations since its earliest days. However, the established intrinsic approach has undergone rebranding in recent years, being repositioned as viral, buzz, guerrilla or stealth marketing. Advocacy has shifted from reflecting genuine support, satisfaction and enthusiasm from a public relations perspective to being amplified or accelerated by a marketing approach of sponsoring and incentivizing customers, or influencers, for their endorsement.

This can be seen, for example, through social networking platforms where rather than using public relations to build communities with real interest in a product, organization or brand by creating compelling content and engagement, promotional campaigns are conceived involving competitions or other initiatives that require people to 'like' a brand regardless of their actual preferences. This gaming approach lacks credibility and reflects a focus on quantity rather than the quality of endorsement. The credibility of social media channels has been negatively affected by organizations seeking anonymously to influence search engine results, amend entries on Wikipedia, or create fake reviews on Amazon or Trip Advisor. In December 2011, the Bureau of Investigative Journalism published a report in which it claimed the public relations consultancy Bell Pottinger boasted of its ability to manipulate online coverage to reduce the impact of negative issues.

Rather than seeing relationships with influencers as a natural process inherent in both mass media and personal influence practices within public relations, there is an increasing tendency to manipulate, control and manage the outcome of such engagement. This may reflect a more marketing-oriented perspective, where an exchange relationship based on payment for access to media coverage has dominated practice. In public relations, more traditionally communal relationships have been developed, generating media coverage and word of mouth through understanding news values, building contacts and telling compelling stories. However, lack of recognition of the innate strengths of public relations practitioners as 'invisible persuaders' (Mitchie 1998), alongside the increasing power of online communications, has led to a more commercial approach. For example, blogger outreach initiatives have replaced the slower approach of building relationships with the immediate gratification of advertising, sponsorship and 'pay-to-play' approaches. This can be seen in the development of online forums for mothers from self-help groups into million pound businesses such as Mumsnet, sought out by politicians and brands for endorsement, which is increasingly offered under commercial terms. In turn, there are public and political calls for such financial arrangements to be made apparent or even legislated.

There is an irony in the shift towards organizations and individuals seeking more control over communications at a time when social media challenges this approach. The emerging online environment is frequently viewed as terrain that is in need of taming by legal regulation (Kohl 2007) or self-regulatory commercial forces (Price and Verhulst 2005). There is also a notable tension between the Internet as somewhere 'fostering conversation and connection between people' (Levine 2009: 25) and the 'commercialization of cyberspace' (Curran and Seaton 2003: 235). This echoes the debate about public relations as caught between the 'aggressive, competitive, hyperbolic, selling mind-set' of marketing and a 'more conciliatory, peacemaking approach' (Hutton 2001: 206).

The credibility issue relates to ensuring that an organization (or individual) earns a good reputation ('the result of what you do, what you say and what others say about you': CIPR 2012), reflecting delivery on 'the promise that makes a brand meaningful' (Abbing 2010: 32). In other words, promotional messages should reflect the reality of experience. This also positions public relations as responsible for creating and managing a compelling and credible organizational narrative using traditional and/or online platforms to build relationships within the wider promotional culture.

Public relations and promotional culture

There has been little consideration of public relations within promotional culture literature. However, Wernick's (1991) extension of promotional discourse beyond advertisements sees L'Etang (2006b) identify public relations within this thesis. The antecedents of public relations are traced in the US to circus promotion, with P. T. Barnum presented as a 'brash huckster' (Harris 1981: 3) and 'master publicist' (Crable and Vibbert 1986: 98) from the nineteenth century. In the UK, L'Etang (2004) identifies professional origins of the field in local government-sector publicity campaigns of the 1930s. The involvement of public relations can be seen in these cultural developments in terms of the promotion of mass entertainment and the promotion of mass public compliance.

Kilborn (2006: 188) argues: 'PR can be regarded an integral part of the "promotional culture" which has become a significant feature of contemporary Western societies'; citing Miller and Dinan (2000: 27–28), who see the work of 'promotional professionals' thus: 'PR and public affairs have seeped into the very fabric and decision-making in Britain and in the European political arena'. Public relations is identified by Hesmondhalgh and Baker (2011: 103) alongside marketing in affecting 'creative-commercial relations' by controlling the circulation (distribution) of cultural products. This sees public relations as influencing 'creative outcomes' (Hesmondhalgh and Baker 2011: 104) – for example, within the music industry, a process, it is argued, that has 'quickly alienated "editorial" (creative) staff'. Journalism is presented as a creative process which is not only commercialized by external public relations practitioners, but also by those working in-house within publishers who seek to influence and promote publications as brands.

Moloney (2000: 31) notes that the rise in civic and commercial pluralism (which he links to 'the pervasiveness of PR in contemporary UK society') led to 'more media businesses and more media marketing ... aimed at readers, listeners and viewers' (Moloney 2000: 56), which in turn further fuelled the demand for and 'reliance on PR material'. As a consequence of this increasingly commercial spiral within media relations, news and other editorial content can be seen as a product in its own right and promoted as such. For example, television channels not only create adverts that are broadcast to promote various programmes, they use public relations to gain coverage within other programmes (including news reports), mainstream print media and social media channels. Going further, the way in which the BBC *Top Gear* programme has created a global market for the television show, spawned a magazine, website and live event, as well as generated fame (and commercial benefits) for its presenters, demonstrates the 'many-sided inter-relatedness of promotional messages' (Wernick 1991: 94), which extends into the products, and personalities, featured within the *Top Gear* stable. The promotional culture even led to a court case involving exposure of the identity of the anonymous racing driver behind The Stig, a fictional character who had been heavily marketed as a *Top Gear* product, particularly to children (including Stig avatar items in virtual reality games such as *Gran Turismo 5*). The anonymity of the character can be seen as a critical promotional feature with the exposure of the identity of the original Stig (wearing black) by a newspaper and the legal dispute involving an autobiography revealing the identity of the second Stig (who wore white). Media coverage of the revelations acted further as promotional messages for the *Top Gear* brand. Controversy relating to the programme and its most contentious presenter, Jeremy Clarkson, again generates headlines that promote the BBC *Top Gear* brand and all its commercial offshoots.

Similarly, a network of promotional associations is created by the appearance of the *Top Gear* presenters in adverts or through their other journalistic and promotional work. Companies, and their public relations teams, also seek to connect their promotional messages to the *Top Gear* network of communications. Perhaps most famously was the move in 2009 promoting the start of a new BBC *Top Gear* series which involved a £1 million Ferrari FXX driven by The Stig, who was unmasked as Formula One racing champion Michael Schumacher, just ahead of the announcement of his return as a Ferrari driver. The car, one of only 30 produced, is a unique promotional product, having been presented to Schumacher by the company on his earlier retirement and featuring a distinctive visual appearance. Public relations is uniquely able to organize and maximize the promotion of such stunts on many different levels, before, during and after their occurrence.

Wernick (1991) notices this mutual interconnection of promotional messages in the eighteenth century, albeit on a smaller scale. Indeed, there is a long history of using celebrity and mega-spectacles within the media to serve its own promotional purposes. Images of the decorated Christmas trees belonging to Queen Victoria and Prince Albert were promoted in the *Illustrated London News* in 1848, creating public interest in this form of celebration (Rappaport 2003). In organizing the Thousand Mile Trial spectacle in 1900 to change opinions and promote understanding of motor cars (Bennett 2000), Claude Johnson of the Automobile Club enlisted the support of the *Daily Mail* newspaper to provide publicity, underwrite costs and contribute a substantial prize fund. Taking the concept further, the Tour de France was conceived in 1903 as a promotional idea by *L'Auto* magazine, although its originators could not have foreseen the breadth of promotional connections (both positive and negative) the event would establish as a standalone brand into the twenty-first century. L'Etang (2006b) has specifically considered the links between public relations and sport within promotional culture. She highlights a role for public relations practitioners in the 'primary definition' (L'Etang 2006b: 387) of 'events, issues and other actors' – that is, in the way in which professional sports are presented and promoted, which reduces the media to 'secondary definers'. This control of narrative underpins the tensions between media and public relations practitioners as a result of an increasing promotional culture. Furthermore, in presenting public relations as a cultural intermediary, L'Etang (2006b: 388) argues that it plays a role in 'the commodification of lifestyles, values and relationships', particularly in the context of professional sports.

Applying Bourdieu's concept of capital to public relations, Ihlen (2009) considers that the commodification of communications means significant financial resources are required to ensure adequate presence in the market system of free speech. While such privileged access is available to those who can afford professional public relations counsel, online media developments 'may act as a counter-weight to the influence of economic capital' (Ihlen 2009: 71) within contemporary society. They also contribute towards the expansion of the web of interconnected promotional messages. In addition to 11 million likes for the official *Top Gear* Facebook site at the start of April 2012, there are dozens of unofficial pages, each promoting the brand.

Ethical concerns

Positioning public relations within a promotional culture context raises concerns about ethical practice. The term 'PR disaster' is routinely used to indicate 'anything that could catalyse embarrassing or negative publicity for a given organization' (McCusker 2006: 311), implying that the discipline is responsible when issues have not been addressed effectively (in the opinion of the critics), resulting in unwanted attention. Public relations is blamed regardless of the origins of the problem.

In some cases, poorly conceived promotional activities themselves necessitate crisis management. For example, an advertisement to promote the Cadbury's Temptations chocolate brand on India's Independence Day in 2002 included a map highlighting a contested area of Jammu and Kashmir with the slogan 'Too good to be true'. This caused an international outcry, which was repeated in 2011 by a race row regarding a UK advert that offended the supermodel Naomi Campbell by appearing to compare her to a chocolate bar called Bliss. With Cadbury's now owned by the US conglomerate Kraft, calls for a US boycott by the campaign group Operation Black Vote ensued. Criticism of promotions can also be a promotional tactic for charities, activists and pressure groups. For example, the Food Commission contributes towards media reports and complains to regulators in order to raise the profile of its activities while challenging the actions of food companies. Here we have an example of an organization using an underdog public relations strategy to counter economic brand power and promote its own interests. Similarly, grassroots campaigns can be mobilized (or emerge organically) to challenge large companies. Facebook groups have successfully achieved a change of direction from brands such as Marks and Spencer and HSBC, although in the case of Cadbury's Wispa brand, the public relations consultant Mark Borkowski was involved in promoting a small underground movement calling for the chocolate bar's return into an online movement. This is an example of what critics claim is the ability of public relations to 'manipulate while it remains invisible' (Stauber and Rampton 1995: 16). Yet, when seen to be active, public relations efforts may be labelled a 'PR exercise', reflecting 'a situation of communication with no substance within it' (Green 2007: 215).

Bowen (2010: 570) argues communications helps to 'examine matters in depth' with 'an ethical vision for the role of public relations in building collaborative decisions and appreciating publics'. However, she notes little ethical training within the field below senior practitioner level, and the regular occurrence of contentious practices such as 'dishonesty, vociferous advocacy, spin or manipulation' (Bowen 2010: 571). This does not contend that promotion itself is unethical, although Hallahan (2010) notes 'when critics refer to questionable public relations practices, they are usually referring to the *publicity* aspects of public relations'. The distancing of public relations from publicity and, by implication, from promotion reflects the earlier discussion relating to definitions and the relationship with marketing.

It is not clear to what extent public relations is involved in marketing campaigns that create promotional difficulties for companies. Perhaps there is little strategic input (reflecting a lack of communication between marketing and public relations), or public relations may operate at a tactical level only. Any pre-crisis management systems (Jaques 2010) in place would appear to omit consideration of issues caused by promotional activities. There is also the possibility that organizations deliberately seek out controversy and see public relations' role in crisis management as part of the promotional campaign. This is evident with the airline Ryanair, which routinely attracts complaints for its advertising and promotions. In February 2012, the Advertising Standards Authority banned two adverts featuring female flight crew dressed in underwear. These had been placed in the *Guardian*, *Independent* and *Daily Telegraph* newspapers, which would appear to have been chosen to increase the likelihood of complaints rather than for their advertising merit in reaching typical Ryanair customers. Controversial advertising is a promotional strategy the airline has used before, alongside deliberately provocative statements (e.g., plans to show pornography and remove toilets on flights) from Chief Executive Michael O'Leary to generate considerable media attention.

Whether or not public relations is a promotional industry remains debatable, even when it reflects promotional practices and can be seen as contributing towards, and a consequence of, an increasingly promotional culture. This topic has not been studied to a great extent within the public relations literature (L'Etang 2006b), where a relationship perspective is presented as both normative and positivist reflection of practice, most notably embodied in the field's dominant Model of Excellence (Dozier et al 1995). Although this should not preclude using persuasive messaging to build relationships or resolve conflict (Grunig 2001), promotion tends to be relegated alongside publicity or press agentry within marketing PR (Kitchen 1997) and to be more evident in 'tactical training' (Hallahan 2010: 524), rather than considered an essential component of public relations as a strategic management function.

Public relations within a converging communications context

Convergence as a way of life

In many ways, public relations practitioners have always recognized a convergence context for communications in terms of engaging with multiple stakeholder groups through a wide range of channels (both direct and mediated). For example, the need to coordinate internal communications (with employees), lobbying (with politicians) and public information (through media relations) is reflected throughout routine public relations practice. Similarly, public relations practitioners have accommodated the emergence of radio, television, websites and social media in addition to print and direct channels over the past century. Such flexibility is part of the DNA of public relations.

Public relations has a long history of working with many influencers such as journalists, celebrities, academics, experts and community leaders. To these have been added bloggers and others who offer online third-party endorsement. Contact has continued to be made in building face-to-face relationships, alongside the use of the telephone, with telexes, letters and faxes being replaced by email, texts and social media networking. Consequently, a typical public relations programme is likely to integrate various methods, channels and sources of communication in order to engage with a range of stakeholders and publics. Nevertheless, the online communications context provides a new dimension of convergence with regard to global reach and immediate access. In addition, it enables content to be aggregated by a complex dynamic network of public and private relationships, which challenges the gatekeeper role that has largely been occupied by public relations practitioners on behalf of organizations and journalists within wider society.

An expert bridging role

The ease by which individuals and organizations can connect to disseminate and share information or express opinions online presents a mainly uncontrolled environment. With their experience in anticipating and reacting to emerging issues, engaging with independent influencers and managing crisis situations, the role competencies of public relations practitioners (Gregory 2008) position the occupation to take advantage of this online public sphere, where 'private people come together as a public' (Habermas 1989, cited by L'Etang 2008: 107). The free-for-all nature of online communications potentially creates more of a need for informed gatekeepers, with public relations equipped to connect organizations and their publics.

Kim and Ni (2010: 49–50) present a 'strategic management paradigm' where public relations 'bridges gaps of interests and stances on problems between an organization and its environment by communicating interactively and proactively'. This is contrasted with a role as a buffer, used to prevent or control access to information, which Kim and Ni (2010: 49) report as reflecting '*tactical* and *technical* messaging efforts' where 'reputation, brand, image, and identity, are the ultimate goals of public relations activities'. This suggests public relations expertise is required for proactive issues and crisis management within the contemporary communications context where online and offline channels converge.

The function also acts as an internal facilitator to help organizations respond to the challenges presented by online communications. Gregory (1999) identifies three relevant phenomena:

- transparency – how organizations' activities are made more visible (openness in communications);
- porosity – how organizations are increasingly leaky, with digital information easily distributed internally and externally.
- agency – how others can change information, acting as positive or negative influencers in endorsing or challenging a message.

Working with human resources and senior management, public relations needs to develop a realistic policy and undertake training to cover employees' engagement (personally and professionally) with social media channels. It is unlikely to be reasonable to ban use entirely, but guidance is needed to clarify issues such as confidentiality, privacy and protection of the organization's reputation. Risks to the organization (and employees) need to be determined and minimized, while recognizing that, as with other forms of communication, mistakes may happen.

At the same time, public relations should work with information technology (IT), customer relations, external consultancies employed to undertake social media activities, and other relevant functions to put together an effective issues-monitoring process for all online communications. This needs to be connected to research and knowledge management, as well as crisis preparation procedures. The requirement is for qualitative monitoring of social and other online media, alongside existing public relations evaluation of traditional media and influencer commentary. In particular, early identification of potential issues, the volume and reach of discussion, along with analysis of those engaged in originating and disseminating information should be the responsibility of public relations practitioners in their expert bridging role. Such a proactive approach offers an opportunity to engage others rather than reflect 'surveillance' (L'Etang 2008: 86) where organizations seek to exert power over those being investigated.

Complexity and crisis management

A promotional approach in society is evident in the tendency within public relations to focus on creating, communicating and monitoring key messages. Simplification of the content of communications reflects a view that publics are more likely to engage in low elaboration (Petty and Cacioppo 1986) of information, reacting emotionally through the peripheral processing of superficial aspects. Sound bites are more readily recalled rather than informed debate or explanation of complex matters. This stage-managed approach is not new as Lippmann (1922: 11) observed: 'great men, even in their lifetime, are usually known to the public only through a fictitious personality', which has been created by professional communicators. Today this is evident when public relations practitioners act as ghost-writers for blog posts or Twitter accounts, alongside script-writing, media training and other techniques used to present a particular image.

Organizations, guided by public relations practitioners, use rhetoric in part as a response to increasingly hostile media. Debates comprise one-sided arguments in which parties seek to win rather than engage in dialectical communications. Frequently, organizations are presented as villains in the context of narrative journalism, while their own communications offer heroic narratives. It is essential that public relations advisers prepare executives for such confrontations, although resorting to simplified messages potentially undermines public understanding of complex matters. Ironically, when gaffes are made (such as BP's Tony Hayward, who infamously said he wanted to get his life back at the height of the disastrous oil spill in the Gulf in 2010 or Gerald Ratner, describing his company's products as crap two decades earlier), the organization is described as having poor PR. This encourages greater control rather than addressing the increasing needs for excellent communication competencies at the highest level in the modern risk society (Beck 1992). Indeed, when a CEO is a charismatic or skilled communicator, there is suspicion of style over substance.

One issue affecting the role of public relations practitioners, or media-trained executives, as the corporate mouthpiece is that greater authenticity and expertise are expected within the context of an instantaneous communications environment. It is impossible for public relations practitioners to be cognisant in any depth across all aspects of an organization's operations. In the time taken to verify information, 'the immediacy and interconnectedness of mobile, online and social media are able to amplify what might otherwise be issues of low or no significance' (Yaxley 2011: 154).

The implication is that complicated issues need to be communicated directly by functional experts. This raises the importance of a public relations mind-set within organizations by which a natural voice is heard, but potential issues are anticipated and avoided. Rather than reflecting a promotional approach, the relationship context discussed above becomes more important. An organization needs to gain trust and manage a reputation for being adept in its area of responsibility rather than simply promoting an image that lacks credibility. This is particularly necessary when many issues cannot be addressed by simple statements and require publics, and influencers, to engage in understanding rather than immediately reacting to emerging situations.

The more complicated nature of the modern converging communications context necessitates a new approach involving public relations acting 'to equip key managers with the capabilities, flexibility and confidence to deal with sudden and unexpected problems/events – or shifts in public perception of any such problems/events' (Robert and Lajtha 2002: 181). Gilpin and Murphy (2008) advocate a model based on establishing strong relationships and robust knowledge of the organization, as well as developing competencies in intuition, active sense-making, sensitivity to change and rapid decision-making. This reflects a shift towards improvisation and away from rational planning – echoing the more open context of online communications where attempting control is problematic.

Apologia as a promotional phenomenon

In an era of social media, crisis situations appear to inflate, burst and dissipate at a greater pace than ever. It has never been easier to promote awareness of a problem to a global audience through social networks and online multimedia channels. The term 'clicktivism' has been coined to reflect the promotional nature of such activism, which seeks to raise funds, stimulate online debate and generate public action (e.g., through online polls and protests).

At the same time, such grievances can be observed immediately using computerized systems to monitor specific keywords. This emphasizes convergence between public relations and consumer relations where responses to individual problems need to be recognized as public, something that used to be the case only with issues affecting high-profile individuals or reported to the organization by journalists. Effective management of even minor problems can be seen to offer promotional opportunities, although it is important to solve underlying causes rather than focus on managing public perceptions to issues, In an era of online communications where anyone can gain global public attention, it is difficult to prevent negative issues from arising. Seeking to prevent disclosure (using tactics where connections, manipulation, threats or legal restraints are employed) is also likely to backfire, with online exposure of such approaches presenting an individual or organization in a much worse light and exacerbating any issue.

Another crisis management tactic that has become a promotional phenomenon is the high-profile apology. Aristotle originally conceived the term '*apologia*' as 'the rhetoric of self-defense, image-repair or crisis management' (Campbell and Huxman 2003: 293). Today the act is a public spectacle, rather than reflection of contrition. For example, Tiger Woods faced demands for a public apology following exposure of his marital infidelities, where, arguably, this was a private rather than a public relations issue (Sowell 2010). From a public relations perspective, *apologia* is used to promote the client's perspective and forms part of an integrated communications approach that may include public advertising, as well as presenting information directly to internal and external stakeholders.

Lazare (2005: 7) observes an 'apology phenomenon' in modern media, reflecting what he asserts are pseudo-apologies, where sorrow is expressed conditionally rather than reflecting responsibility (Hearit 2001). The role of the public apology as promotional performance is emphasized in Corbett's statement (1988: xi): 'What perversity is there in the human psyche that makes us enjoy the spectacle of human beings desperately trying to answer the charges levelled against them? Maybe secretly, as we read or listen, we say to ourselves, "Ah, there but for the grace of

God go I.'" Such apologies reflect public demand for retributive power over organizations and celebrities, who are forced to embarrass themselves as a form of public entertainment.

The hand of promotional public relations may be involved in generating such apologies. Activist groups, for example, commonly use confrontation, mass rallies, shock tactics and other techniques to pillory a high-profile organization in the court of public opinion. Punishment is frequently subversive treatment of an organization's brand icons through social media. For example, during the Gulf of Mexico oil crisis of 2010, Greenpeace launched a campaign using social media photography site Flikr to redesign BP's Helios logo (which had been famously redesigned by corporate identity firm Landor in 2000 to reflect a strategic shift 'Beyond Petroleum'). Greenpeace sought to show the company was 'up to their necks in tar sands and deepwater drilling' with the redesigned logo to be used in an 'international campaign against the oil company'.

Convergence of promotion and counter promotion

Brill and Marrocco (2011) identify the emergence of a third sector since the 1980s, comprising more than 180,000 registered charities, alongside social enterprises, community interest companies (CICs), trade unions, political parties and educational institutions within civil society. These types of organizations operate in an increasingly pluralistic world, where they compete for public attention as well as funding and other forms of support. As such, the third sector – frequently in partnership with the public and/or private sectors – is part of the promotional culture, using promotional methods (particularly public relations) to promote causes or particular behaviours. An integrated communications approach would tend to be led by the public relations function in such organizations, according to Hutton (2001), with many of the largest not-for-profit concerns reflecting sophisticated brand management strategies and considerable investment in promotion and campaigning activities.

Public relations within the third sector may be thought of as acting in the public interest by promoting matters of concern onto the media, public, corporate, policy and social media agendas. This involves creating issues-related campaigns that 'bring topics before the public so that they can be discussed' using publicity techniques and 'symbolic action' (Taylor 2001: 8). This territory reflects the convergence of public relations and social marketing. McKie and Toledano (2008: 319) consider that a marketing approach in this arena has negative effects such as reallocating 'resources away from disadvantaged and at risk groups', as well as a tendency to undertake 'expensive advertising campaigns' rather than build 'sustaining relationships'. They believe the involvement of public relations expertise enhances the productivity of social projects.

Convergence in this context raises several issues. First of all, not-for-profit organizations are using promotional techniques to reflect a more modern approach, mimicking those of the commercial sector and necessitating a need to invest resources in marketing and public relations rather than service delivery. A more promotional perspective seeks out narratives that offer stronger stories to gain attention and stimulate action. It also risks objectifying those affected by the causes that are being promoted. This can be seen in the documentary film *Pink Ribbons Inc* (Gombita and Lunney 2012), which questions 'the manufactured messages and "breast cancer culture" of hope and optimism, promoted by charitable foundations'. The issue here arises from the promotional agenda of corporations who engage in cause marketing by seeking out charities and not-for-profit organizations with whom they wish to associate their brand. Causes are likely to be selected for their promotional value to the brand, while promotional activities will probably be chosen to benefit the corporation, rather than reflect the needs of the charitable partner. This results in the simplistic use of cause-related symbols (such as the pink ribbon) to promote products and corporate brands without stimulating discussion about the underlying issue, or acknowledging the real-world experiences of those affected by the relevant cause. Staff and other resources will be required within the organization to manage the relationship and campaigns involving commercial partners, which is likely to put further focus on promotion rather than the cause.

Conflict is inherent in the use of promotional techniques to promote behaviour and counter this promotion when considering social issues. This can be seen, for example, in partnerships between cancer charities and organizations (such as cosmetic companies) whose products may contribute towards the cause of cancer. It can also be hard to distinguish between campaigns that seek to promote both sides of an issue. For example, alcohol awareness campaigns use the same techniques as promotions for alcoholic drinks. Promotional messages can also have the opposite effect to that sought; for example, in seeking to raise awareness of the dangers of websites promoting anorexia, the existence of such sites, and their 'thinspirational' slogans, is being promoted.

Celebrities and spectacles as public relations promotional techniques

Turner et al (2000: 30) discuss the use of events in public relations as presenting both a 'promotional opportunity – and a particular kind of experience'. This demonstrates how relationship-building increasingly converges with publicity-oriented aspects of public relations. For example, media attending events organized by public relations practitioners are being entertained and given an experience, as well as, or sometimes instead of, being provided with information. This can be seen in the longstanding relationship developed between Audi and the Elton John Aids Foundation. Audi creates special models to be auctioned at the annual fundraising White Tie & Tiara Ball, which is attended by A-list celebrities and high-profile media. In 2010, the company donated a pink Audi A1 designed by British artist Damien Hirst; in 2011, two chromed R8 Spyders were auctioned, raising almost $1 million. As a promotional activity, Audi is able to build relationships with celebrity influencers and media contacts, as well as gaining publicity and a reputation for social responsibility in donating to a worthy cause. The car itself has less media value than the associations with celebrities, who are viewed as essential to the publicity process (Turner et al 2000). Again, this tactic is not new in public relations, with the New York publicist Benjamin Sonnenberg famously organizing lavish parties at his Gramercy Park home in the mid-twentieth century (Barmash 1983).

Likewise, publicity stunts have a long history as a promotional technique utilized by public relations practitioners. Borkowski (2000: 7) highlights how 'past masters of the art' set up 'situations which are so intriguing and so bizarre that they are irresistible to the press'. From the use of animals to protest movements, stunts continue to attract public and media attention. Indeed, Basen (2012) considers the 2011 Occupy movement as a promotional phenomenon, both in terms of its brand value and how organizations have sought to identify themselves with it. For example, the Pepsi advert at the 2012 Super Bowl aligned the drink with the general public, not the 1 per cent elite, echoing the Occupy message. The *Wall Street Journal* (2011) reported the irony of tax-avoiding celebrities visiting Occupy camps, as well as a fashion shoot being held by the *Evening Standard* newspaper (owned by Russian billionaire Alexander Lebedev) at the Occupy London site 'to celebrate the "radical chic" of the protest movement'.

Kellner (2003: 2) connects the use of staged events and media imagery to the 'society of the spectacle' concept proposed by Guy Debord in the 1960s. He considers how media spectacles are increasingly constructed around sporting events, political occurrences and items of news. Daniel Boorstin pointed out the notion of pseudo-events and celebrities who are famous for being famous in the early 1960s (Turner et al 2000). Since then, almost all types of media and public relations have adopted both approaches in attracting attention. This can be seen in the appointment of celebrities to produce policy recommendations for government, and the reporting in the *Financial Times* (2012) and other serious media of the launch of a bacon-themed coffin by Seattle-based J&D's Foods as a promotion for its mayonnaise and an entry into the customized casket market. The fact that it is not clear whether this is an April Fool's joke or a serious business development highlights the increasing difficulty of distinguishing genuine from pseudo-news.

Conclusion

Although the argument that public relations is a promotional industry is contentious, the field is closely entwined with an increasingly pluralistic society within which promotional trends affect its practice. This can be seen in all sectors of society where policies and causes are promoted using the same techniques as products and services. The unique contribution that public relations brings in an era of communications convergence is an understanding of how mutually beneficial relationships ensure credibility and authenticity, which is missing in marketing-oriented exchange relationships.

The value of public relations in anticipating potential issues and managing crisis situations reflects competence in engaging with multiple stakeholders through a variety of channels. Public relations is well placed to take advantage of online technologies where practitioners need to act in an expert bridging role.

At the same time, public relations facilitates promotion and counter-promotion, using techniques such as the use of celebrities and pseudo-events which further contribute towards an increasingly promotional culture in society. As such, this affects the level of knowledge and debate in the public sphere, particularly around complex issues.

One outcome of the increased convergence discussed in this chapter could be that the future of public relations as a distinct discipline is under threat. However, the experience of Simon Sproule, Nissan Motor Company corporate vice president, global marketing communications, illustrates the opportunity presented for those with a professional public relations background. Sproule began his career as a press officer for Ford of Britain, gaining international experience before heading up a global marketing operation established at Renault-Nissan (Sachs 2011). In integrating marketing communications, media relations, investor relations, corporate social responsibility (CSR) and internal communications, Sproule emphasizes a need to break down a silo mentality and create a 'new profession' (Sachs 2011: 91), which will 'become the norm rather than the exception'. He argues for public relations practitioners to become integrationists if they are to develop successful careers.

Bibliography

Abbing, E. R. (2010) *Brand-Driven Innovation*, Lausanne: AVA Publishing.

Barnash, I. (1983) *Always Live Better than your Clients: The Fabulous Life and Times of Benjamin Sonnenberg, America's Greatest Publicist*, New York, NY: Dodd, Mead.

Basen, I. (2012) *Featured Documentary: Occupy Next*, http://www.cbc.ca/thesundayedition/documentaries/2012/04/01/occupy-next, accessed 2 April 2012.

Beck, U. (1992) *Risk Society: Towards a New Modernity*, M. Ritter (trans.), London: Sage.

Bennett, E. (2000) *Thousand Mile Trial*, London: Fountain Press.

Bernays, E. L. (1961) *Your Future in Public Relations*, New York, NY: Richards Rosen Press.

Borkowski, M. (2000) *Improperganda: The Art of the Publicity Stunt*, London: Vision On Publishing.

Bowen, S.A. (2010) 'The Nature of Good in Public Relations: What Should Be Its Normative Ethic?', in R. L. Heath (ed) *The Sage Handbook of Public Relations*, 2nd edition, London: Sage.

Brill, P. and Marrocco, C. (2011) 'Not-for-Profit Public Relations', in A. Theaker (ed) *The Public Relations Handbook*, 4th edition, Abingdon, UK: Routledge.

Camlot, J. (2008) *Style and the Nineteenth-Century British Critic: Sincere Mannerisms*, Aldershot, UK: Ashgate Publishing.

Campbell, K. K. and Huxman, S. S. (2003) *The Rhetorical Act: Thinking, Speaking and Writing Critically*, 3rd edition, Belmont, CA: Thomson Wadworth.

CEBR (Centre for Economics and Business Research Ltd) (2005) *PR Today: 48,000 Professionals; £36.5 Billion Turnover. The Economic Significance of Public Relations*, http://www.cipr.co.uk/sites/default/files/CIPR%20full%20report%20-%20November%204%202005.pdf, accessed 1 March 2012.

CIPR (Chartered Institute of Public Relations) (2012), *What is PR?*, http://www.cipr.co.uk/content/careers-cpd/careers-pr/what-pr, accessed 1 March 2012.

Corbett, J. E. (1988) 'Foreword', In R. R. Halford (ed) *Oratorical Encounters: Selected Studies and Sources of Twentieth-Century Political Accusations and Apologies*, New York, NY: Greenwood Publishing Group.

Crable, R. E. and Vibbert, S. L. (1986) *Public Relations as Communications Management*, Edina, MN: Bellwether Press.

Curran, J. and Seaton, J. (2003) *Power without Responsibility: The Press, Broadcasting, and New Media in Britain*, Abingdon, UK: Routledge.

Cutlip, S. M., Center, A. H. and Broom, G. M. (2000) *Effective Public Relations*, 8th edition, Upper Saddle River, NJ: Prentice Hall.

Davies, N. (2008) *Flat Earth News*, London: Chatto & Windus.

Dozier, D. M., Grunig, L. A. and Grunig, J. E. (1995) *Manager's Guide to Excellence in Public Relations and Communication Management*, Mahwah, NJ: Lawrence Erlbaum Associates.

Financial Times (2012) 'J& D's Foods Wants Slice of Coffin Market', http://www.ft.com/cms/s/0/a3120a4c-7a82-11e1-9c77-00144feab49a.html#axzz1qzGlGKJd, accessed 2 April 2012.

Gilpin, D. R. and Murphy, P. J. (2008) *Crisis Management in a Complex World*, Oxford: Oxford University Press.

Goldman, E. F. (1948) *Two-Way Street: The Emergence of the Public Relations Counsel*, Boston, MA: Bellman Publishing.

Gombita, J. and Lunney, M. (2012), *Pink Ribbons, Inc. – Rage against the Marketing Machine's 'Shiny, Pink Success Story'*, http://www.prconversations.com/index.php/2012/02/pink-ribbons-inc–rage-against-the-marketing-machine's-shiny-pink-success-story, accessed 1 March 2012.

Gorkana (2011) *2011 PR Census*, PR Week/PRCA.

Green, A. (2007) *Creativity in Public Relations*, 3rd edition, London: Kogan Page.

Greenpeace (2010) *What's Behind BP's Logo*, http://www.greenpeace.org.uk/files/tarsands/logo-competition.html, accessed 1 March 2012.

Gregory, A. (1999) *How the Internet Radically Alters Public Relations Practice*, Institute of Public Relations/Public Relations Consultants Association, Internet Commission Report.

——(2008) 'Competencies of Senior Communication Practitioners in the UK: An Initial Study', *Public Relations Review*, vol 34, no 3, pp215–223.

Grunig, J. E. (2001) 'Two-Way Symmetrical Public Relations: Past, Present and Future', in R. L. Heath (ed) *The Handbook of Public Relations*, Thousand Oaks, CA: Sage.

Grunig, J. E. and Hunt, T. (1984) *Managing Public Relations*, New York, NY: Holt, Rinehart and Winston.

Hallahan, K. (2010) 'Being Public: Publicity as Public Relations', in R. L. Heath (ed) *The Sage Handbook of Public Relations*, 2nd edition, London: Sage.

Harris, N. (1981) *Humbug: The Art of P. T. Barnum*, Chicago, IL: University of Chicago Press.

Hearit, K. M. (2001) 'Corporate Apologia: When an Organization Speaks in Defense of Itself', in R. L. Heath (ed) *The Sage Handbook of Public Relations*, 2nd edition, London: Sage.

Hesmondhalgh, D. and Baker, S. (2011) *Creative Labour: Media Work in Three Cultural Industries*, Abingdon, UK: Routledge.

Hope, C. (1941) *Publicity is Broccoli*, New York, NY: The Bobbs-Merrill Company.

House of Commons Health Committee: Twelfth Report (2011) http://www.publications.parliament.uk/pa/cm201012/cmselect/cmhealth/1048/104803.htm, accessed 1 March 2012.

Hutton, J. G. (2001) 'Defining the Relationship between Public Relations and Marketing: Public Relations' Most Important Challenge', in R. L. Heath (ed) *The Handbook of Public Relations*, London: Sage.

Ihlen, O. (2009) 'On Bourdieu: Public Relations in Field Struggles', in O. Ihlen, B. van Ruler and M. Fredriksson (eds) *Public Relations and Social Theory: Key Figures and Concepts*, Abingdon, UK: Routledge.

Jaques, T. (2010) 'Embedding Issue Management: From Process to Policy', in R. L. Heath (ed) *The Sage Handbook of Public Relations*, 2nd edition, London: Sage.

Johnson, S. (1751) *The Rambler*, Longman, accessed via Google eBook.

Kellner, D. (2003) *Media Spectacle*, London: Routledge.

Kilborn, R. (2006) 'A Marriage Made in Heaven or in Hell? Relations between Documentary Filmmakers and PR Practitioners', in J. L'Etang and M. Pieczka (eds) *Critical Perspectives in Public Relations*, Mahwah, NJ: Lawrence Erlbaum Associates.

Kim, J.-N. and Ni, L. (2010) 'Seeing the Forest through the Trees: The Behavioural Strategic Management Paradigm in Public Relations and Its Future', in R. L. Heath (ed) *The Sage Handbook of Public Relations*, 2nd edition, London: Sage.

Kitchen, P. J. (1997) 'The Interaction between Public Relations and Marketing', in P. J. Kitchen (ed) *Public Relations, Principles and Practice*, London: International Thomson Business Press.

Kohl, U. (2007) *Jurisdiction and the Internet: A Study of Regulatory Competence over Online Activity*, Cambridge: Cambridge University Press.

Kotler, P., Armstrong, G., Saunders, J. and Wong, V. (1999) *Principles of Marketing*, 2nd edition, Upper Saddle River, NJ: Prentice Hall.

L'Etang, J. (2004) *Public Relations in Britain: A History of the Professional Practice in the 20th Century*, Mahwah, NJ: Lawrence Erlbaum Associates.

——(2006a) 'Public Relations as Theatre: Key Players in the Evolution of British Public Relations', in J. L'Etang and M. Pieczka (eds) *Critical Perspectives in Public Relations*, Mahwah, NJ: Lawrence Erlbaum Associates.

——(2006b) 'Public Relations and Sport in Promotional Culture', *Public Relations Review*, vol 32, no 4, pp386–394.

——(2008) *Public Relations: Concepts, Practice and Critique*, London: Sage.

Lazare, A. (2005) *On Apology*, New York, NY: Oxford University Press.

Lehr, D. (2012) *Public Relations: Why It Matters ALL the Time*, http://www.proactive communications.com/index.php/2012/02/public-relations-why-it-matters-all-the-time, accessed 1 March 2012.

Levine, R. (2009) 'But How Does It Taste?', in R. Levine, C. Locke, D. Searls and D. Weinberger (eds) *The Cluetrain Manifesto: 10th Anniversary Edition*, New York, NY: Basic Books.

Lippmann, W. (1922) *Public Opinion*, New York, NY: Harcourt, Brace.

Lynn, S. (1992) *Samuel Johnson after Deconstruction: Rhetoric and the Rambler*, Carbondale, IL: Southern Illinois University Press.

McCusker, G. (2006) *Public Relations Disasters: Talespin – Inside Stories and Lessons Learnt*, London: Kogan Page.

McKie, D. and Toledano, M. (2008) 'Dangerous Liaison or Perfect Match? Public Relations and Social Marketing', *Public Relations Review*, vol 34, no 4, pp318–324.

Miller, D. and Dinan, W. (2000) *A Century of Spin: How Public Relations Became the Cutting Edge of Corporate Power*, London: Pluto Press.

Mitchie, D. (1998) *The Invisible Persuaders*, London: Bantam Press.

Moloney, K. (2000) *Rethinking Public Relations: The Spin and the Substance*, Abingdon, UK: Routledge.

——(2006) *Rethinking Public Relations: PR Propaganda and Democracy*, 2nd edition, Abingdon, UK: Routledge.

Petty, R. E. and Cacioppo, J. T. (1986) 'The Elaboration Likelihood Model of Persuasion', in L. Berkowitz (ed) *Advances in Experimental Social Psychology*, vol 19, New York, NY: Academic Press.

Price, M. E. and Verhulst, S. G. (2005) *Self-Regulation and the Internet*, The Hague: Kluwer Law International.

Rappaport, H. (2003) *Queen Victoria: A Biographical Companion*, Santa Barbara, CA: ABC-CLIO.

Robert, B. and Lajtha, C. (2002) 'A New Approach to Crisis Management', *Journal of Contingencies and Crisis Management*, vol 10, pp181–191.

Sachs, M. L (2011) *The Changing MO of the CMO: How the Convergence of Brand and Reputation Is Affecting Marketers*, Vermont: Gower Publishing.

Somerville, I. and Ramsey, P. (2011) 'Public Relations and Politics', in A. Theaker (ed) *Public Relations Handbook*, 4th edition, Abingdon, UK: Routledge.

Sowell, T. (2010) *Dismantling America: And Other Controversial Essays*, New York, NY: Basic Books.

Springston, J. K. and Lariscy, R. W. (2010) 'The Role of Public Relations in Promoting Healthy Communities', in R. L. Heath (ed) *The Sage Handbook of Public Relations*, 2nd edition, London: Sage.

Stauber, J. and Rampton, S. (1995) *Toxic Sludge Is Good for You*, Monroe, ME: Common Courage Press.

Taylor, M. (2001) 'Public Relations in the Enactment of Civil Society', in R. L. Heath (ed) *The Sage Handbook of Public Relations*, 2nd edition, London: Sage.

The Bureau of Investigative Journalism (2012) *PR Uncovered: Top Lobbyists Boast of How They Influence the PM*, http://www.thebureauinvestigates.com/2011/12/05/pr-uncovered-top-lobbyists-boast-of-how-they-influence-the-pm, accessed 1 March 2012.

Turner, G., Bonner, F. and Marshall, P. D. (2000) *Fame Games: The Production of Celebrity in Australia*, Cambridge: Cambridge University Press.

Wall Street Journal (2011) 'Rich Getting Hip with the "Radical Chic" of Occupy', http://online.wsj.com/article/SB10001424052970203960804577239071752882192.html, accessed 1 March 2012.

Wernick, A. (1991) *Promotional Culture: Advertising, Ideology and Symbolic Expression*, London: Sage.

Yaxley, H. (2011) 'Risk, Issues and Crisis Management', in A. Theaker (ed) *Public Relations Handbook*, 4th edition, Abingdon, UK: Routledge.

PART II
Media in Context

6

THE CHANGING RELATIONSHIP BETWEEN MEDIA AND MARKETING

Jonathan Hardy

One of the most powerful ways of approaching an understanding of media is to examine how media content and services are financed and paid for. How media are financed not only affects the amount of money that can be invested, but also involves relationships between payers and suppliers that influence what content is provided.

Advertising has been an integral part of the financing of all modern mass media. Sometimes advertising has been the principal source of finance, as in commercial free-to-air television and radio. In other cases, advertising finance has subsidized the costs of media for consumers, as in newspaper and magazine publishing. The processes summarized as *convergence* and *digitalization* have vastly increased the supply of media so that more media are chasing advertising finance in competitive struggles between different media forms and vehicles. These struggles involve relations of dependence between marketers and media that, in turn, affect the fabric of content. In the current phase, across most media systems, a key trend is intensifying *integration* of media and advertising, exemplified by product placement. Another, arguably even more profound, shift is also under way, the *dis*-integration of media and advertising. The arrangement whereby advertisers subsidized media content in order to reach target audiences and prospects is breaking down. Online and mobile communications provide marketers with opportunities to reach, track and target individuals more (cost) effectively, and in environments such as social media, e-commerce and search that lie outside media content vehicles. Both patterns are present and are, in fact, related in convergent media today.

This chapter maps key changes in media, focusing on media–advertising relationships. It asks what the transformations of digital media convergence have meant for the relationship between media and advertising? How are advertiser-funded business models adapting to new media contexts? The following section considers key features and ways of understanding media convergence. The next examines how media are adapting to changes in consumption and advertising finance, including efforts to promote each converging medium to advertisers. The changing relationship between media and marketing also needs to be understood in relation to the promotion of media brands themselves and the increasingly multimedia promotion of content and services. This is examined before a final section, which invites consideration of some of the critical issues and problems identified in the interaction and integration of media and marketing.

Media convergence

As noted in the Introduction to this book, media convergence – the coming together of different technologies and industries to create new ways of producing, distributing and using cultural goods and services – began in earnest during the late 1980s, although the term was used in its modern sense from the 1950s. By 2005 convergent media devices and services were being incorporated within people's daily lives, reaching a majority of adults in advanced economies by 2010.

Definitions can help us to describe processes, but they also make claims. The term media convergence has been applied to a great range of processes and practices; but it is more fruitful to disassemble rather than merely conflate them. Technological convergence remains the most manifest dimension; however, to understand the various components and the issues that arise, the term needs unpacking. In a celebrated formulation, Murdock (2000) delineates three convergence processes: the convergence of cultural forms as formerly distinct forms of expression, such as musical sounds, texts and images, can be combined and recomposed; the convergence of communication systems as historically separate networks and platforms can start to carry the same kind of services; and the convergence of corporate ownership as firms have sought to occupy lucrative positions right across the value chain, linking content creation, production, distribution and retail of services. Others, including Garnham (1996), provide longer lists encompassing convergence across production, circulation and consumption, while the UK regulator Ofcom (2006) identifies device convergence (accessing different services from the same device), billing convergence and platform convergence.

A key issue in academic and policy debate has been the manner in which technological, industrial and sociocultural aspects of convergence have featured in explanations of the context, agency and direction of changes in media cultures and systems. Without seeking to resolve such important divisions here, we can identify three main tendencies: technicist/neoliberal; industrial/political-economic; and prosumer/culturalist.

Technicist/neoliberal

The central importance of technological innovation and adaption has led to accounts that privilege technology as the driver of change. Such approaches are critiqued as technological determinism by perspectives that highlight the social shaping of technology and, more recently, by accounts of *soft determinism* that emphasize the close interaction of technological and social adaption (Livingstone 2010). Technicist explanations tend to align with neoliberalism in accounts which focus on the opportunities for capitalist innovation and renewal through a new digital economy.

Industrial/political-economic

The technicist view has been strongly criticized by scholars who argue that far from being a 'natural' process driven by technological innovation, media convergence has involved important policy changes, allowing media companies to expand through cross-ownership and to operate under regulatory arrangements that have been liberalized at the behest of corporate business interests. The process is commonly known as deregulation; but critics argue that it is better described as liberalizing re-regulation, since the core dynamic is the re-engineering of regulations to favour private market actors. This perspective, focusing on the reorganization of media businesses, has come from scholars who emphasize the wider political-economic and social context for convergence, and who highlight the significance of regulatory changes that permitted and favoured corporate consolidation and marketization.

Prosumer/culturalist

A third approach emphasizes changes in cultural consumption and use. Convergence is not merely a process of technological innovation or business reorganization, but a cultural process involving profound shifts in power as consumers participate, co-create and publish. The opportunities to engage in media companies' multimedia activities, following transmedia promotional campaigns across platforms, are viewed as liberating creative experiences by some culturalists (Jenkins 2008) and regarded as strategies for exploitation by others (Fuchs 2011; Turow 2011; see Hardy 2011). Analyses of convergence culture thus range from celebratory accounts of digital democratization, in which the erosion of differences between media production and consumption presages consumer sovereignty, to ones that are more sceptical and critical about the extent to which 'participation' and empowerment are facilitated under capitalism and within specific configurations of state and market control. The best work points to the contradictions and tensions between corporate power, co-creation and the counter-power arising from social uses of networked communications, and thus the potentialities and constraints of convergent communications (see Castells 2009; Fuchs 2011; Curran et al 2012).

As this brief survey indicates, one set of issues concerns the relative weight given to understanding processes of media production and consumption. Another concerns the manner in which the implications of changes for citizens and consumers are understood and evaluated. It is useful, then, to keep in mind the range of convergence processes occurring within and across technology, industry, markets, media forms and genres, cultural practices and communications behaviour.

Key features of media convergence: Convergent media and changing market conditions

The production, distribution and consumption of communication services have been transformed by the rapid emergence and adoption of digital technologies. Reviewing the 'digital decade' of 2000 to 2010, the UK regulator Ofcom (2011: 27) summarized the substantial changes:

- The majority of homes have connected to the Internet.
- Faster broadband connections have become available [with greater choice of supplier].
- There has been huge growth in consumption of mobile voice and data.
- The vast majority of homes have adopted digital, multichannel TV.
- Digital radio services now make up over a quarter of all radio listening.
- Smartphones are enabling people to access the Internet while on the move.

A snapshot of the UK communications market today shows how far digital communications have been adopted and integrated within the lives of those able to afford them. Virtually all of the 77 per cent of homes with a computer have an Internet connection (Ofcom 2011: 19). By 2011, nearly all TV homes had digital TV (96 per cent), and three in ten mobile owners used a smartphone handset. The functionality of smartphones affects people's other leisure activities, with over half (55 per cent) of adults claiming to be doing less of these (Ofcom 2011: 48). Sixty-eight per cent of teenage smartphone users claimed to have reduced time spent on other activities such as playing games on a console/PC (30 per cent), taking photos with a camera (30 per cent), using a PC to access the Internet (28 per cent), watching TV (23 per cent), and reading books (15 per cent) (Ofcom 2011: 58).

Digitalization is pervasive: all media now involve digital technologies in at least some stages of production, distribution and consumption. Media convergence has meant the coming together of three traditionally separate sectors: telecommunications, broadcasting and computing. To that core triad, we must add publishing and entertainment sectors. Traditionally, media have been separately organized with regard to the businesses involved in provision, the technologies of production and distribution, the manner of regulation and governing values (such as what it means to be a professional, abiding by industry codes of conduct, etc.), the relationship with consumers, and social expectations regarding the services provided. Yet, media have also been interwoven throughout their history and various kinds of 'convergence' long predate digitalization – for instance, in the transfer of performers, and promotion, between theatre, film and television. Yet, the on-going convergence of broadcasting, telecommunications, computing and the wider entertainment/leisure sectors has generated new media forms and the integration of previously distinct forms. The converging sectors have led to devices and services that combine features of the telephone, television and computer, most notably the Internet, allowing the combination and 'remediation' of all forms of communication and content (Bolter and Grusin 2000).

The Internet lies at the core of convergence and the broader transformations of media and advertising. From the mid-1990s the World Wide Web became the platform for an expansion of media content, principally text and graphics, but also sound, reaching an ever-increasing corpus of Internet users to become a mass medium. From around 2003 to 2004, what became designated as Web 2.0 highlighted the significant expansion of services and modes of usage. With the shift from low-bandwidth dial-up access to increasingly high-bandwidth broadband, more users could access increasingly 'rich' audio-visual material and use the emerging tools for social communication with subscription-based, 'always on' connectivity via Internet service providers (ISPs). The principal features of Web 2.0 are interactivity, user-generated content (UCG), co-creation, participation and social media, which integrate features of mass and interpersonal communication and blur the distinction between personal communication and the 'broadcast model of messages sent to nobody in particular' (Meikle and Young 2012: 5). Social media involve creating and sharing a profile, and making and interacting with contacts. The first services with these characteristics, such as SixDegrees.com, emerged around 1997; but today a handful of social media brands dominate, amongst which Facebook is currently pre-eminent globally, although Sina Weibo and Renren are amongst the platforms that reach an estimated 513 million Chinese 'netizens'.

Discourses of Web 2.0, like convergence, need unpacking. Web 2.0 has become convenient shorthand for key characteristics of co-creation and communion in digital communications, but it was also a skilful marketing effort to reaffirm the digital future after the dot.com crash, which saw dramatic falls on the NASDAQ index of technology stocks precipitated in March 2000 (Cassidy 2002). Web 2.0 has most often applied to online participatory culture, the rise of blogging, content sharing, co-creation and social networking. However, it also served as part of a rhetoric of exhortation to businesses to reorganize their activities to compete effectively under new conditions. For Tim O'Reilly (2005) and similar commentators, Web 2.0 focuses on e-commerce and describes 'business models for convergence built around database management, customization personalization, automation and participatory affordances for users' (Meikle and Young 2012: 66).

Facebook illustrates both new conditions and challenges for media as well as problems that tend to be discounted in more celebratory accounts of user empowerment. Facebook users must accept operating terms that give Facebook ownership of all (non-copyrighted) material created and posted on the site. Facebook's business model is principally based on advertising finance, although it draws additional revenue from games and apps.[1] Facebook offers advertisers targeted advertising based on 'demographic factors such as location, age, gender, education, work history and the interests people have chosen to share on Facebook'. A corporate spokesperson told a BBC reporter (Cellan-Jones 2012):

> Facebook offers the most targeted advertising of any medium. If your business is selling alloy wheels in Manchester, then you can deliver your adverts to men aged 20–30 who live within 10 miles of the city and like Top Gear and Max Power.

Facebook also offers so-called sponsored stories, where marketers can purchase 'stories' created when someone likes or comments on a page, and send these to other people who are either friends of the person or connected to the page. Clicking 'Like' allows marketers to use the user's Facebook name and profile picture in ads appearing in friends' news feeds. Adult users cannot opt out of being featured in sponsored stories and can only act by restricting whom they share their activities with. Facebook distinguishes sponsored stories from advertising messages, yet while associated with people's own communication, these stories can be generated by corporate pages' activities and distributed to networks of friends to appear in news feeds. Offering forms of editorial promotion and promotion via people's own comments, recommendations or engagement, sponsored stories have been described as a way in which Facebook 'turns users into spokespeople for companies and products in ads that are broadcast to their friends' (Hill 2012). Previously in 2009, Facebook agreed to pay $9.5 million to charities to settle another class action concerning Beacon, the company's system for monitoring and publishing users' purchases, which caused a storm of protest over breaches of privacy.

The formulation Web 1.0/2.0 has its supporters, with Spurgeon (2008: 112) finding it more helpful than the imprecision inherent in discussions of old and new media. However, the progression from Web1.0/2.0 is overly stagist and misleading in failing to capture the complex co-presence, adaption and interaction of different properties. What it does capture, albeit crudely, is the Internetization of media. The Internet is altering the core dynamics of media by changing the way in which they are distributed and consumed. In addition, while the impact of Internetization on business practices varies, it also involves shifts in thinking and disposition, in business culture as well as strategy. As one report enthuses (PwC 2011):

> … the [entertainment and media] industry has crossed a psychological and behavioral tipping-point – moving from the 'old normal', of essentially traditional business with a growing digital element, to a 'new normal' where digital is acknowledged as the central driver of future operating models, consumer relationships and revenue growth. While digital currently accounts for just over a quarter of total industry revenues, it will account for 58.7 percent of all growth in spending during the next five years.

Web 2.0 also signals important shifts in thinking and practice from a more push-oriented publishing model of web-content towards greater interactivity and co-creation associated with wikis, blogs and social media. Those shifts are very evident and important; but emphasizing them can obscure the various ways in which media content providers have sought to manage adaption to new conditions.

Change and conjunctures in convergent media

To appreciate the unevenness and complexity of convergence, some correctives and qualifications are needed. The early expansion of the Internet was accompanied by waves of techno–utopian rhetoric. This gave way to more sober assessments, after the dot.com crash; but the underlying promise and presumptions of digitalization remain deeply embedded. In both strong and weak versions, many accounts are stagist, conceiving a transition from old to new, from 'traditional' media to new 'digital' media. Such an account is almost irresistible since change is the stuff of life, the new is often radically transformative, and the evidence of rapid change and obsolescence is evident across the technological revolution. Big brands such as Netscape, online clothes retailer boo.com and SixDegrees.com have burned brightly yet briefly across the digital firmament. The problem arises when such change is totalized and generalized. The notion of a break between old and new media, a radical disjuncture, has been critiqued because it obscures the complexity and unevenness of change (Andrejevic 2004).

Without question, there are and will continue to be manifest disjunctures: the digital revolution is disrupting all media industries and upturning firms and business models. Reading a book on a tablet device is a radical disjuncture from reading a conventional paperback book. Yet, while the publishing industry has been hugely disrupted and the direction of change towards eBooks may be irreversible, there is nevertheless a co-presence of forms of books, illustrating adaption and co-mingling of elements. This means that instead of disjuncture it may be more illuminating to consider conjuncture. Conjuncture from the Latin *conjungere* means to join together. A conjuncture is a combination of events, a particular state of affairs; but it also has a more specific meaning of a critical combination of circumstances or events producing a crisis. McChesney (2007) argues that we are in the midst of a critical juncture in communications that shares characteristics with previous critical junctures, such as occurred with the development of radio during the 1930s and the rise of popular social movements challenging mass media in the 1960s and 1970s, in which 'the old institutions and mores are collapsing' and alternative paths for development are actively debated. These are 'relatively rare and brief periods in which dramatic changes were debated and enacted drawing from a broad palette of options, followed by long periods in which structural or institutional change was slow and difficult' (McChesney 2007: 9).

Media change and consumption

Media consumption patterns confound stagist accounts by showing the co-existence of rapid and radical shifts with relatively stable engagements with media as measured by expenditure and time spent. Television is a prime example. Despite predictions that the rise of new media would lead to a decline in TV consumption, television viewing increased during the decade of 2000 to 2010 in the UK and elsewhere. The continuing success of television arises from enhancements in the television viewing experience, in hardware (equipment) and software (content and services). The television offer has also been enhanced for many through the take-up of new technologies: high-definition television (HDTV), large flat screens, surround sound, 3D, interactive and Internet-enabled TV, and the adoption of new ways to watch time-shifted programming on fixed and mobile devices. More viewers now access TV programmes via the Internet and mobile devices, as well as digital video recorders (DVRs) and games consoles for catch-up services. Globally, almost as many web users view online videos each day as watch TV (24 per cent, compared with 27 per cent). Multi-screening is a major growing trend with half of tablet users checking their social profile while watching TV. Nevertheless, consumption patterns show the persistence of linear broadcasting viewing. The typical young adult in the US watched almost 137 hours of traditional TV per month, compared with 31 hours of time-shifted TV, in 2011 (Admap 2012).

Media businesses

The Internet has been a hugely disruptive technology. Many analysts view this as heralding fantastic opportunities not only for new services and new relationships between suppliers and users, but for a dramatic expansion in provision. The Internet, it has been argued, creates a more level playing field in which innovative newcomers nimbly leapfrog over slothful incumbent firms because the advantages of the latter diminish. There are powerful supporting examples of innovation from enterprises such as Google, Amazon, Tencent and Twitter. Yet, the presumption that new conditions generally favour market entrants over incumbent firms has been wide of the mark. There is clearly too much diversity to reduce this to any simple pattern; but understanding some of the reasons why established media businesses have tended to prevail is a vital corrective to earlier claims, such as Negroponte's (1995: 57) that established big media would dissolve into an array of cottage industries.

Accounts of the radical transformation of media markets have presumed that the technology would shake up existing suppliers. A new digital economy would 'kill scarcity and create opportunities in abundance' (Jarvis 2009: 59). This 'new economy' thesis failed to take adequate account of the continuing economic advantage of corporate size. Digitalization has involved a very significant cascade of challenges and risks for media businesses, but also opportunities and ways of capitalizing on strengths. Existing media firms have had advantages of available content, established brand identities, developed markets and consumer relationships, and sunk investments in infrastructure and know-how. Large corporations have had the benefits of financial resources, bigger budgets and greater access to capital than small companies. Big companies can enjoy greater economies of scale, reducing the unit costs of production. Another important benefit for multimedia conglomerates has been economies of scope where activities in one area can lead to savings in another. Producing content that can be repurposed in other forms, with the efficiency benefits of shared costs and shared marketing is an integral feature of contemporary media production and distribution. Large firms can generate economies of scale and scope arising from the sharing of services, cross-selling, integrated marketing and cross-promotion (Hardy 2010). Large firms can assemble and retain concentrations of expertise and resources that assist the launch of new products and services. They can seek to undermine under-resourced competition by temporarily lowering prices and by exploiting their marketing and promotional advantage. They have greater resources to acquire, or create partnerships with, promising young companies that possess the digital capabilities they need. Yet, the new economy business literature is full of stories of Davids slaying Goliaths, of nimble, unencumbered newcomers snatching shares of people's time and money from the lumbering feet of ossified incumbents. There are certainly advantages to set against those of large firms and plenty of examples of innovation across markets. There is an enormous growth in the capacity for content creation and distribution. What is much less evident, however, is that the major firms supplying professional mass media content have been displaced.

In Chris Anderson's (2009) influential analysis, the Internet enables a wider inventory of goods to reach small niche markets in place of the winner-takes-all strategies and advantages of large firms. Applied to media goods, the 'blockbuster' strategy that dominated in the mass media era can be challenged by a 'long tail' of niche provision. Anderson sees this as ushering in a new era of cultural diversity where the constraints that led producers and retailers to concentrate on a small selection of hits gives way to a cornucopia of goods circulating in near-perfect markets where supply and demand can be matched at much less cost than before by means of the Internet and digitalization. There is plausibility and evidence for the long tail thesis. It fits the growth of online retailing well and the massive expansion of a digitalized back catalogue of content such as music that would until recently have been much less available. However, there are various flaws in the account when applied across the media. It underestimates the persistence and effectiveness of blockbuster strategies. It downplays the vital role of marketing and branding in making content attractive and visible. Above all, it fits retail and certain kinds of media content well, but 'Talk about the long tail or narrowcasting is irrelevant to online markets where the barriers to entry remain high' (Hindman 2009: 100) and where there are high first-copy costs for content production such as newspapers, magazines, film entertainment and other expensive audio-visual products.

For media content industries, neither winner-takes-all nor long tail strategies offer a satisfactory account as elements of both co-exist. The long tail celebrates consumer empowerment through effective competition. Winner-takes-all is one facet of corporate systems geared towards reducing threats to profitability, including competition. Given the inherent uncertainties of popularity and taste and the increasing volatility felt in media markets, it is particularly useful to examine risk and risk management in order to understand contemporary firms' behaviour (Croteau and Hoynes 2006; Hesmondhalgh 2007). Second, it is useful to examine how media firms have sought to adapt to new conditions with varying degrees of success. As Meikle and Young (2012: 40) summarize, media industries 'develop by responding to the possibilities offered by the affordances of communications technologies. In some cases they incorporate these into their existing business; in others, they significantly change the scope and prevailing uses of the technology, and in doing so change the scope and prevailing uses of their own business.' The impact of digitalization upon media industries, while profound, has been uneven. The notion that new media is replacing (or has replaced) old media is true in some markets and sectors, but is inaccurate and misleading when applied across the media as a whole.

Media finance

Media finance is another critical indicator of continuity and change in media markets. On the one hand, there are enormous challenges to the future financing of media, reaching crisis in some sectors such as printed newspapers. On the other hand, it is important not to exaggerate the current impact of change across media markets. In the UK, despite enormous changes over the last decade, industry revenues have remained stable overall. According to Ofcom (2011: 28), total annual communications industry revenue in 2010 was £53.4 billion. This figure is remarkably similar to the (inflation-adjusted) revenue of £54.3 billion in 2000. Reductions in advertising revenue in some media sectors have been gradual rather than precipitate. Finally, while the shift in advertising finance from traditional 'offline' media towards the Internet and digital media is the key dynamic reshaping media systems, it important not to exaggerate, or generalize, the impacts to date across different media. According to Zenith Optimedia (2011), by 2013, the Internet will overtake newspapers to become the world's second largest medium. Yet television, radio and outdoor media are expected to maintain their shares while the Internet gradually erodes the advertising shares of newspapers and magazines.

Traditionally, some media have been financed principally by consumer sales (music, cinema, book publishing); but commercial mass media (newspapers, magazines, radio and television broadcasting) have been dependent on advertising for a share of revenue. In some cases, advertising finance has been the principal source of funding (free-to-air (FTA) commercial broadcasting). In other cases, such as newspapers and magazines, advertising finance has supplemented sales income, averaging 50 to 60 per cent for magazines and 80 per cent for newspapers, according to Bettig and Hall (2012: 164). The ability of papers to attract both sources of finance, and the ratio of advertising to sales finance, has had an important bearing on the nature of content and competition amongst newspapers (Sparks 1999). Advertising has thus served as a subsidy system for media. As an important critical tradition of scholarship has examined, advertising finance, the outcome of the multiple decisions of marketers, has served as a *de facto* licencing system for advertising-dependent media, shaping which media vehicles would be granted largesse for reaching audiences attractive to advertisers and which punished by market decisions for catering to less valued audiences (Baker 1994; Gandy 2000; Curran 2011: 153–167).

Over the last 20 years the shift in advertising expenditure from traditional media to the Internet has undoubtedly had enormous repercussions. However, it is important to place this in the broad context of changes affecting media finance. Before the Internet, markets such as television, radio, newspapers and periodical publishing were characterized by expansion of supply and increasing competition for revenue. The proliferation of commercial television channels increased competitive pressures before the challenges of rich audio-visual content via Internet-enabled technologies.

Over the last two decades the means by which advertising communications take place has changed dramatically (Assael 2011). Today, marketing communications take place across an increasing variety of platforms, including mobile. The Internet, experienced largely through the World Wide Web, e-commercial and email via PCs in the 1990s, has expanded into networked services and social media available across mobile devices and multifunctional interfaces such as games consoles and smart television sets. The Internet itself has variously affected different media. At a general level, the shift of audiences' media consumption to the Internet has meant that advertisers have followed, and allocated their spending accordingly. In the UK, Internet advertising expenditure surpassed the total spent on radio advertising in 2006 (IAB 2006). According to the Interactive Advertising Bureau (IAB), online advertising now accounts for the largest single component of the UK ad market (27 per cent). Over one quarter of all UK advertising spending is on the Internet. Internet advertising expenditure grew by 16 per cent in 2010 to over £4 billion, accounting for 26 per cent of total advertising spend in the UK, marginally ahead of television. Internet advertising also showed the strongest compound growth rate of 16.7 per cent between 2005 and 2011, although cable TV also grew by 4 per cent, while the other media sectors fell. In 2011, £4.8 billion was spent on Internet advertising, greater than television at £4.2 billion and press at £3.9 billion (WARC figures cited in Ofcom 2012: 13).

For the US, in 2011, broadcast television (network, syndicated and spot TV revenue) retained the highest share of advertising finance at $38.5 billion, followed by the Internet ($31.7 billion), cable television ($30 billion), newspapers ($20.7 billion), magazines ($18 billion), radio ($15.2 billion), outdoor ($6.5 billion), video games ($1 billion) and cinema ($0.7 billion) (IAB 2012). Internet advertising revenues ($31.74 billion) were up 22 per cent from the $26.04 billion reported in 2010. Mobile advertising increased 149 per cent in 2011, with $1.60 billion spent compared to $0.64 billion in 2010 (IAB 2012). In the UK, mobile advertising increased by 121 per cent in 2010 to reach £83 million, and grew to £203 million in 2011; mobile revenue grew sevenfold since 2008 during a period in which the proportion of adults using mobiles to go online increased from 20 to 39 per cent (Ofcom 2012: 13).

Internet advertising has generated profound challenges for media business models (although both advertising and media have adapted). The Internet enables advertising to be aggregated with content in new ways, as the growth of banner ads, interstitials, rich media and other advertising formats demonstrates. Yet, one of the most profound challenges for media arises from the opportunities to disaggregate media and advertising. In traditional print publishing, advertising appears within the physical product whose production, and usually also distribution, is controlled by the publisher. Advertising is separated from the editorial content, but integrated within the physical product. The marketer pays the publisher to carry the advertisement.

On the Internet, advertising can be successfully decoupled from media content. While advertisers can pay to place advertising alongside online media content that is controlled by publishers, they can take advantage of the way in which content and services are assembled online. The impact has varied across advertising forms and purposes. In print publishing, a classic division is between display and classified advertising. Classified advertising includes small advertising of items for sale, services or recruitment advertising, with information laid out by the publisher in a fixed format and generally appearing in a distinct section of print publications. The second main type, display advertising, includes text and artwork (images and logos) that is arranged by the advertiser and sent to the publisher where it is placed adjacent to media content. Local newspapers have been heavily dependent on advertising for automobiles and housing, both classified and display ads. During the 1990s websites such as Craigslist (US) and Rightmove (UK) began to erode the classified advertising market that had been dominated by local newspapers, with competition from other print publishers. In the UK, between 2000 and 2008, the Internet's share of classified advertising grew from 2 to 45 per cent, while the local and regional press share fell from 47 to 26 per cent, and national newspapers' share fell from 14 to 6 per cent (Office of Fair Trading 2009: 13). Online display advertising, paid advertising placements using graphical or audio-visual elements, has also expanded, broadly in line with bandwidth capacity.

The main entry points for Internet activity are search engines which take approximately half of online advertising revenues. With increasing competition for the remainder, the outcome has been ever-greater efforts by online publishers to accommodate advertisers' demands (Turow 2011). The way in which Internet advertising has developed has led to pressures on all media to provide the same levels of tracking, measurement, performance and pricing. There has been a shift from pricing based on audience size (cost per million) to performance-based pricing for advertising, especially online. According to the IAB (2012), performance-based pricing has been the prevalent pricing model since 2006, reaching 65 per cent in 2011. Google influenced this shift towards performance- and transaction-based pricing. Whereas most publishers charge a fee for displaying an advert, Google charged advertisers only if a person clicked on an advert adjacent to search results. Google rapidly secured over 50 per cent of all online advertising in the US, with other online publishers turning to new types of organizations such as online advertising networks, data providers, and data exchanges to help them compete for the remaining 50 per cent (Turow 2011: 10).

Media and advertising

This section reviews changes and their implications across converging media in a little more detail. In challenging conditions, each medium seeks to promote benefits for advertisers. Many advertising textbooks summarize the strengths and limitations of each medium from the perspective of advertisers. Rather than reproduce that material here, this section takes a different route by focusing on selected trade bodies, whose principal role is to promote their respective medium to marketers. These are a valuable source for research, both as resource and topic. This section focuses on the UK, but includes international data and addresses trends evident across comparable media systems.

We can distinguish between specific media brands (media vehicles) and media channels such as TV, radio and mobile (Hackley 2010: 139). The trade bodies, financed by companies active in the market, promote the medium or channel for its intrinsic merits and benefits over other media. These bodies also emphasize how the channel can serve as part of the marketing mix and as a vital component of integrated marketing strategies. Such claims increasingly focus on integration with the Internet, mobile and other 'new' media. Whether as vehicles or channels, media seek to demonstrate that:

1   They have content or services that attract the users who are attractive to marketers.
2   The channel has intrinsic advantages that are distinctive and indispensable.
3   They are able to demonstrate promotional effectiveness and cost effectiveness.
4   They can provide the data analysis and precise targeting desired by marketers.

Newspapers

In most markets printed newspapers sold to the public have seen an inexorable decline in sales, and with that advertising revenue. The main exception has been free newspapers distributed in cities, which have provided a profitable advertising vehicle reaching commuters, including those whose consumption of other offline media tends to be light. Newspaper publishers have sought to build their brands and readership online. After initial experimentation most papers moving online during the 1990s offered free content, with only elite and business papers pursuing a route of charging for content on a subscription or itemized basis. However, in the mid-2000s, News Corporation led efforts to establish more general subscription models.

Publishers have faced falling readerships and falling ad revenue, but also changing consumer habits. A small but growing number of consumers now access news on mobile devices, particularly smartphones. According to the National Readership Survey (Q1, 2011, cited in Green 2011), 3.8 million adults in the UK (8 per cent of the population) were viewing publisher content via tablets, e-readers or apps. While most news remains 'free' online, publishers are investing in paid-apps in the hope of encouraging standalone subscriptions or bundling a combination of print and online content offers. Yet, a Reuters Institute survey (Rainey 2012) found that only 4 per cent of people in the UK had ever paid for digital news, compared to 12 per cent in Denmark and between 6 and 8 per cent elsewhere.

So-called 'legacy' publishers (those that originated in the print world) have adopted a variety of different strategies to try to manage business change and the transition to new platforms and markets. Newspapers established digital versions and adopted strategies ranging from paywalls and subscriptions or, alternatively, like *The Guardian*, promoting open journalism, as discussed in the Introduction to this volume. Moving online has opened up new revenue streams from advertising. However, the revenue generated tends to be considerably smaller per reader than for print editions. Online advertising is also often sold well below the rate card value (Turow 2011). Fierce competition drove down the price newspapers could charge advertisers; cost-per-thousand impressions (CPM, where M = mille, 1000 in Roman numerals) and online ad charges were tiny compared to the rates charged to reach print readers. The huge inventory of freely available content, the culture of free, and efforts to build bands and audiences online meant that news publishers have struggled to cover costs of online content services.

The US Newspaper Association of America (NAA) in 2011 reported the 17th successive quarterly year-on-year decline in newspaper advertising expenditure and the lowest dollar spending figure since the first quarter of 1983. Paid circulation had fallen by 26 per cent from its 1990 peak. The migration of advertising from offline media to the web has contributed to the closure of many American news-papers (including centuries-old city papers such as the *Tucson Citizen*, founded in 1870 and replaced by a much smaller Internet-only publication in 2009), editorial budget cuts, and a 20 per cent reduction in the number of journalists employed in 2009 compared to 2001. In the UK, 106 local newspapers closed during the period from January 2008 to September 2009 (Curran 2011: 111). One report (OECD 2010) found that UK circulation fell by 25 per cent between 2007 and 2009, second only to the US at 30 per cent. Online advertising contributed a 'miniscule' proportion of total revenues, just 4 per cent in 2009. The report concluded 'no business and/or revenue sharing models have been found to finance in-depth independent news production. This raises questions as to the supply of high-quality journalism in the longer term' (OECD 2010: 4). The rise of web-based media and new journalistic production has not compensated for newspapers' decline because they have failed to secure an adequate revenue stream to sustain them. According to Curran (2011: 24), 'over the long term, the internet may well rejuvenate jour-nalism, especially if it is accompanied by constructive public policies. But the cumulative decoupling of advertising from news production which brought about the rise of the Internet also poses a major problem that is likely to endure.'

In the UK, national newspaper circulations have fallen by more than one third since 2003 (Fenton 2010). However, the collapse in newspaper circulation is not a consistent pattern globally and there are notable counter-trends. Global printed newspaper circulation (including free titles) was 7.7 per cent higher in 2009 than it had been five years earlier. Declines in mature markets are being countered by growth in African and Asian markets, notably India, according to the World Association of Newspapers (2009), which estimates that around 37 per cent of the world's adult population read a newspaper on a regular basis. More consistent is the decline in total advertising revenue for newspapers as a media channel. ZenithOptimedia (2011) estimates that total global spending on newspaper advertising will hit around $93 billion in 2013, $10 billion less than in 2000. In the US, consumer magazines' advertising revenue fell from $20.3 billion in 2006 to $15.6 billion in 2009; newspapers' ad revenue declined from $46.6 billion in 2006 to $24.8 billion in 2009 (Turow 2011: 114). The decline was attributable, in part, to the deep recession in the general economy from 2008, but also reflects a long-term shift of advertiser spending from traditional media advertising to online and word-of-mouth advertising.

Over the years, newspaper trade bodies have promoted key strengths of their medium for advertisers, including:

- high coverage (either locally, regionally or nationally, depending on the country);
- targetability – e.g., reaching specific localities or groups of people such as commuters;
- immediacy and short campaign lead times;
- high engagement (reading is an inherently engaging activity);
- flexibility of sizes and formats;
- space to communicate detailed messages;
- the ability to produce tear-off ads/coupons;
- space to feature telephone numbers and website addresses, enabling rapid response.

(Green 2011: 3)

While these remain salient, newspapers have been repositioning themselves to make a positive case for online effectiveness as print circulations dwindle. In May 2012 the UK-based Newspaper Marketing Agency rebranded itself Newsworks. According to its new chief executive, Rufus Olins, the change reflected newspapers now needing to see themselves as 'newsbrands', delivering content over a range of platforms – computers, smartphones and tablets – as well as print. The rebranding promoted the message that while print sales have declined, 'newsbrands' have increased their net daily audience by some 2 million adults over the last five years, from 22.6 million in 2007 to 24.4 million in 2012, with research indicating increased time spent reading online. However, as Turow (2011) shows, online publishers are under increasing pressure to prove their utility to media buyers, as the concluding section of this chapter discusses.

Television

Television remains the dominant medium for both factual and entertainment audio-visual content. The infrastructure and experience of television viewing has improved considerably for those able to afford high-definition and Internet-enabled TVs, along with DVRs, Blu-ray or other HD players. However, commercial television has faced increasing pressures to retain advertising finance in conditions where total advertising spending is static or falling and where the number of channels competing for that finance continues to grow. The outcomes and effects of this struggle on programme content and output are the subject of fierce debate.

In the UK, annual spending on broadcasting channels by advertisers declined over the decade, falling from £5.9 billion in 2000 to £4.5 billion in real terms in 2010. The steepest fall occurred in the second half of the decade, with some recovery in 2010 on the previous year. This partly reflected a contraction in advertising expenditure during a recessionary period; the proportion of total advertising expenditure devoted to TV remained largely uncharged (30 per cent in 2000 and 29 per cent in 2010) (Ofcom 2011: 97). Nevertheless, annual advertising spending (excluding sponsorship and branded content) fell and the proportion of TV revenue generated by advertising also fell from 35 per cent in 2005 to 30 per cent in 2010 (Ofcom 2011: 97). Growth recovered somewhat in 2010 and 2011, with advertising revenue expanding across commercial stations and the public service broadcasters' (PSB) portfolio channels, although among the commercial PSB's main channels only the lightly regulated Channel 5 saw growth in 2011 (up 30 per cent to £281 million) (Ofcom 2012: 117, 139).

The main way in which FTA commercial television has been financed has been through spot advertising during programme breaks or block advertising. This model has been changing under conditions that predate digitalization. The subscription model was adopted by US cable channels during the 1970s and took off with satellite TV in the 1980s. However, it was not until 2008, in the UK, that subscription revenue for multichannel television overtook advertising revenue. As a percentage of total UK TV revenue, subscription revenue increased from 35 per cent in 2000 to 41 per cent in 2010. By 2011, the gap between the share of TV industry revenue generated by advertising (£3.6 billion) versus subscription revenue (£5.2 billion) widened. While much smaller in revenue terms, the other significant growth area has been in online TV revenue, which grew from £11 million in 2006 to £229 million in 2011, with the free-to-view (advertising-financed) business model accounting for £134 million of that total.

The traditional form of advertising via spots between programme segments has been the subject of intense discussion since the 1970s. Dire predictions of imminent collapse have been confounded by a more gradual decline in spot advertising revenues, but served a function in widespread industry lobbying for relaxations on the regulation of marketing communications on television. Marketers have pushed to extend marketing opportunities beyond designated advertising into programme surrounds (sponsorship) and into programmes themselves via advertiser-financed content, product placement and brand integration. Whereas broadcasters and programme-makers tended to resist these pressures in accordance with regulation, self-regulation, professional norms and cultural values, from the 1990s they have become increasingly willing advocates. Some have argued that integrating brand communications within media content is a necessary response to the declining effectiveness of spot advertising, a necessary means of financing audio-visual production; further, with branding pervasive, 'It is inevitable, and even natural, that movie and broadcast entertainment scenes reflect this cultural reality' (Hackley 2010: 173). For critics, product placement permits brands to pay for presence in ways that can damage the editorial integrity and independence of information, the artistic integrity and autonomy of fiction and entertainment, and grants marketers an influence over content decisions that is damaging for media cultures and for democracy (Hardy 2010).

The US Federal Trade Commission (FTC 2005) defines product placement as 'a form of promotion in which advertisers insert branded products into programming in exchange for fees or other consideration'. There is nothing new about the integration of advertising and media content. Product placement in movies can be traced back to the Lumière films of the 1890s and was well established in the Hollywood studio system by the 1920s (Eckert 1991; Newell et al 2006). Placement takes a variety of forms from the incidental presence of brands, to verbal endorsement and sophisticated 'brand integration', such as the Halliburton security case dominating an early episode of *Lost* – what the *Economist* called 'product placement to die for'. Product placement increased in US films from the 1970s, where it is largely unrestricted, and in television, especially cable but also network, from the 1990s where self-regulation has weakened and rules on sponsorship disclosure have proved ineffective. In the first quarter of 2008, TNS Media Intelligence found that brand appearances, in the form of product placement (PP) and integration, averaged 12 minutes and 8 seconds per hour in primetime on network TV, in addition to 14 minutes of commercial breaks (Hardy 2010: 235).

The UK, like other European systems, established rules for advertising that were designed to ensure that advertising finance did not influence the content and editorial decisions of broadcasters. The 1954 Television Act, which set up commercially funded TV in the UK, authorized the clear separation between programmes and advertising and required the new regulator, Independent Television Authority, to ensure compliance. The act prohibited any material which was or appeared to be 'supplied or suggested by any advertiser'. There were early problems and challenges, notably the advertising magazines in which characters in settings such as pubs endorsed and advertised branded goods (Murdock 1992). These were banned after 1963, after which separation principles were largely upheld, despite increasing pressure to extend brand communications. For instance, in August 2005, Channel 4 was fined £5000 for promotions of Red Bull on a daytime chat show, *The Richard and Judy Show*.

The situation changed when European regulation permitted product placement in 2007. The Audiovisual Media Services Directive, which replaced the Television

Without Frontiers Directive (established in 1989 and revised in 1997) permits member states to allow product placement, except in news, current affairs and children's programmes, subject to requirements that such programmes are identified to viewers and that editorial independence is maintained. This liberalization was the outcome of formidable lobbying by advertisers and commercial media groups, although challenged by cultural bodies, consumer groups, media trades unions and civil society networks. After lengthy debates and policy reversals, the UK government authorized product placement in legislation in 2010 (Hardy 2010).

Far from being inevitable or evolutionary, the liberalization of product placement in Europe marked a victory for commercial over societal interests. In the UK, before he was replaced by a more compliant minister, Culture Secretary Andy Burnham rejected product placement, following a consultation, arguing: 'There is a lack of evidence of economic benefits, along with very serious concerns about blurring the boundaries between advertising and editorial' (DCMS 2009). In an earlier speech (Burnham 2008) he said: 'I think there are some lines that we should not cross – one of which is that you can buy the space between the programmes on commercial channels, but not the space within them.' Critics of media integration argued that product placement undermined transparency in marketing communications; but even where viewers did know when they were being sold to, another key criticism was that programme agendas and editorial decisions risked being distorted for commercial purposes in order to maximize the opportunities for placing products. A related critique came from creative workers, especially in the US, who had experienced the intensification of brand integration. According to David Young, director of the Writers Guild of America, West (2005, 2008), 'Product integration goes far beyond the long-standing practice of using real commercial products as props. It forces professional television writers to disguise commercials as story lines and destroys the line between advertising and editorial content.'

Promoting television

In 1987, new agency Howell Henry Chaldecott Lury (HHCL) launched itself with an infamous advert in the trade press depicting a couple making love on a sofa with the TV on. The slogan was: 'According to current audience research, this couple are watching your ad. Who's really getting screwed?' The campaign so annoyed its early client, the commercial broadcaster Thames Television, that the agency was promptly sacked. Demonstrating advertising effectiveness and competing for ad spending has always been challenging; but seeing how the case is made today offers important insights into media–advertiser relationships. In the UK the lead body promoting TV to advertisers is Thinkbox, whose key claim is that television delivers a higher return on investment (ROI) than any other medium. Such a claim carries particular importance given that television remains the most expensive medium. Thinkbox commissioned a study by PriceWaterhouseCoopers that examined data for over 700 brands in various markets to conclude that TV delivered the highest return of any medium: £4.5 million per £1 million spent (Thinkbox 2012). A follow-up study compared sales and profit impact during the period of 2006 to 2011 across five forms of advertising: TV, radio, press, online static display and outdoor. It found TV advertising is 2.5 times more effective at creating sales uplift per equivalent exposure than the next best performing medium (press) (Thinkbox 2012).

Thinkbox's website summarizes various studies into the effectiveness of television, the links between creative execution and ROI effectiveness, and highlights key medium attributes, including excelling at creating emotion, linking and generating fame. Television remains preeminent in delivering mass audiences and event viewing. During the 2009 Super Bowl (a global media event), Hollywood studios spent an estimated $3 million for each 30-second spot promoting ten movies, including *Monsters vs. Aliens* (2009), *G.I. Joe* (2009), *Star Trek* (2009) and *Transformers 2* (2009) (Eller 2009). However, marketers want greater brand integration in place of 'interruption' advertising to counter ad-avoidance from zapping, time-shifting and online viewing (McAllister 1996; Lehu 2009; Hardy 2010).

One indication of how this is likely to develop comes from Zeebox, a British company whose founders include the former chief technology officer for the BBC iPlayer, Anthony Rose. Zeebox is a social television website and app for mobile devices that provides contextual information second by second as people watch TV, including which of their friends are watching the same shows at the same time. Zeebox also provides instant information on adverts, including links to websites and other content, providing augmented information on what is seen and heard within the broadcast. Brands featured in programmes as well as ads can appear simultaneously on screens with hyperlinks to brand content and e-commerce.

Cinema

Despite predictions of terminal decline, cinema has reinvigorated its offer against the attractions of home viewing. The Cinema Advertising Association (CAA) is a trade body that promotes, but also clears and vets, cinema advertising in the UK. According to the CAA, an estimated 174 million were expected to visit the cinema worldwide in 2010. Amongst the attractions of cinema for advertisers are the lowest ad avoidance of all media, greater impact, and reaching audiences that include light consumers of other media such as TV. According to the CAA, 'cinema continues to be the most impactful of all media not only due to the size of the screen and surround sound but with consumers being actively engaged in the experience, captive, willing and have "opted in" to an experience' (CAA 2012). The CAA (2012) promotes the 'event' nature of film and the social interaction connected with this experience:

> The film is a focal point for social interaction and offers a shared experience which fuels talkability. With the fragmentation of other media, this collective

experience and personal opinion is fuelling new 'watercooler' moments as well as conversation on social media sites online such as Facebook and Twitter. These digital platforms are in turn fuelling admissions as networks for word-of-mouth are significantly larger and faster than previously.

Internet and mobile media

Digital media also have trade bodies that promote their respective claims to advertisers. One such body is the Interactive Advertising Bureau (IAB), another is the Mobile Marketing Association, which promotes advertising 'tailored to and delivered through wireless mobile devices such as smartphones (e.g. Blackberry, iPhone, Android), feature phones (e.g., lower-end mobile phones capable of accessing mobile content), and media-tablets (e.g., iPad, Samsung Galaxy Tab)' (IAB 2012: 22). Typically, mobile marketing communications takes the form of static or rich media display ads, text messaging ads, search ads, or audio/video spots, appearing within mobile websites or applications, text messaging services or mobile search results. According to a report by Google (2012), 56 per cent have performed mobile search after seeing an ad in offline media. Based on interviews with 1000 UK adults (18 to 64 years old), the study found that 84 per cent of users noticed mobile ads.

The various media are seeking to adapt to the accelerating migration of consumers and advertisers online. In the West, advertising finance has suffered under a prolonged recessionary period triggered by the banking crises of 2008. Alongside this cyclical decline, deeper structural shifts are under way. Newspapers and printed periodicals face collapsing revenues with uncertain efforts to monetize content online. Audio-visual media is more buoyant overall, but with ever-increasing competition for the media-buying decisions of large advertising oligopolies. One of the drivers of media conglomeration has been the effort to offer media buyers integrated packages across multimedia portfolios. Media have also consolidated to build and cross-promote their brands and properties. The changing relationship between media and advertising is intimately connected with the growing importance of media promotion.

Media promotion

Although attracting advertisers remains of paramount importance for ad-dependent media, promotion and advertising by media themselves have become ever-more important as brands compete across fast-changing markets. Content is increasingly multiplatform, with redistribution and repurposing across a variety of digital media; providers seek to move users to profitable sustained consumption while facing intensifying competition across product, platform, delivery and consumption markets. Media promotion of its own and allied content is the glue binding a vast web of media communications; 'content about content' has been identified as the fastest growing sector of content creation (Deuze and Stewart 2011: 7).

A useful distinction in marketing communications is between owned, earned and paid-for promotion. Paid-for promotion includes advertising, sponsorship and product placement. Earned media includes editorial coverage, achieved through public relations activity, on mass media and social media channels such as Twitter, Facebook and LinkedIn. Owned media are the vehicles belonging to the marketer or content creator themselves.

Media promotion is becoming more strategically important in the context of multiplatform content distribution. Content is repurposed across books, films, television, music, games and merchandise, and cross-promoted across news media, magazines and promotional tie-ins with marketers and retailers. Channel 4 television illustrates key trends. It began as a public service, commercially funded television channel in 1984, expanded into film finance and created a digital film channel (initially subscription only) and then a growing portfolio of digital channels, established websites, a video-on-demand (VOD) catch-up service, mobile content services (such as Channel 4 News), and began simulcasting its Channel 4 TV service online from June 2006. During the 2000s, Channel 4 has repositioned itself as a multimedia distributor of content. CEO David Abraham, addressing a UK media industry convention in January 2012, spoke of 'leading a surge into multi-screen programming and maximising the distribution of our content across still proliferating digital platforms'. He added:

> We are re-tooling our self-funded commercial model by investing in more direct connections with our audiences and engaging viewers ever more deeply. We will pioneer the use of data to innovate our advertising model – in turn contributing to future investment in content.

During the 2000s, television executives began to speak of 360 degree commissioning, creating content that can be repurposed for other platforms, including mobile phones, the Internet, radio and digital channels. In 2011, Channel 4 created a new role of commissioning editor: convergent formats with the brief to develop creative formats for Internet-connected televisions and other devices. They appointed Anna Cronin who had previously managed competitions and promotions for GMTV and then worked for ITV on consumer-facing multiplatform projects such as the *X Factor* and *Britain's Got Talent*. A key aspect of her role 'will be to showcase new formats to internal and external stakeholders to help demonstrate their creative possibilities, helping establish Channel 4 as the most creative innovator in content for the convergent era' (Channel 4 2011). Channel 4's *The Bank Job* (2011–2012), created by Endemol, involved a 'two-screen experience' of TV competition and gaming, promoted through an elaborate campaign involving 'guerrilla' stunts suggesting bank heists in front of Christmas shoppers and an integrated marketing campaign to drive viewers to the online game that supports the show.

The growing strategic importance of media promotion is a key factor in the greater integration of media and advertising. At a corporate level, media and advertising agencies have engaged in mergers and joint ventures (Bettig and Hall

2012: 165), although alongside such corporate interlocking there has also been corporate disaggregation and de-convergence involving the proliferation of smaller specialist creative and media planning agencies (Spurgeon 2008: 104). Alliances include the billion dollar deal in 2006 for Google to become the exclusive provider of search and keyword targeted advertising for News Corporation's Fox Interactive Media Group (Dwyer 2010: 19). At senior management level in media businesses there has been an enhanced valuation placed on marketing experience. Operationally, media promotions have won enhanced professional status and resources to accompany their strategic importance so that television promotions are planned and executed like major ad campaigns (Hardy 2010, 2011). Yet, the most compelling illustrations of the merger of media and marketing remain the super-narratives of filmed entertainment.

Prometheus, Ridley Scott's prequel to *Alien*, exemplifies the multimedia promotional strategies adopted for modern blockbusters. The strategy by 20th Century Fox, a subsidiary of News Corporation, included viral videos, teasers and elaborate additional stories and content for transmedia storytelling. A viral video showed a mock presentation made at the TED (Technology, Entertainment and Design) conference by the owner and founder of the Weyland Corporation (the corporation driving the plot in *Prometheus* and in the original *Alien* franchise). A social media campaign included elaborate Facebook pages based around the fictional corporation; another focused on the *David8* android (played by Michael Fassbender). The movie trailer first aired on UK television on Channel 4 (during *Homeland* on Sunday 29 April 2012), and included a Twitter feed with the hash-tag *#areyouseeing this*. Those who visited the site and sent messages or Tweeted using the hash-tag then had the chance to see their tweets feature, if selected, on a second airing of the trailer, in the following ad break. The trailer was played simultaneously online, on Channel 4 and on Zeebox, the powerful social TV app. According to one of the agencies involved, word-of-mouth consultancy 1000 Heads, the ad campaign reached 15 million Twitter users, with more than 4000 tweets posted about the film on that first night (IAB 2012). Eray Galip, Creative Solutions manager at 20th Century Fox's media agency Vizeum, said: 'We are delighted with this activity which kicks off our marketing campaign; it fits perfectly with our strategy in terms of amplifying the anticipation and conversation that has already started for *Prometheus*' (IAB 2012).

Prometheus is an example of a synergistic entertainment franchise and strategy for 'total entertainment' (Grainge 2008). It illustrates the integration of media and marketing through synergistic efforts to achieve visibility for media brands and maximize profits from transmedia super-narratives (Wolf 1999). Whether such corporate promotion is viewed as enabling immersive pleasure or as strategies for exploitation, or a complex mixture of both are important issues for analysis (Hardy 2010, 2011). More immediately, they illustrate aspects of the broader interlinking of media and marketing within the logics of multimedia production and promotion. Multimedia content production, advertising finance and promotion needs all drive a logic of 'collaboration' between content providers and marketers.

Conclusion

The characteristic relationship of media and advertising in mid-twentieth-century media was integration with separation. Advertising was integrated in the sense that it was physically combined with the media product. In newspapers and magazines, adverts appeared alongside editorial; in linear television, spot (or block) advertising appeared in designated breaks within or between programmes. While advertisers controlled their commercial communications, media firms controlled the packaging and distribution of the ad-carrying media. Media and advertising were kept separate on the whole. There have always been opportunities and pressures to integrate; but the principles of separation were generally upheld by journalists and by creative professionals in television, supported by managers, underpinned by self-regulatory codes of conduct in both media and advertising and subject to stronger statutory regulation in some sectors, such as UK broadcasting.

In both ad-dependent print media and television, there was an institutionalized effort to capture the benefits of ad finance while protecting the quality, integrity and independence of media speech. This drew on a combination of values derived from democratic, consumer welfare, artistic and cultural concerns. Media and advertising should be separated to ensure that consumers know when they are in a selling environment and to ensure that advertisers should not be the principal arbiters of media content and provision.

Media and advertising integration is by no means a new phenomenon and has a long history across all media forms. Yet, arguably the most profound change in the twenty-first century is that the commercial digital environment has brought increased pressures from marketers, met with increased accommodation by media. The emergent forms are *integration without separation*, but this co-exists with trends towards *disaggregation* of media and advertising. While these trends are in some senses diametrically opposed, they both reflect a new shift towards marketer power in an era of increased competition for, and dependence on, advertising finance.

Like integration, disaggregation of media and advertising takes various forms with different consequences. The most challenging feature is that advertising is much less dependent on media vehicles than in traditional models. Content matters, since it attracts the consumers that advertisers seek to reach. However, marketers have much greater opportunity to reach consumers without subsidizing or accommodating media content providers. The intermediary role of media creating an audience to sell to advertisers is being undermined, in part because the production and distribution of physical goods are expensive ways to reach audiences, and in part because of the advantages of new ways to reach target consumers. As search illustrates, advertising can be connected to media content but flow to search engines. This highlights the decoupling of media production and distribution and the fragmented way in which content is accessed. As Turow (2011: 117) states: 'consumers no longer typically confront media products as unified branded products or programming flows. Many read individual newspapers articles, listen to individual songs and view individual program episodes unmoored from a "channel" that has been constructed by the content-creating firms.'

Advertisers can link advertising to search and users' activity online so that advertising follows people's profiles rather than being bundled with media content. The greater range of opportunities to reach target consumers also diminishes the value and exclusivity of mass media vehicles. There is still a value in content that attracts prospects desired by advertisers; but the affordances of digital communications and targeting are driving marketers to demand that they pay only the actual costs of delivering an advert onto a selected platform (Turow 2011). Consequently, the traditional subsidy supporting the news, information or entertainment surrounding advertisements is set to diminish, with truly profound consequences for democratic communication resources, public media and cultural pluralism.

Advertising integration and disaggregation trends are obviously contrary tendencies: the embedding of advertising within content and the disembedding of advertising from content publishing and packaging online. Yet, both tendencies spring from the same underlying dynamics and reflect responses to increasing dependence of media on advertising finance. Taking advantage of the competition among web creators and distributors, 'media buyers are eroding the power of Web publishers and causing them to play by advertisers' new rules to survive' (Turow 2011: 112).

Note

1 In 2011, Facebook's ad revenue was $3.1 billion, out of a total revenue of $3.7 billion, but 56 per cent of that came from the US where overall growth was slowing, and Facebook has struggled to generate ad revenue from its fast-growing mobile platform (Raice 2012).

Bibliography

Abraham, D. (2012) Speech to the Oxford Media Convention, http://www.channel4.com/info/press/news/david-abraham-speech-to-the-oxford-media-convention, accessed 30 January 2012.

Admap (2012) *Adstats: TV Advertising* (June), London: WARC.

Anderson, C. (2009) *The Longer Long Tail: How Endless Choice Is Creating Unlimited Demand*, London; Random House.

Andrejevic, M. (2004) *Reality TV: The Work of Being Watched*, Lanham, MD: Rowman and Littlefield.

Assael, H. (2011) 'From Silos to Synergy: A Fifty-Year Review of Cross-Media Research Shows Synergy Has Yet to Achieve Its Full Potential', *Journal of Advertising Research, 50th Anniversary Supplement*, vol 51, no 1, pp42–48.

Baker, C. E. (1994) *Advertising and a Democratic Press*, Princeton, NJ: Princeton University Press.

Bettig, R. V. and Hall, J. L. (2012) *Big Media, Big Money: Cultural Texts and Political Economies*, Lanham, MD: Rowman and Littlefield.

Bolter, J. D. and Grusin, R. (2000) *Remediation: Understanding New Media*, Cambridge, MA: MIT Press.

Burnham, A. (2008) Secretary of State speech to the Convergence Think Tank, 11 June. http://webarchive.nationalarchives.gov.uk/+/http://www.culture.gov.uk/reference_library/minister_speeches/5192.aspx, accessed 19 February 2013.

CAA (Cinema Advertising Association) (2012) 'Power of Cinema', http://www.dcm.co.uk/why-cinema/why-cinema-works/the-power-of-cinema, accessed 18 June 2012.

Castells, M. (2009) *Communication Power*, Oxford: Oxford University Press.

Cassidy, J. (2002) *Dot.Con*, London: Penguin.

Cellan-Jones, R. (2012) 'Facebook Q&A: The Network Justifies the Cost of Its "Like" Adverts', 13 July, http://www.bbc.co.uk/news/technology-18816674, accessed 13 July 2012.

Channel 4 (2011) 'C4 Appoints Commissioning Editor Convergent Formats', http://www.channel4.com/info/press/news/c4-appoints-commissioning-editor-convergent-formats, accessed 1 July 2012.

Croteau, D. and Hoynes, W. (2006) *The Business of Media: Corporate Media and the Public Interest*, Thousand Oaks, CA: Pine Forge Press.

Curran, J. (2011) *Media and Democracy*, London: Routledge.

Curran, J., Fenton, N. and Freedman, D. (2012) *Misunderstanding the Internet*, London: Routledge.

DCMS [Department for Media, Culture and Sport] (2009) 'Preserving standards will be cornerstone of UK media services', News Release 11 March, London: DCMS.

Deuze, M. and Stewart, B. (2011) 'Managing Media Work', in M. Deuze (ed) *Managing Media Work*, London: Sage.

Dwyer, T. (2010) *Media Convergence*, Maidenhead, UK: Open University Press.

Eckert, C. (1991) 'Carole Lombard in Macy's window', in C. Herzog and J. M. Gaines (eds) *Fabrications: Costume and the Female Body*, London: Routledge.

Eller, C. (2009) 'Studios Struggle to Rein in Movie Marketing Costs', *Los Angeles Times*, 20 April, http://articles.latimes.com/2009/apr/20/business/fi-ct-movies20, accessed 23 July 2012.

Fenton, N. (ed) (2010) *New Media, Old News*, London: Sage.

FTC (Federal Trade Commission) (2005) Letter from Mary K. Engle, Associate Director for Advertising Practices, FTC, to Gary Ruskin, Executive Director, Commercial Alert, 10 February, http://www.ftc.gov/os/closings/staff/050210productplacemen.pdf.

Fuchs, C. (2011) *Foundations of Critical Media and Information Studies*, London: Routledge.

Gandy, O. (2000) 'Race, Ethnicity and the Segmentation of Media Markets' in J. Curran and M. Gurevitch (eds) *Mass Media and Society*, 3rd edition, London: Arnold.

Garnham, N. (1996) 'Constraints on Multi-Media Convergence', in W. Dutton (ed) *Information and Communication Technologies*, Oxford: Oxford University Press.

Grainge, P. (2008) *Brand Hollywood: Selling Entertainment in a Global Media Age*, London: Routledge.

Green, A. (2011) *Understanding Newspaper Audiences: WARC Best Practice*, (December), London: WARC.

Google (2012) *Our Mobile Planet: UK*, http://www.mmaglobal.com/research/our-mobile-planet-uk, accessed 29 June 2012.

Hackley, C. (2010) *Advertising and Promotion*, London: Sage.

Hardy, J. (2010) *Cross-Media Promotion*, New York, NY: Peter Lang.

——(2011) 'Mapping Commercial Intertextuality: HBO's *True Blood*', *Convergence,* vol 17, no 1, pp7–17.

Hesmondhalgh, D. (2007) *The Cultural Industries*, London: Sage.

Hill, K. (2012) 'Facebook Will Pay $10 Million to Make Its "Sponsored Stories" Problem Go Away', *Forbes*, 18 June, http://www.forbes.com/sites/kashmirhill/2012/06/18/facebook-will-pay-10-million-to-make-its-sponsored-stories-problem-go-away, accessed 30 June 2012.

Hindman, M. (2009) *The Myth of Digital Democracy*, Princeton, NJ: Princeton University Press.

IAB (Interactive Advertising Bureau) (2006) *Fact Sheet: Online Adspend – First Half 2006*, http://www.iabuk.net/research/library/iab-adspend-factsheet-h1–2006, accessed 30 June 2012.

IAB (2012) *IAB Internet Advertising Revenue Report, 2011 Full Year Results, April 2012*, http://www.iab.net/insights_research/industry_data_and_landscape/adrevenuereport, accessed 18 June 2012.

Jarvis, J. (2009) *What Would Google Do?*, London: Harper Collins.

Jenkins, H. (2008) *Convergence Culture*, New York, NY: New York University Press.

Lehu, J.-M. (2009) *Branded Entertainment*, London: Kogan Page.

Livingstone, S. (2010) 'Interactive, Engaging but Unequal: Critical Conclusions from Internet Studies', in J. Curran (ed) *Media and Society*, London: Bloomsbury.

McAllister, M. (1996) *The Commercialization of American Culture*, London: Sage.

McChesney, R. (2007) *Communication Revolution*, New York, NY: The New Press.

Meikle, G. and Young, S. (2012) *Media Convergence: Networked Digital Media in Everyday Life*, Basingstoke, UK: Palgrave.

Murdock, G. (1992) 'Embedded Persuasions: The Fall and Rise of Integrated Advertising', in D. Strinati and S. Wagg (eds) *Come on Down?*, London: Routledge.

——(2000) 'Digital Futures: European Television in the Age of Convergence', in J. Wieten, G. Murdock, and P. Dahlgren (eds) *Television across Europe: A Comparative Introduction*, London: Sage.

NAA (Newspaper Association of America) (undated) Home page, www.naa.org, accessed 30 June 2012.

Negroponte, N. (1995) *Being Digital*, Philadelphia, PA: Coronet.

Newell, J., Salmon, C. T. and Chang, S. (2006) 'The Hidden History of Product Placement', *Journal of Broadcasting & Electronic Media*, vol 50, no 4, pp575–594.

O'Reilly, T. (2005) 'What Is Web 2.0?', http://oreilly.com/web2/archive/what-is-web-20.html, accessed 24 July 2012.

OECD (Organisation for Economic Co-operation and Development) (2010) *News in the Internet Age: New Trends in News Publishing*, Paris: OECD.

Ofcom (2006) *The Communications Market 2006* (UK), London: Ofcom.

——(2011) *Communications Market Report* (UK), London: Ofcom.

——(2012) *Communications Market Report* (UK), London: Ofcom.

Office of Fair Trading (2009) 'Review of the Local and Regional Media Merger Regime', www.oft.gov.uk/shared_oft/mergers_ea02/oft1091.pdf, accessed 20 July 2012.

PwC (PriceWaterhouseCoopers) (2011) *Global Entertainment and Media Outlook 2011–2015*, www.pwc.com/outlook, accessed 29 June 2012.

Raice, S. (2012) 'Days of Wild User Growth Appear Over at Facebook', *Wall Street Journal*, 11 June, http://online.wsj.com/article/SB10001424052702303296604577454970244896342.html, accessed 12 June 2012.

Rainey, V. (2012) 'Germans Buck Trend with Love of Newspapers', 9 July, http://www.reuters.com/article/2012/07/09/us-media-survey-idUSBRE8680GD20120709, accessed 19 February 2013.

Sparks, C. (1999) 'The Press', in J. Stokes and A. Reading (eds) *The Media in Britain*, London: Macmillan.

Spurgeon, C. (2008) *Advertising and New Media*, London: Routledge.

Thinkbox (2012) 'TV Is at the Heart of Advertising Effectiveness', http://www.thinkbox.tv/server/show/nav.1182, accessed 26 May 2012.

Turow, J. (2011) *The Daily You: How the New Advertising Industry Is Defining Your Identity and Your Worth*, New Haven, CT: Yale University Press.

US Federal Trade Commission (2005) 'Product Placement and Adults', http://www.ftc.gov/os/closings/staff/050210productplacemen.pdf, accessed 30 June 2012.

Wolf, M. (1999) *The Entertainment Economy*, London: Penguin.

World Association of Newspapers (2009) 'World Press Trends: Advertising Revenues to Increase, Circulation Relatively Stable', http://www.wan-press.org/article18612.html, accessed 23 July 2012.

Writers Guild of America, West (2005) 'Entertainment Guilds Call for Industry Code of Conduct or FCC Regulation for Product Integration in Programming and Film', News Release, 14 November, New York, NY: WGA.

——(2008) David Young, Executive Director Writers Guild of America, West. Letter to Campaign for Press and Broadcast Freedom, 22 October.

Zenith Optimedia (2011) *Adspend Forecast Update April 2011*, http://www.zenithoptimedia.com/zenith/zenithoptimedia-adspend-forecast-update-apr-2011, accessed 1 July 2011.

7

MEDIA CONVERGENCE AND NEWSPAPERS

Daniel Lee

Background and overview

Walk into any newspaper almost anywhere in the world and 'reader interaction' will be one of the buzz phrases. Newspapers have always wanted to get readers involved to make them feel part of the product, to encourage loyalty; but the Internet and social media have heightened the editorial need to be seen to be working with, not giving news to, the readers. Look at *The Guardian* newspaper's statement on interaction with readers in its editorial guidelines, available freely on the Internet (*The Guardian* Editorial Code, August 2011 edition). It says:

> Our most important relationship is the one we have with our readers and site users. Courtesy applies whether an exchange takes place in person, by telephone, letter or email. The company recognises that communication online, eg in blogs and social media domains, can be more informal, brisk and, where a debate is underway, combative – but journalists should be mindful of the guidelines on blogging and social media available on GNM's internal Really Social Media site.

The Really Social Media site guidelines are, you will note, available on the Guardian News and Media's (GNM's) *internal* site. There is, of course, nothing wrong with keeping some of the editorial guidelines behind closed screens. Before the Internet, all of them would have been sitting on a shelf somewhere in *The Guardian*'s offices unseen by any reader; but now it seems odd, evidence of a strain between the need to keep readers feeling part of the organization, engaged with it socially, and a need to run a professional news organization by keeping some of the levers and pulleys behind the curtain. There is clearly a strain between the need to be social, 'informal, brisk and … combative' and the need to maintain these professional standards, which are covered more in the internal site. The more one reads the statement, the more revealing it appears. What does the writer mean by 'most important relationship'? Surely the relationships with contacts who give the journalists stories must be as important, because without them there would be no newspaper and, therefore, no readers or site users. What about relationships with experts, staff and freelance contributors? And what about the 'readers and site users'? Even the description of the customers is becoming oblique, no longer describing the simple process of reading, but moving back a stage to the more generic phrase, site user, which could mean anything from a reader to a video viewer, podcast listener, game player, contributor to a comment section or someone actually helping the newspaper create its core product – news stories – by providing research through a crowd-sourcing section, a video clip or photograph. The list lengthens almost by the day.

Of course, *The Guardian* is not alone in finding that the Internet and media convergence have thrust it into a schizophrenic position: torn between the need to be credible and professional and the need to publish a story or enter a debate with Internet site users as quickly as a reader can pick up a mobile phone camera or tweet. You will find similar confusion in many newspapers around the world. Convergence and the Internet offer more newsgathering and publication opportunities than ever before; but how can one take advantage of these openings without running away from the core business: newspapers?

Yet, the trick of balancing professionalism with the need to gather and publish news quickly while interacting with the audience is not as new as one might think. From early on, readers were asked to send stories through to newspapers, sometimes in exchange for subscriptions. In other words, they became correspondents. The line between professional journalist and reader was blurred. In his 'History of Newspapers' (1994), Mitchell Stephens quotes an example of this written by Benjamin Franklin in the *Pennsylvania Gazette* in 1729: 'Our Country Correspondents are desired to acquaint us, as soon as they can conveniently, with every remarkable Accident, Occurrence, &c fit for public Notice.'

There has always been, and is always likely to be, a need to know the news because human beings are social animals and like to know what their neighbours are doing and because many people have personal, political and/or business reasons for finding out who's buying, attacking or forming alliances with whom (Stephens 2007). As defined by the *Shorter Oxford English Dictionary* (2007), this information (news) is: 'New things, novelties; information … about important or interesting recent events.' News itself has remained the same from the start. It is the means of disseminating news that has changed over the years. Messengers and group meetings were the usual means of communicating the news. Handwriting was used for early newsletters (tipao) for officials in China during the Han dynasty (202 BCE to 221 CE) and also in Rome (approximately 59 BCE). After woodblock printing, moveable type printing was introduced in China (1045), followed by Johannes Gutenberg's development of a similar process in Mainz, Germany, in the mid-fifteenth century. William Caxton set up his Westminster Press in England in 1476 and the Venetian *Gazetta* turned to print from the late sixteenth century. The ability to reprint a page numerous times relatively quickly aided the distribution of news and, therefore, later newspapers beyond anything that would have been possible relying on handwriting. Soon a news industry was developing. Printing 'constituted part of the social and economic changes that would create conditions in which printed news and early versions of journalism could emerge and then flourish' (Conboy 2004: 9). People increasingly talked about current affairs (coffee house debates were examples of this) and the widening availability of printed material helped to extend literacy.

Needless to say, monarchs and political leaders recognized the power of the press from early on, restricting its freedom while using its influence to peddle their own propaganda. Printing required specialized equipment which was not widely available. This meant that at the same time as making mass circulation possible, it became easier for leaders to take control of production in various ways, including censorship, licensing and taxes. Henry VIII took almost complete control of printing by the mid-sixteenth century, but the sales of newsletters giving valuable information to merchants were still beginning to flourish. News was beginning to flow outside of the established order, foreshadowing a similar development with the converged and Internet-based media operating outside the rules of the traditional media today. There was also another form of convergence. A variety of types of news publications, from reports of proceedings of various societies to lists of local events, were starting to coalesce. Broader publications covering more than one type of issue were beginning to develop. In England, in the wake of the Civil War and abolition of the Court of Star Chamber in the mid-seventeenth century, print papers gained more freedom from political control and became a key part of the ensuing debates. Despite political restrictions, newspapers were being born around the world: in Antwerp there was the *Relation* (1605); in France there was the *Gazette* (1631); in America there was *Publick Occurances* (1690); in England there was what is considered to be the country's first daily newspaper, *The Courant* (1702); and in Japan there was the *Yokohama Mainichi Shimbun* (1871). Other restrictions on press freedom remained in England until the end of press taxation in the mid-nineteenth century, which had made many types of press advertising uneconomic. At the same time, improving education provision during the nineteenth century spread literacy and, therefore, increased the potential newspaper-reading population. Perhaps most importantly, other industrial developments aided printing speed and the process began to progress towards a form of mass communication that we might recognize today.

The Cambridge History of English and American Literature (1907–21) details the enormous leaps forward in the nineteenth century:

> Prior to 1814, not more than 750 impressions an hour could be obtained from one machine. In 1814, John Walter, the second of that name who owned *The Times,* showed that, with the aid of steam, newspapers could be

printed at the rate of 1,100 copies per hour. By the end of the century, one cylindrical press could print, at the rate of 25,000 copies per hour, journals twice the size of those issued at the beginning of the century. Further, when a mould of a page of type has been taken, the printer can cast plates for about a dozen presses.

All good news for the industry. However, sales never covered the costs of a commercial newspaper operation and, according to Curran and Seaton (2010: 3), 'the growth of newspaper profits, largely from advertising, supposedly rescued the press from its compromising dependence on state or party subsidies'. Advertising has been seen as 'the midwife of press freedom'. Newspapers were delivered from the clutches of the political parties to the hands of newspaper barons, the only people wealthy enough to own and run the expensive equipment needed for mass production. On top of this, to win a mass circulation, cover prices had to be reduced so that as many people as possible could afford the paper. *The Daily Mail*, launched by Alfred Harmsworth (later Lord Northcliffe) in 1896, in the wake of a similar movement in the US, was at the forefront of this trend in the UK. At half a penny, its price was half as much as many other newspapers, which meant it was dependent on attracting advertising to survive. The cover price alone would not keep it going. With slogans such as 'The Busy Man's Daily Newspaper' or 'A Penny Newspaper for One Halfpenny', a focus on a simpler, shorter style to appeal to the widest possible market, and the use of innovations such as the banner headline (right across the page), it established a new norm for the popular press. Other routes were restricted or bleak; a high cover price with a small circulation or reliance on political control, which is what happened to, for example, the left-wing *Daily Herald*. After re-launching with a promotion campaign, its circulation rose for a year to 1920; but that meant its costs also rose due to more newspapers to print and deliver and with no advertising to pay for the increasing expenditure. Eventually, its survival was only assured when the Trades Union Congress (TUC) and the Labour Party took it over two years later.

UK newspapers that have managed to survive, to date, without overt political control include *The Observer* (launched in 1791), reflecting the concerns of the period with the slogan 'Unbiased by prejudice – uninfluenced by party'; *The Times* (published as the *Daily Universal Register*) (1785); *Daily Telegraph* (*The Daily Telegraph & Courier*) (1855); and *The Guardian* (published as *The Manchester Guardian*) (1821). In the US, long-term fixtures include *The New York Sun* (1833), which cost 1 cent and is often considered the start of the penny press, and *The Washington Post* (1877).

Whereas journals and magazines tend (and tended) to reflect on or collate event details from elsewhere, often in longer articles (*The Gentleman's Magazine*, established 1731) or run specialist content (*Lloyd's News* – now *Lloyd's List*, established 1692), up-to-the-minute general interest news and fast-changing events were the lifeblood of newspapers. Speed and, linked to this, ready access to sources were always key factors.

The latest technology was always a key part of the process. The development of the telegraph aided the speed of story-gathering in the mid-nineteenth century. In terms of production, for most of the history of modern newspapers, typesetters would use metal typecasts to print. This meant large numbers of people needed to be employed to arrange the type and operate the presses, which kept printing papers expensive and restricted the commercial viability of newspapers. By the early 1980s, this was changing fast with desktop publishing (DTP). A personal computer could be used to typeset documents, drastically reducing the number of people needed to produce a newspaper. Eddie Shah (*Today* newspaper) and Rupert Murdoch (the *Sun*, *News of the World*, *The Times*, *The Sunday Times*) took advantage of the flexibility offered by DTP to create a slimmed-down newspaper operation. Murdoch dismissed 5500 people and continued publishing his newspapers in a new plant at Wapping, bypassing print-workers (members of the National Graphical Association (NGA) union). He won a long and bitter industrial dispute with the unions, and all newspapers would feel the effects of a new, more commercially focused era.

Of course, technological advances did not only help newspapers. The birth of public radio broadcasts in the early twentieth century and then TV a few decades later distracted readers from newspapers. If you got your news on the radio or TV, there would be less interest in a newspaper. More recently, of course, the growth of the Internet towards the end of the twentieth century and so far in the twenty-first century has severely punctured the newspaper business model. News alerts and reader interaction may come from any number of media organizations, not just traditional newspaper publishers, via desktop computers or mobile devices, such as laptops, iPads or BlackBerrys. There is a paradox. It has never been easier or cheaper to publish, certainly using the web, but this has led to an almost unlimited number of competitors to newspapers sucking in the pot of advertising money that first remained unchanged and has now shrunk as a result of the worldwide recession. The size and expense of the operation needed for publishing newspapers, for so long seen as the enemy of commercial success, turned out to be an unlikely friend. It restricted access to industry ownership to all but a few wealthy proprietors, and through them it limited entry to a select group of professional journalists. Since newspapers were always reliant on this advertising money, it follows that they have been particularly badly hit by its diffusion.

Media consultant and former *Financial Times* Labour correspondent Charles Leadbeater (2012) details the changing landscape over the past 25 years graphically in an edited version of his blog:

> Looking at the media industry was like looking at a large open beach strewn with a few very large boulders. These boulders were the big media companies. High fixed costs, industrial relations, regulation, limited spectrum – all created the conditions for high barriers to entry. Anyone trying to set up a significant new media business could be seen from a long way off.

Now imagine the scene on this beach five or ten years from now. A few big boulders are still showing. But several have been drowned by a growing tide of pebbles. People are coming to the beach in droves leaving pebbles. This is the new media business: a beach of pebbles. The big new media companies – Google, YouTube, Facebook, MySpace – deal in pebbles: they aggregate them, navigate you through them, link them together. The commercial trick is to work out how to make money from pebbles rather than boulders. Money may still be made on the beach but it will be in smaller, more distributed pockets as well as few, smaller numbers of large pockets. You need to become the best beachcombers in the business.

Whereas writers or broadcasters used to be limited by their chosen media, this is much less the case today. On the Internet, if it works, it can be used. There are more opportunities than ever before for journalists and others to express themselves and exchange information. Fast newsgathering and quick publication have always set newspapers apart from other forms of publishing, and converged media and the Internet offer this *par excellence*. But how do journalists and newspaper proprietors make sure that their product gets noticed on that crowded beach, and that it is credible, ethical and legal? How do journalists make it pay?

The changing business model and scrutinizing power

It is accepted wisdom now that media products are ephemeral. Many commentators seem to assume that this is something new and forget about the old adage: 'Today's newspaper is tomorrow's fish and chip wrapping.' Thanks to health and safety concerns about print and chemicals rubbing off on the haddock, this is no longer literally true, but for a long time it was accepted by newspaper journalists as a cry against preciousness in the editorial process. 'Don't be a prima donna', the reporter might be told, when her article was chopped in half. 'It'll be tomorrow's fish and chip paper.' Of course, this was not meant to imply that the paper had no value. To the contrary, it emphasized the key selling point of a newspaper: that it contained the latest report on any important and interesting recent event so yesterday's edition would be worthless because you would want today's edition. The problem is that this selling point is no longer the sole preserve of newspapers. In the age of a converged media industry, everyone, from the back-bedroom zealot and citizen journalist to the middle-aged hack, can gather news and distribute it almost instantaneously. This was not the case even when radio and TV made inroads into newspaper territory. Quite often newspapers, because their reporters needed little equipment compared with their broadcast colleagues, would be able to report more quickly from a wider range of scenes. Taken together with rising post-war living standards and less legal and political control for the print press in many countries, such as the UK, US and most of Europe, this meant newspaper circulation remained more robust than expected until towards the end of the twentieth century, despite the rise in TV ownership.

The rising star of the newspaper is easy to track until it begins to plummet in the latter part of the twentieth century. In 1782, one newspaper in Britain was published to 110,000 inhabitants; in 1821, one to 90,000; and, in 1832, one to 55,000 (*The Cambridge History of English and American Literature* (1907–21)). In 1950, in the UK, there were 573 newspapers in circulation for each 1000 people in the population, whereas in 1996 there were 332 per 1000 people (Norris 2000). Overall, there were similar falls in circulation elsewhere – for example, in the US, where the circulation fell from 342 per 1000 to 212 per 1000 in the same period. However, there have been some exceptions. In Germany, circulation rose from 242 to 311 per 1000 people (Norris 2000).

Not that lack of sales alone is enough to undermine the newspaper business model. From early on in the nineteenth century, advertising was paying the bulk of the cost of production, with increasingly specialized journalists and ever-more sophisticated machines. 'To support such changes in the structure of journalism, the requirements of large sums of capital investment meant a greater than ever dependence on circulation combined with advertising revenue' (Conboy 2004: 112). This business model has remained dominant until the present day, but it has become more and more difficult to sustain in a converged, digitized, Internet-influenced media industry. The advertising spend is spread too thinly and both mainstream news and raw information is too readily available through numerous devices, such as iPads, mobile phones and, of course, desktop computers, for many people to continue to pay for a newspaper. On top of this, websites such as *The Huffington Post* make a success in large part out of aggregating content from the sites of other publications, stealing their users in the process.

Locals and regionals

In all this, local and regional newspapers in the UK have probably suffered more than their national counterparts and their importance for communities is frequently underestimated and eclipsed by their bigger, noisier national cousins. As well as performing a valuable service for the local community, local and regional newspapers have traditionally been a main route into journalism for many reporters. They learn the key elements of journalism, from building contacts and verifying reports of events to understanding the audience and storytelling. Many national media stories have also started life as reports in the local press.

There are about 1300 local and regional newspaper titles published by 87 publishers in the UK, according to a 2010 House of Commons Culture, Media and Sport Committee report called *The Future for Local and Regional Media*. Publishers include Trinity Mirror, GMG, Newsquest and Archant. The biggest player is Johnston Press with 241 titles and a total circulation of 4.5 million. The House of Commons (2010) report says:

> Local newspapers, and more specifically the journalists who work on them, also underpin the national news industry forming the bottom layer of what

has been described as the 'news pyramid' as John Fry, Chief Executive of Johnston Press, explained to us: 'Locally we create the bottom layer of that pyramid. We have 11,000 journalists around the country and they create huge numbers of local stories. People further up the pyramid then take some of them and develop them. At BBC News what they do every day is they come into work. They buy the local newspaper. They look on our websites and they select from that.'

Fry's statement is interesting because it illustrates how local, regional and national newspapers have always been an integral part of a wider media network, a relationship that has become even more entwined as a result of convergence. Nevertheless, circulation and advertising for locals and regionals have fallen off a cliff. For example, *The Western Mail* sells 26,000 copies (2012), having sold 94,000 copies in 1979 (Audit Bureau of Circulations 2012). UK local and regional newspaper advertising revenues dropped from £2.8 billion to £2 billion between 2002 and 2008, while at the same time online advertising revenues rose from £0.2 billion to £2.8 billion (House of Commons 2010).

Reflecting the position throughout the local and regional press, the Commons report says that 'in March 2009, Johnston Press reported a loss of £429.3 million, compared to a profit of £124.7 million in the previous year' (House of Commons 2010). There were 60 local newspaper closures and 1500 job losses between May 2008 and May 2009, according to the National Union of Journalists (NUJ). The report highlights other trends that threaten the local press and local accountability, particularly the number of local authority publications that are 'competing with commercial local newspapers'. Claire Enders, chief executive of Enders Analysis, told the committee that she 'expected up to half of the 1,300 titles to close within five years' (House of Commons 2010). *Private Eye*'s Rotten Boroughs column is often far ahead of local newspapers in revealing local corruption.

At first sight, this might all be blamed on the Internet and convergence; but the picture is far more complex. After sales of local and regional newspapers started to fall during the 1970s, unions were tamed, minimizing irresponsible and costly industrial action, but also often leaving journalists on poor contracts and salaries and susceptible to bullying from above. Classified advertising boomed and, buoyed by this false dawn, regionals and locals borrowed too much to expand and failed to respond quickly enough to the growth of the Internet. To compound their difficulties, they cut their journalism to try to preserve their profits, reducing the quality of their product and probably driving down sales even more.

Local newspapers have been developing an online presence to catch up with the changes, but they are struggling. Now, local journalism is often being provided through publications such as hyper-local websites, which grow out of and focus on neighbourhoods rather than industrial concerns that spread coverage top down over a whole town or region. Whether or not this could provide a model for a commercially viable industry is still an open question. Does this matter for effective public journalism, scrutinizing local political and other decision-making, if the people researching and writing the material are doing it in a balanced and credible way? Arguably not. Arguably, without the need to rely on advertising, it could be better than it was before.

Nevertheless, in response to the crisis in local and regional newspapers, some traditional proprietors have asked for there to be a relaxation of the rules on cross-media ownership. For example, there is a national '20 per cent' rule:

- No one controlling more than 20 per cent of the national newspaper market may hold a licence for Channel 3.
- No one controlling more than 20 per cent of the national newspaper market may hold more than a 20 per cent stake in any Channel 3 service.
- A company may not own more than a 20 per cent share in such a service if more than 20 per cent of its stock is, in turn, owned by a national newspaper proprietor with more than 20 per cent of the market.

(Dwyer 2010: 101)

This may prop up newspapers, but at what cost for journalism standards and freedom from bias? In any event, this is unlikely to become a popular option in the light of the revelations at the 2012 Leveson hearings into phone hacking and other newspaper misconduct, increasingly focusing on the problems of Murdoch's far-reaching media empire.

A business model for the future

Newspapers, from local to national, are desperately trying to find a new business model. Freesheets, publications distributed without customer payment, or paywalls, asking users to pay for access to the newspaper's website, offer two ways forward. In terms of circulation, freesheets represent a qualified success story. Broadly speaking, their business model assumes that people are less likely to pay for general news that they can get for free on the Internet and elsewhere but that they will still read the paper if it is free. The theory is that increased advertising will follow a rising circulation to more than offset the lost cover price income. Train commuters were and are a key part of the equation for freesheets in London, the UK's biggest single market area. The millions of train, Tube and bus travellers in the capital provide a captive market, which is why the positioning of newspaper bins next to station entrances is so important. In 2006 in London there were three freesheets: *London Lite* (a free version of the paid-for *Evening Standard*, published by Associated Newspapers), *Metro* (also published by Associated Newspapers) and *The London Paper* (published by the Murdoch-owned News International). Effectively, there was a battle for readers between the two corporations. In fact, *London Lite* was called *Standard Lite* when it was launched in 2004 and its change of name in 2006 was widely seen as a spoiler aimed at News International's freesheet launched that year. Associated Newspapers attracted critics who argued that its freesheets were, in effect, taking readers from its paid-for *Evening Standard*. However, the strategy appeared to work. *The London Paper* couldn't match the competition even though its free circulation was 100,000 more than the figure for *London Lite*, which was just over 400,000 in July 2008. After recording a turnover of £14.1 million with a pre-tax loss of £12.9 million in the year to 29 June 2008, it closed in September 2009 (Brook 2009). Just a month later *The Evening Standard*, which was by then mostly owned by Alexander Lebedev (also *The Independent* newspaper owner) and his son Evgeny Lebedev, made itself free. *London Lite* announced it would close later in the same year.

Critics argued that in its new guise, *The Evening Standard* would have to reduce its quality; but they were confounded in 2010 when the paper won the Grand Prix prize at the prestigious *Media Week* awards and was named Media Brand of the year. Perhaps in recognition of this continued quality control, the paper's readership has also continued to rise. In the year October 2010 to September 2011 the paper's readership was 1,557,000, according to the National Readership Survey. This was up from 1,439,000 during the same period in the previous year.

Bearing in mind that advertising became *The Evening Standard*'s sole source of income, many critics thought its financial base would be unsustainable. Here, again, the critics were confounded. As Peter Preston, ex-editor of *The Guardian* and now a media commentator, explains:

> ... advertising began to improve. Volume was up; so, by 60%, was yield. Readership surveys showed the free Standard, giving away 600,000 a day, had an audience of 1.4 million or so – hugely increased. It used to sell 1,600 copies a day at Oxford Circus; now it could distribute 20,000 free. It costs about £1.1m to produce the Standard over a week, and the paper, on current form, can bring in about £1.1m from advertising to meet those bills.
>
> *(Preston 2010)*

The Evening Standard looks like it has so far made a success of its transfer to being free, but this did cost the lives of two other papers in its region. It is this latter part of the picture that is more typical around the world, according to a 2011 World Press Trends survey by the World Association of Newspapers and News Publishers. It showed that 'free newspapers took a big hit in 2010 – a drop in total distribution to 24 million copies from a high of around 34 million in 2008'.

The Evening Standard is, however, something more. It is a reminder that globally the audience for newspapers is bigger than it is for the Internet. This is likely to change in favour of the latter, but it is still worth remembering. *The Evening Standard* is also an example of newspapers playing the Internet at its own game: using free distribution to increase the number of readers and, therefore, advertising yield. In this restricted way, if a newspaper is free it has until now had an advantage over most electronic platforms because of its portability and the ease with which it can be scanned. This advantage is, however, disappearing with the rising access to increasingly versatile iPads, e-readers and other mobile devices. But, and this is a big but, people are often migrating from paper to screen, while staying with the same brand. Again, the 2011 *World Press Trends* survey shows that worldwide:

> Daily print newspaper circulation declined from 528 million in 2009 to 519 million in 2010, a drop of about 2 percent. But what has been lost to print has been more than made up by digital newspaper readers. Digital audiences are typically a third of print readership. So against a 2 percent decline, digital growth is significantly greater.
>
> *(World Association of Newspapers and News Publishers 2011)*

Looked at in this context, *The Evening Standard* example appears to lead the way in showing that a quality product with a recognized brand will still attract plenty of readers. It is the money, as ever, that is the key issue. But the above survey adds: 'In Europe, internet advertising rose 14 per cent from 2009, compared with 9 per cent for TV [the biggest advertising medium by money], while newspaper advertising fell 1 per cent' (World Association of Newspapers and News Publishers 2011) For the time being, *The Evening Standard* may be breaking even; but, as can be seen from the world picture, this may not be a business model that can be widely applied for any significant length of time. Some other way needs to be found to pay for the product. This was stressed by World Association of Newspapers and News Publishers CEO Christoph Riess, speaking at the World Editors' Forum in Hamburg in 2010: 'Whatever form the newspaper takes, it will remain the dominant media force in the world.' But he added that for digital material, a way must be found to get readers to pay: 'Will paid content generate revenue? It's not a question of yes or no. It's a question of how. In order to survive, we have to do it' (Riess 2010).

It is not surprising that newspapers want to try to get Internet users to pay for access. Live blogs, data mining, data visualization, crowdsourcing and other innovations have all attracted new users. A look at one month's Audit Bureau of Circulations electronic figures from May 2011 is striking. In May 2011, the number of daily users of the *Mail Online* jumped by 21.4 per cent to 4,365,716, and the number of monthly unique users grew by 21 per cent to 77,250,993. For guardian.co.uk, the figures show an 18 per cent daily user increase to 2,827,677 and a monthly figure of 51,383,937. At telegraph.co.uk, the number of daily users jumped by 13.25 per cent to 2,188,745 and there was a 14 per cent rise in monthly unique browsers to 43,796,963 (cited in Deans and Halliday 2011). Paywalls are an obvious way to get payment for the product: charge the user. The big problem with paywalls is that they tend to reduce the readership, which lessens the attraction of the site for advertising. This, in turn, makes the site even more dependent on people paying for access; but it takes a lot of subscriptions to pay for the production of a newspaper, even if the production of actual paper is taken out of the equation for a product that is increasingly circulated online. The other downside to the paywall is that it tends to undermine relationships between journalists and users, a key factor in sourcing, researching and delivering stories; enabling journalists to enhance their profile; and making users feel part of a community. Many see these relationships as central to building and maintaining any media brand, as *The Guardian* code, looked at earlier in this chapter, showed. But the picture of whether a paid-for or free approach is best is blurred, according to Dan Sabbagh's Organ Grinder Blog in *The Guardian*. He says: 'What is clear is that those who wanted to swear by either free or paid-for online news have been proved wrong. So far, the internet, a large place at the best of times, appears to be big enough for both models' (Sabbagh 2011).

In February 2012 Gannett, a major US newspaper publisher and owner of the British publisher Newsquest, created paywalls for all of its American titles, except *USA Today*. Readers will be allowed a limited number of free views and they will then have to pay for access. The Gannett move follows other stories of limited success. *The Times* paywall, launched in mid-2010, seems to have had some promising results over its first year. News Corporation, the owning company, announced that 101,036 had signed up for a monthly subscription, raising a relatively modest total of £10.5 million of extra revenue. The figures show that 35,000 people read the paper on an iPad daily. There are some suggestions that the paper may relax access so that people will be able to read some articles, perhaps those linked from Facebook pages (Sabbagh 2011).

In October 2011, after setting up a paywall in March of the same year, the *New York Times* said it had 324,000 paid digital subscribers, a rise of 40,000 on the previous quarter. It made a profit of $15.7 million compared with a loss of $4.3 million for the same period in the previous year. It announced that it had more than 1 million digital subscribers (including people buying other editions, such as Kindle and print, with website access as well) (*New York Times* 2011). The *New York Times*'s paywall allows non-subscribers to read a set number of articles before they have to pay, unlike London's *The Times*'s paywall, which blocks all unpaid access. There is a tense relationship between print and web for newspapers. Revenue from the *New York Times*'s circulation grew by 3.4 per cent to $237 million, but ad sales fell 8.8 per cent to $262 million (*New York Times* 2011). The company identified revenues from its paid digital products as 'helping to offset a decline in print copies sold across the News Media Group' (*New York Times* 2011). Subscribing to both the print and the web version may be cheaper than subscribing to the web version only (800,000 print subscribers link their accounts to NYTimes.com to get free access). Similarly, a subscription to the website of other newspapers, such as *The Boston Globe* (which set up a paywall in October 2011), often costs more than a subscription to the print paper and print subscribers get free access to all digital content. This is because advertising customers pay a higher price for advertising in the print version of the newspaper than they do on its Internet sister (or, perhaps, offspring might be a more accurate metaphor). Effectively, payment for Internet access is used to subsidize the print version to attract more advertising, underlining the difficult reality that, fundamentally, the newspaper business model has not changed. It is still dependent on advertising.

Both the *New York Times* and the London *Times* are, of course, general reader-ship newspapers, which makes it difficult for them to charge for material that is available for free elsewhere. When a newspaper has specialist content, this tension is less apparent. People subscribe to *The Wall Street Journal* and *The Financial Times*, for example, because they publish valuable financial news required for readers to do their jobs and make their profits, and that news is not available at all or in the same depth in any or many other places. Bill Mitchell, head of Entrepreneurial and International Programs at the Poynter Institute, explains:

> I think that the idea of charging today for something that was free yesterday is fundamentally a non-starter, economically. The user really needs to see evidence of new value. A niche publication offers the user the opportunity to get content that either helps them do their job better, because it's focused on their area of employment, or really addresses a personal passion. But I think this doesn't close the door to general interest publications because most are made up of a number of niches.
>
> *(Mitchell 2011)*

Mitchell (2011) favours a mixed approach. He says:

> I think the so-called 'leaky' wall [part pay, part free] is the best bet as opposed to a hard wall. With an emerging business model like this, flexibility is really critical and the metered or 'leaky' wall enables flexibility across many fronts. It enables the publisher to shape the terms of the two fundamental experiences that it offers to its customers: the paid experience and the free experience.

He adds:

> I think that some of the strategies that are beginning to make up overall a hybrid revenue approach include ideas about membership. In some ways, you can think of membership as an enhanced subscription relationship. A membership in a news organisation might involve things like regular events. It might involve the opportunity to host free classified ads if you're selling your piano or buying a second car. User-generated advertising will reduce some of the production costs for advertising initiatives. That will open up the area of advertising to small business owners who traditionally have been priced out of the market for most publications.

Canadian media commentator Matthew Ingram (2011) points to what he calls 'another promising strategy'. The publisher needs to look at the newspaper 'not as a thing that you need to charge readers for, but as a platform for data and infor-mation that you can generate value from in other ways – including by licensing it to developers and other third parties via an open API [application programming interface].' *The Guardian* in the UK and *USA Today* are both experimenting with this approach. Meanwhile, according to William F. Baker in the *Columbia Journalism Review* (Baker 2012), a possible third way could be emerging in Bratislava, where '[a company has chosen] a cable TV-style payment system, in which users pay once to get access to a range of premium content'.

Launched in 2011, *Piano Media* gives subscribers a flat-fee single login to online content from all nine of Slovakia's leading news publishers. In addition, without paying any subscription, everyone can get limited, or metered, access for free. The company says it has exceeded profit expectations and not driven people away from the sites. But Baker (2012) warns: 'To say that *Piano* has solved the paywall puzzle would be a stretch. One of the biggest reasons for its success may be Slovakia's linguistic isolation from the rest of the world. With ... little Slovak-language competition from outside the nation's borders, readers would seem to have little choice.' Furthermore, 'data from six months of *Piano*'s experiment has revealed that readers who decide to pay are not motivated by concern for access to specific content. Rather, they decide to pay because they want to be the kind of person who values intellectual work and pays for it, and because they like paying just once for access' (Baker 2012: 2). In other words, there is a market for people who value unfettered access to newspaper online content for its own sake to form their views, to understand the world and to make a range of decisions on everything from films and food to wars and politicians.

And this brings us to one of the most important elements, if not the most important element of the journalism and convergence debate, according to media commentator Roy Greenslade, professor of journalism, City University London (Greenslade 2010): 'I'm not worried about the fate of newspapers, but the fate of journalism. How can we preserve a public service that, not to be too pompous about it, is a key – arguably the key – bulwark of our democracy?' Greenslade adds that there can be little doubt that *The Times*'s and News International's initiative:

> ... has more do with commerce than public service. But there is a logic to the link between making profit and providing editorial content. After all, it is a business model with a history in Britain running back more than 150 years. In trying to attract consumers are we failing to address citizens? Clearly, the audience is gradually drifting away from paid-for print papers. If people also turn away from online papers that offer serious, quality editorial, the likely outcome is a damaging democratic deficit. We cannot afford to allow that to happen.
>
> *(Greenslade 2010)*

All of which brings the story back to what happens inside the newspaper office. Not only are people turning away from newspapers, but newspapers are also reducing their content and cutting staff, risking quality and depth of coverage. They know that cost-cutting can reduce their losses or even help them to turn a profit. According to the Audit Bureau of Circulation figures in the UK in the year to April 2012, for example, *The Telegraph's* daily circulation fell by 7.9 per cent and the *Sunday* dropped by 6.3 per cent. During the same period, *The Times's* circulation fell 11.6 per cent and its *Sunday* sibling's dropped 10 per cent. However, according to Peter Preston (a former editor of *The Guardian* and now a media commentator) writing in *The Observer* (Preston 2012), *The Telegraph's* operating profits remained reasonably stable, dropping from approximately £60 million in 2010 to nearly £56 million in 2011, but *The Times's* losses have fallen drastically. 'Two years ago, [its] losses, as posted at Companies House, were £87.7m. Last year, July to July, that became £45m. And now it's shrunk again, to £11.6m' (Preston 2012).

Another threat to quality, depth and coverage comes from the concentration of newspaper ownership in fewer hands that has worked in tandem, with convergence and its accompanying no-holds-barred aggressive commercial environment. If there is little competition, where will be the incentive for producing an engaging, bold product or one that challenges powerful elites and investigates injustice? News is clearly much more available than ever before through websites and social media; but newspapers are still a key element in liberal democracies for credible expertise, in-depth analysis and persistent scrutiny of power. Social media and numerous websites perform a vital function in providing access to information and transparency, but newspapers verify what they offer and provide context and sense.

Changed working practices for the future

One of the first effects on newspapers is their continually shrinking staff, reflecting the falling readership and weak ad revenue. According to Preston (2012) in *The Observer*:

> So where does the Barclays' [David and Frederick Barclay, owners of *The Telegraph*] consistent profitability come from? [C]osts are relentlessly driven down. The daily and *Sunday* together employ around 500 editorial people (under half the *New York Times* comparison). Some subediting tasks are outsourced to Australia. Any new editorial venture, online or off, has to be deemed profitable almost from the word go. If you wonder why the daily seems a bit short on features, you're told that a proper features section would lose £4m a year, so no dice.

As we have seen earlier in this chapter, the defining elements of a newspaper are present in the name: news + paper. Just to confuse things a bit, let's start with the second part of the definition first. Paper is simply a means of delivery. If instead of its literal meaning we take this to mean delivery through text and still pictures, then convergence makes a lot more sense. The strength of emotion for paper, fetishising it or treating it as totemic, is understandable. It has, after all, formed the basis for communicating culture for a long time, but newspapers have always been ephemeral (tomorrow's fish and chip paper, etc.). This doesn't change if newspapers are delivered electronically. Electronic delivery can only add to what newspapers can offer: audio, video, polls, reader comment, audience interaction plus in-depth text.

The first part of the definition remains unchanged. People still want news (timely, up-to-the-minute, relevant stories), and that is unlikely to change. Inherent to this element of the definition, it has always been the case that newspapers have had to make sure the news makes sense to their readers, otherwise they lose them. As part of this function, newspapers have always gone further than word of mouth, radio or TV in providing explanation and context. As we have seen earlier in this chapter, this has always been one of their selling points. Whereas radio and TV excel at giving the audience the opportunity to consider the credibility and feel of an event or person from sound and/or moving vision, text and still pictures excel at delivering detail, analysis, data and reflection. Consider a TV broadcast full of statistics and complex analysis. It wouldn't work. Text, on the other hand, is still the most flexible, effective way of delivering complex material because it allows the reader to check backwards and forwards to compare comments, quotes and figures, to refresh the memory during a long article. Added to this, for heavily descriptive articles, text allows the reader to imagine and form her or his own feelings of what is being described, an interactivity that is often forgotten. This can make a text-based piece more personal and engaging to the reader, user or audience than any film or audio. None of this should be seen as undermining video, audio or digital interactivity, but rather as a call to use all forms of creativity, including text, to best effect to complement each other. This is now possible for newspaper organizations. Consider a newspaper full of audio and moving vision. Harry Potter fantasy? Not now. That's currently available on any tablet. Technological advances may have created chaos in the news industry, but they are also freeing newspapers of the need to rely on paper. Today a newspaper organization can offer much of what a TV or radio broadcaster can offer plus the detail and analysis of text. Newspapers are recognizing this, as can be seen from mainstream names, such as *The Guardian* and *The Telegraph*, deciding to become what they call 'digital first'. In other words, the first target for their reporting will be for electronic formats. The focus, however, has to be news. Otherwise there is no distinction between a newspaper and a periodical. As organizations with expert editors, correspondents and reporters with bulging contacts books (the foundation stone upon which any reporting career is built), newspapers are still in a strong position for providing the up-to-the-minute news that most other media organizations just do not have the resources to deliver.

There is, of course, a catch. Just as newspapers can offer audio and video, broadcasters can now offer text. So we revert to another basic distinguishing feature of the newspaper: the journalist who specializes in researching and writing news for text. Most journalists will tend to specialize or excel in only one or perhaps two forms of communication (text, audio, video, photography, interactivity), even though they may need to learn to produce material across all five to an adequate standard. This is likely to remain the case in the future. Some people sound or look better than others in video or audio; some people construct a written sentence or an argument with style, others plod; some people are good at interacting, others freeze. The audience tends to reflect these divisions. People tend to have a preference for how they want to receive different types of news. Consumers are likely to prefer to receive news of a football match with video; analysis is likely to be more thorough in text and debates; and discussions are likely to be more engaging with the interactivity of the Internet. And if the creatives and audiences work this way, it is likely that news organizations will continue to develop to reflect this: some specializing in text, some in audio or video. Interactivity, however, will remain constant. And why not? Twitter, Facebook, reader comments and crowdsourcing are powerful ways of newsgathering and distribution. Just think of *The Guardian*'s reporting of the MPs' expenses scandal and consider how its website facility for readers to investigate MPs (http://mps-expenses.guardian.co.uk/), comparing and contrasting invoices, facts and figures, kept that story running. This is good news, and the continuing questions about the most viable business model will be answered, even though there may be more pain on the way.

As well as the new world of the newspaper being one delivered largely electronically and complemented with audio, video and interactivity, what other good news is there? In the UK, the freedom of the web has helped to stimulate a debate about restrictive laws, such as defamation (a government Defamation Bill, sponsored by Kenneth Clarke at the Ministry of Justice, is now before parliament); people are not so prepared to accept 'the truth' handed down on tablets of stone by anyone – doctors, scientists or journalists; everyone can reveal stories, which improves public transparency.

The *Shorter Oxford English Dictionary* (2007) definition of a journalist is: 'A person who earns a living by writing for or editing a newspaper or periodical. Also, a reporter for radio or television.' The same OED defines a newspaper as 'containing news, frequently with photographs, features, advertisements, etc'. So we can assume that a newspaper journalist combines both elements: earns money primarily from writing news. But to fulfil that critical part of the definition – 'earns a living' – journalists need to offer something more than their readers can provide for themselves. Yet, journalists, along with other major institutions, may have a struggle. In 2010 Grant Blank (2010) of the Oxford Internet Institute evaluated statistics from a 2009 institute report, *The Internet in Britain*, to show that 'people providing internet services' won the trust of 39 per cent of people, compared with 30 per cent for major corporations and 28 per cent for newspapers (Dutton et al 2009; Blank 2010). In other words, people trust the Internet more than newspapers. Newspapers will be on the Internet as well as in print, of course, but the shift in people's attitudes is clear. Government came out even worse, with the backing of just 20 per cent of people; but 2009 was the year the expenses scandal broke. Banks and newspapers are likely to fare worse after recent financial debacles and the hacking outrage at the Murdoch empire.

It is hard for news reporters to spend time on producing decent material today. Journalists frequently produce three times more material than 20 or 30 years ago

(Lewis et al 2008). A reporter may be expected to attend an event, file 100 words for the web straight away, take some pictures, record audio, film video and then file updates later in the day. It used to be a question of interviewing people and filing a story in the pre-digital world. The increased workload is a key factor in what *Guardian* journalist Nick Davies (2008) and BBC journalist Waseem Zakir, who first coined the term, call 'churnalism' (Harcup 2008): reprocessing press and PR copy with little or no independent investigation or verification. This cannot go on. Journalists, especially news journalists, need to offer a professionalism that is not usually available elsewhere. What shape is it or what shape should it take?

Journalists working on newspapers, delivered electronically or on paper, need to verify, make sense of, bear witness to and investigate stories. 'These four over-lapping functions should be the pillars of trust' (Brock 2010). If the idea of a daily text-based delivery of news is to survive, responsibility and credibility are likely to be key parts of the struggle to survive as an industry. The Leveson Inquiry (2012) has revealed shoddy and often criminal working practices: from hacking mobile phones to harassing and bullying people, that may have enabled some newspapers to sell more copies on the back of sensation in the past, but will only undermine the credibility of the industry for the future. It may be that these practices were focused on certain aggressively commercial papers, such as the now defunct *News of the World*; but the whole industry is affected. As we have seen in this chapter, and as the Leveson Inquiry has revealed, key factors for newspapers exercising what Conservative leader Stanley Baldwin in 1929 called 'power without responsibility, the prerogative of the harlot throughout the ages', include ensuring that there is not a concentration of too much ownership in the hands of one or a few indivi-duals; adequate industry bodies, such as the National Union of Journalists, to keep a check on proprietor power; and a regulator that, unlike the current Press Com-plaints Commission, is seen to be effective for complainants, fair to journalists and independent of the press (especially the part of the press that considers commercial considerations above everything and it must also be independent of the state if journalism is to function as it should). We've been here before, with, for example, the Press Council, which lasted from 1953 to 1991, shortly after the Calcutt Report in 1990 considered press invasions of privacy.

A lack of responsibility means draconian regulation is more likely and it under-mines public trust. And, unlike in 1991, this public trust is now critical for the survival of the newspaper industry. Back then there was no web publishing to compete with the press barons. Now regulation is more difficult: how do you control the Internet without undermining the freedom that makes it so useful? Furthermore, credibility is even more important and perhaps harder to maintain in the face of the breadth and quantity of information available on the web. In the middle of this overwhelming amount of information, public trust is fundamental for what some see as the emerging role of a new type of journalist. On his blog The Buttry Diary, Steve Buttry (2012), director of community engagement and social media, Digital First Media, says:

The gatekeeper days of journalism were fun. But they're over. And they weren't as good as we remember them. If journalists aren't gatekeepers, what are we?

We are:

Watchdogs. We still need to keep an eye on the powerful institutions and people of the community. But we're not the only watchdogs. When we fall down on the job, blogs, interest groups and citizen advocates will bark where we should be barking.

Storytellers. Stories still help people understand their world and their communities. We can and should tell our stories with photos, videos, audio, animation, games, maps, databases, timelines, data visualization and interactive graphics.

Fact-checkers.

Aggregators and curators. We listen and highlight the most reliable and meaningful voices.

Investigative journalists.

I'm sure that's just a starter list. The transformation of journalism is a work in progress, and I presume it will be for the rest of my career and longer.

And the transformation in the journalistic approach needs to go right back to the start, says Charlie Beckett (2009), director of Polis, in the department of media and communications at the London School of Economics: 'Journalism education should not just be about training students to do what people used to do. Journalism education must be about challenging the role, value and nature of news media.' Traditional roles have certainly been challenged by Josh Halliday of *The Guardian*, Dave Lee of the BBC and Conrad Quilty-Harper of *The Telegraph*. They are a few of the many young news journalists who point to their blogs (still text, don't forget) as being key to their success. They emphasize the need for young journalists to build themselves as a brand. Is this the future for newspaper journalists?

Clay Shirky (2010), a media consultant and New York University academic, considered *The Times*'s paywall in a blog called '*The Times* Paywall and Newsletter Economics':

> *The Times* has stopped being a newspaper, in the sense of a generally available and omnibus account of the news of the day, broadly read in the community. Instead, it is becoming a newsletter, an outlet supported by, and speaking to, a specific and relatively coherent and compact audience. Is this the future for newspapers?

Is the future, then, with the hyper-local? Perhaps, according to Greenslade (2012). In an article headlined 'The future of journalism is bright as hacks go hyperlocal', he says:

First, as the [*Evening Standard*] proves ... the paid-for newspaper model is not the only way to build an audience for quality journalism. Second, the financial problems facing large publishing chains do not mean people are turning their backs on the papers and websites they produce. Third, newsprint newspapers are not the only platform to provide an audience with news and information. Fourth, consider this paradox: local journalism is showing every sign of reinventing itself by going back to the past. News Corporation, the owning company announced that 101,036 had signed up for a monthly subscription, raising a relatively modest total of £10.5 million of extra revenue. The figures show that 35,000 people read the paper on an iPad daily.

He refers back to nineteenth-century news press ventures that struggled to survive because of the cost of producing newspapers and contrasts this with the cheapness of publishing content on the web today. There are a number of success stories, he says, of people setting up news websites or blogs covering local areas and issues that have been deserted by the mainstream press, such as councils and community meetings. One example has 'spawned a monthly newsprint publication' (Greenslade 2012). 'In other words, online has generated print ... we are in the foothills of this new hyperlocal enthusiasm and my hunch is it is a pointer to a fertile future for journalism – and for the people' (Greenslade 2012). Optimism, indeed. Is he right?

Whatever happens in the future, newspapers are no longer likely to return to being one-way custodians of the so-called truth. There always was some sort of interactivity in newspapers. Readers' letters have always been an important part of encouraging reader loyalty through a feeling of being part of a debate. But this has now become much more fluent. There is now a continuous conversation between the journalist and the audience. Often, neither may get the final word, and it is worth remembering that even good old Socrates distrusted writing and preferred dialogue: continuous questioning and answering to get to a true understanding. As part of this, today social networks such as Twitter and other forms of interactivity, already key tools for the journalist, are likely to become even more important for sourcing and alerting people to stories. That's why *The Guardian*'s editorial guide is so keen to encourage social network use and interactivity, and that's why, in 2009, it published a story predicting that it would 'become the first newspaper in the world to be published exclusively via Twitter', ensuring that any story 'can be told in 140 characters' (*The Guardian* 2009). It was, of course, 1 April and this was a joke; but the form of delivery for news is likely to keep changing. One thing is likely to remain unchanged: whatever innovations there are, people are likely for the foreseeable future to want news in a text form; but if the creators and distributors of it want pay for it – whether they deliver their content on paper, on a mobile device or through a desktop computer – they will still need to provide the basics: new, credible, revealing and relevant stories delivered in an engaging, accessible way. Let's call it a newspaper.

Bibliography

Audit Bureau of Circulations (2012) http://www.abc.org.uk, accessed 8 July 2012.

Baker, W. F. (2012) 'A National Paywall that Works', *Columbia Journalism Review*, 14 February, http://www.cjr.org/the_news_frontier/a_national_paywall_that_works.php?page=all, accessed 1 March 2012.

Beckett, C. (2009) 'Journalism Education in a Networked World', *LSE Polis*, 31 October, http://blogs.lse.ac.uk/polis/2009/10/31/journalism-education-in-a-networked-world-polis-in-shanghai, accessed 29 July 2012.

Blank, G. (2010) 'Trust on the Internet Now Exceeds Trust in Other Major Institutions', *Oxford Internet Surveys*, 25 October, http://microsites.oii.ox.ac.uk/oxis/blog/2010/trust-internet-now-exceeds-trust-other-major-institutions, accessed 12 July 2011.

Brock, G. (2010) 'City University Inaugural Lecture: Is News Over?', 17 March, http://www.city.ac.uk/events/2010/mar/is-news-over, accessed 12 July 2012.

Brook, S. (2009) 'The London Paper Set to Close', *The Guardian*, 20 August, http://www.guardian.co.uk/media/2009/aug/20/the-london-paper-close-plan, accessed 16 April 2012.

Buttry, S. (2012) 'Gatekeepers Need to Find New Value When the Fences Have Blown Away', 30 April, http://stevebuttry.wordpress.com/2012/04/30/gatekeepers-need-to-find-new-value-when-the-fences-have-blown-away, accessed 29 July 2012.

Conboy, M. (2004) *Journalism: A Critical History*, London: Sage.

Curran, J. and Seaton, J. (2010) *Power without Responsibility*, London: Routledge.

Davies, N. (2008) *Flat Earth News*, London: Vintage.

Deans, J. and Halliday, J. (2011) 'ABCe: Mail Online Nears 80 Million Monthly Users', *The Guardian*, 23 June, http://www.guardian.co.uk/media/2011/jun/23/abce-mail-online/print, accessed 2 February 2012.

Defamation Bill, http://services.parliament.uk/bills/2012–13/defamation.html, accessed 11 July 2012.

Dutton, W. H., Helsper, E. J. and Gerber, M. M. (2009) 'The Internet in Britain', *Oxford Internet Survey: 2009 Report*, Oxford: Oxford Internet Institute, University of Oxford.

Dwyer, T. (2010) *Media Convergence*, Maidenhead, UK: Open University Press.

Elliott, C. (2012) 'The Readers' Editor on ... the Trouble with Numbers in *Guardian* Reporting', http://www.guardian.co.uk/commentisfree/2012/jan/08/trouble-with-numbers-guardian-reporting, accessed 9 January 2012.

Greenslade, R. (2010) 'Yes, Rupert Murdoch Is Taking a Risk, but Don't Write off His Paywall', *Evening Standard*, 31 March, http://www.thisislondon.co.uk/business/markets/yes-rupert-murdoch-is-taking-a-risk-but-dont-write-off-his-paywall-6799335.html, accessed 1 February 2012.

——(2012) 'The Future of Journalism is Bright as Hacks Go Hyperlocal', *Evening Standard*, 11 July, http://www.standard.co.uk/business/media/media-analysis-the-future-of-jour-nalism-is-bright-as-hacks-go-hyperlocal-7935847.html, accessed 29 July 2012.

Harcup, T. (2008) 'Reporters Need to Ask What They're Not Being Told', *UK Press Gazette*, 18 February, http://www.pressgazette.co.uk/story.asp?storycode=40268, accessed 22 November 2011.

Harris, P. (undated) 'The Story of the *Daily Mail*', www.dmgt.co.uk/uploads/files/The-Story-of-the-Daily-Mail.pdf, accessed 3 January 2012.

House of Commons (2010) The Future for Local and Regional Media, House of Commons: Culture, Media and Sport Committee, Fourth Report of Session, 2009–2010, 24 March, http://www.publications.parliament.uk/pa/cm200910/cmselect/cmcumeds/43/43i.pdf, accessed 20 January 2012.

Ingram, M. (2011) 'If Paywall Is Your only Strategy, Then You Are Doomed', *GIGAOM*, 31 October, http://gigaom.com/2011/10/31/if-a-paywall-is-your-only-strategy-then-you-are-doomed, accessed 20 February 2012.

Leadbeater, C. (2012) Blog, www.charlesleadbeater.net/cms/ ... /Boulders%20and%20Pebbles.pdf, accessed 2 January 2012.

Lewis, J. et al (2008) 'The Quality and Independence of British Journalism: Tracking the Changes Over 20 Years', Cardiff University, http://www.cardiff.ac.uk/jomec/resources/QualityIndependenceofBritishJournalism.pdf, accessed 29 July 2012.

Mitchell, B. (2011) 'Poynter's Bill Mitchell on Paywalls – How to Shape the Paid Experience', *World Media Trend*, http://worldmediatrend.wordpress.com/2011/10/06/poynters-bill-mitchell-on-paywalls-how-to-shape-the-paid-experience, accessed 28 February 2012.

National Readership Survey (2011) http://www.nrs.co.uk/toplinereadership.html, accessed January 2012.

New York Times (2011) 'Company Reports: Third-Quarter Results', Press Release, 20 October, http://www.nytco.com/pdf/3Q_2011_Earnings.pdf, accessed 5 March 2012.

Peters, J. (2011) 'Times Co. Reports a Profit, Aided by Digital Subscribers', *The New York Times*, 20 October, http://www.nytimes.com/2011/10/21/business/media/the-new-york-times-company-reports-a-profit.html, accessed 5 March 2012.

Stephens, M. (1994) 'History of Newspapers', *Collier's Encyclopedia*, http://www.nyu.edu/classes/stephens/Collier%27s%20page.htm, accessed 8 January 2012.

Norris, P. (2000) *A Virtuous Circle: Political Communications in Post-Industrial Societies*, New York, NY: Cambridge University Press.

Preston, P. (2010) '*Evening Standard* Almost in Profit after Going Free', *The Observer*, 13 June, http://www.guardian.co.uk/media/2010/jun/13/peter-preston-evening-standard-free, accessed 10 January 2012.

——(2012) 'If the *Telegraph* Can Turn a Profit, so Can the *Times*', *The Observer*, 15 April, http://www.guardian.co.uk/media/2012/apr/15/telegraph-times-profit, accessed 16 April 2012.

Riess, C. (2010) 'Christoph Riess on the Future of Newspapers: "Paid Content is the Key"', World Association of Newspapers and News Publishers, 8 October, http://www.editorsweblog.org/multimedia/2010/10/christoph_riess_about_the_future_of_news.php, accessed 20 January 2012.

Sabbagh, D. (2011) '*Times* Paywall Tops 100,000 – But Can It Grow Much Further at That Price?', Organ Grinder Blog, *The Guardian*, 3 July, http://www.guardian.co.uk/media/organgrinder/2011/jul/03/times-paywall-revenue, accessed 5 March 2012.

Shirky, C. (2010) 'The *Times*' Paywall and Newsletter Economics', http://www.shirky.com/weblog/2010/11/the-times-paywall-and-newsletter-economics, accessed 1 October 2010.

Shorter Oxford English Dictionary (2007) 6th edition, Oxford: Oxford University Press.

Stephens, M. (2007) *A History of News*, 3rd edition, Oxford: Oxford University Press.

The Cambridge History of English and American Literature (1907–21) (undated) http://www.bartleby.com/224/0405.html, accessed 20 December 2011.

The Guardian (2009) 'Twitter switch for *Guardian*, after 188 years of ink', The Guardian: April Fools, 1 April, http://www.guardian.co.uk/media/2009/apr/01/guardian-twitter-media-technology, accessed 1 October 2010.

——(undated) 'Investigate Your MP', http://mps-expenses.guardian.co.uk, accessed 11 July 2012.

The Guardian's Editorial Code (2011) Updated August 2011, http://www.guardian.co.uk/info/guardian-editorial-code, accessed 9 January 2012.

World Association of Newspapers and News Publishers (2011) *World Press Trends*, http://www.wan-ifra.org/microsites/world-press-trends, accessed 5 March 2012.

8

MAGAZINES AND PROMOTION

Tim Holmes

Magazines have always been associated with promotion. The promotion of self, the promotion of personal interests, the promotion of specialized knowledge, the promotion of commerce: all of these traits have been evident in magazines since their earliest days.

Although the emergence of the magazine as a separate, definable media form is an unresolved area of study, each of the publications commonly claimed as the ur-magazine had links to promotion: *Gynasceum, sive Theatrum Mulierum* ... (1586, Quinn: http://bit.ly/gynasceum) was promoting women's fashions; *Erbaulich Monaths-Unterredungen* (1663, Morrish 2003: 5) was promoting moral and intellectual debate (the title translates as *Edifying Monthly Discussions*); and *Journal des Scavans* (1665, Reed 1997) was essentially an adjunct to publishers' booklists, promoting new titles and authors. Skipping forward 400-odd years, accusations of hyper-commerciality together with associated overt and covert promotion of commodities and lifestyles are levelled against magazines so frequently that citing specific examples is a redundant exercise, although the published works of those in the 'baleful influence' camp of criticism (Holmes and Nice 2012: 124) will stand as witness: Friedan (1963), White (1970), Ferguson (1983), Ballaster et al (1991) – these are just a few of the scholars who have queued up to condemn the magazine for being too magazine like.

But one of the key characteristics of the magazine, and perhaps the major reason for the survival and on-going success of the form, is its value in helping to deliver the promotion of self: personal, cultural and professional identity can be, and are, moulded and reinforced by magazines. The truth of this is easily ascertained by anyone who has ever bought a magazine, and *The Word* (*floreat* 2003–2012) provides a pair of classic examples. For anyone unfamiliar with this independently published music magazine, a few words from Michael Deacon's 'obituary' in the *Telegraph*, which itself makes a point about identity, will help set it in context:

> It was witty, funny, inventive. Unlike its rivals it never lurched into purple prose or self-righteousness. It was thoughtful without being pompous. It welcomed you; it made you feel part of a small but loyal club. It didn't hector, preach or sniff; it conspired with you. From the attention paid to detail, the ingeniousness that went into the headlines and captions, you could tell its creators loved their jobs. You couldn't blame them. More than that, you envied them.
>
> *(http://bit.ly/wordobit)*

The first example concerns an unfortunate choice of cover star. As a magazine, *The Word* was predicated on taste and discernment, on being made to feel part of the 'small but loyal club' Deacon mentions above. Cover stars such as Nick Cave (the first) and Ray Davies (the last) represent core reader interest; but for the September 2003 issue the cover star was female singer-songwriter Dido. I can remember thinking how wrong this seemed at the time: Dido was certainly successful and popular, but surely far too mainstream? It was wrong enough to put me off buying what had become a favourite magazine, and I was not alone in this reaction. As editor Mark Ellen later recalled, that issue remained 'both nailed and glued to the shelves ... metric tonnes of unsold copies were recycled to make confetti, the rest bulldozed into giant landfills all over Kent and Suffolk' (Burrell 2007).

The second example concerns a much more immediate promotion of identity but also helps to explain the reaction to a 'wrong' cover image. School kids in the 1960s would make a point of ostentatiously carrying around the latest, most groovy, furthest out 12 inch LP record for everyone to note and admire; but now that music has been reduced to jewel-boxed CDs and weightless binary digits the printed magazine performs a similar role: a kind of look-at-this-cool-stuff-I'm-reading pose. When I finally spotted someone on the train who was reading a copy of *The Word*, I had to take stock and make a judgement as to whether this looked like an individual whom I felt comfortable being associated with in that 'small but loyal club'. He looked OK, fairly straight but with some important signifiers of coolness, the kind of coolness I understood, so I felt happy to continue my membership.

Although those two examples are anecdotally illustrative, there is plenty of evidence in the literature to confirm this general effect; Hermes (1995), Beetham (1996), Korinek (2000), Consterdine (2002) all emphasize in their findings the highly personal nature of the relationship between the magazine and its readers: or, to be more precise, the *print* magazine. Whether other iterations of the magazine, website, app, social media community, podcast, live events will inspire the same kind of connection has yet to be determined, and on this may hang something very important: the survival of the magazine form.

Before going any further, it is important to ascertain what we mean by the 'magazine form', especially since there seems to be a constant stream of doomsayers foretelling the imminent death of the media as we know them: Steve Smith's prediction in *Min Online* that the magazine industry will lose 35 per cent of its value by 2014 is just one example among many (http://bit.ly/magdoom). At the same time, magazine publishers seem to be coming out of the hibernation they retreated into when the world's finances tanked and are launching new products, even going back to the good old days of launching spoilers to undermine the chances of a rival's success. This happened in April 2012 when Bauer Consumer Media launched *LandScape* and Hubert Burda counter-launched *LandLove*; both magazines were based on German titles and their feature lists and photography were virtually interchangeable (see http://bit.ly/panzer2 for details). Although this return to the heady days of the 1980s, when spoiler tactics were a common practice, seems expensively self-defeating in current economic circumstances, it also indicates that not all publishers feel print is dead and are prepared to spend their money to prove it.

Other sectors have had something of a clear-out. The women's weekly market was revived by Bauer and Burda back in the early 1980s and remained a cash generator for decades; but eventually the more marginal titles had to admit defeat, with *In The Know* (Bauer) and *First* (Emap) among the higher-profile titles to be shuttered. As we have already seen, the music sector became too small to support *The Word* and several long-established business-to-business (B2B) magazines have abandoned print and gone digital only, among them *Media Week* and *The Engineer*. Overall, however, the magazine industry has been surprisingly resilient, with very few headline closures. At the same time, small and independent magazines launched as online sites have gathered enough momentum (and cash) to produce occasional print versions: *Jocks & Nerds* (http://jocksandnerdsmagazine.com) is one such, its mission to explore the relationship between style, culture and history, diversifying from a website to a print quarterly. There is no doubt that appearing in print is still seen as a validating process.

By contrast, and indicative of the confusion permeating the industry, *not* appearing in print can also be a validating process. When the editor of *Good Housekeeping*, Lindsay Nicholson, observed a reader struggling with the online version of the title on an iPhone, it started a chain of events that led to the launch of *Good Ideas*, a magazine that is designed to be viewed primarily on mobile devices but which also appears in print. As you might expect, especially at this stage of the technological development of print-and-app production technology, it looks better on a tablet, where the saturated photography can literally shine, rather than print, where the layout looks very gappy. It also does away with a large amount of the copy found in *Good Housekeeping*, so what the reader/viewer is left with is more like a catalogue (there are live links to suppliers) than a magazine. The relationship between reader, magazine and advertiser is discussed below; but in this context it is interesting to note John Morrish's advice for would-be magazine editors: 'Your obligations to advertisers are met through your relationship with your readers ... . The advertisers pay to join the relationship between reader and magazine, but they do so at a tangent' (Morrish and Bradshaw 2012: 24–25). If one possible future for the magazine is as a variant on the catalogue, this relationship is clearly up for discussion.

There are other, more subtly nuanced, futures under development too. *Good Food* is a magazine from the establishment end of the business, published under the BBC's aegis as a means of capturing the corporation's excellent food-based broadcasting. This apparently conservative background has not stopped it from augmenting the print edition with a website, live cooking shows and exhibitions, an iPad app, a mobile site and, through UKTV, a television channel; there has been talk of a range of branded kitchenware. Although all of these additions offer revenue-generating opportunities, Nick Brett, managing director of the BBC Magazine Unit, is adamant that all developments have been driven by reader demand: his mantra is 'let the reader in' and when the readers say they want to be able to access content in multiple forms and formats, the magazine takes notice. As we shall see, cultural critic Henry Jenkins has something very pertinent to say about this.

On the other side of the tracks, *Vice* magazine started as a hobby for three Canadian men who couldn't find a magazine that reflected their lifestyle. Despite being given away for free in skate and surf shops, rather than sold in newsagents, it now has 19 international editions (including one in the UK), an extensive website, a record label, a film production company (*Swansea Love Story*, a film about the heroin epidemic in South Wales, which received many plaudits), a TV channel to show its incisive documentaries, and an advertising agency. Joanna Fuertes-Knight, whose Girl Eats Food column became a print must-read, now has her own show on Vice.com – surely an example of inter-textuality in practice?

If nothing else, the ability to evolve demonstrated by these two titles indicates that the magazine form is likely to survive; but despite their very different beginnings they both started as print magazines: what if there were some new form that sprang into being after the World Wide Web had been invented? What if such a form was designed to work, as Clay Shirky likes to say, as if the web exists? Well, it is entirely possible that this new form does exist as *The Atavist*. Not exactly a magazine, not exactly a book, not exactly a video, *The Atavist* describes itself as a 'storytelling platform for the digital age', offering 'a new genre of nonfiction, a digital form between long narrative magazine articles and books'. Further on it describes the content as 'inventive, captivating, cinematic journalism' (www.atavist. com: about). Each story is sold individually, following the iTunes principle, and the proceeds are shared between *The Atavist* and the author.

What this suggests very strongly is that hybridity of form is the natural state of digitally accessed content and that previous taxonomies of media are obsolete in the post-Gutenberg era, including those relating to magazines. The conclusion this draws us towards is that a magazine is now more defined by what it does and how it does it than by what it is or what form it takes. Yet, the examples of *Good Food* and *Vice*, chosen not because they are unusual in the diverse multiplicity of their content platforms but because they have reached a similar conclusion from very different starting points, show that when regarded as brands rather than particular entities in specific forms, 'traditional' titles are perfectly capable of responding to the demands of convergence. The brand-extending promotional activities that result from this response are performed in three modes that can be categorised as physical, metaphysical and cyber-spacial.

Physical promotion

I once had the opportunity to ask Felix Dennis, the maverick publishing million-aire and poet, the most important thing to teach magazine students. His answer was 'events', by which he meant the live action functions such as exhibitions or shows magazines put on to strengthen bonds with their readers … and co-incidentally to get the readers to pay for entry to the event while simultaneously getting com-mercial entities to pay to be present in the hope of effecting a profitable meeting with those readers. This is David Abrahamson's definition of the magazine business model given a very literal form:

> … special-interest magazines held the two requirements that continue to be essential for long-term success in magazine publishing: (a) specific informa-tion in a specific form that can be expected to appeal to a definable segment of readers; (b) a group of manufacturers or distributors with the means and willingness to advertise their products and services to those readers. The perceived level of reader commitment to a magazine's subject remains one of the most important aspects of the first requirement. Because they dealt with a single product or activity that was fundamental not only to the editorial material but also to the bulk of advertising, specialized magazines could deliver a specific, highly defined audience to their advertisers. Most successful special-interest magazines relied on a simple editorial formula that supported these requirements.
>
> *(http://bit.ly/abrahamson1)*

Although Felix Dennis may well have been speaking in shorthand, 'events' barely touches on the potential of magazines to use different channels to create new relationships with their readers. All of the examples cited above, personal though they are, tend towards one conclusion: a magazine is a brand. If that is true, then all the knowledge, wisdom and theory of the brand can be applied.

One of the most basic definitions of a brand is that it is a promise: a promise of reliability, quality, continuity and consistency. A Mars bar will always taste like a Mars bar whether you buy it in Land's End or John O'Groats; a bottle of Coca-Cola will always be a bottle of Coca-Cola whether you buy it in New York or Ulaan-baatar. In that sense a magazine is definitely a brand: *Bike* magazine will always deliver motorcycle-related information and entertainment in a particular style; *heat* will never write about celebrities without an edge of mockery and scepticism. Every successful magazine will have something that readers know they will find in every issue.

But that simple promise of quality and consistency can be extended through a positive halo effect:

A halo effect is the 'bias' due to a measure that spills over to another measure (Thorndike 1920). For example, a strong consumer belief about the performance characteristics of a Porsche may spill over onto beliefs about its reliability; or a consumer's overall attitude toward a brand might spill over onto their assessment of specific attributes of that brand (Beckwith and Lehmann 1975).

(Klein and Dawar 2004) (http://bit.ly/haloexplained)

For example, R. J. Reynolds Tobacco decide to aim Camel cigarettes at a rufty-tufty smoker; Camel sponsors a tough motor adventure/expedition/rally; Camel branded clothes identify the people who want other people to think they are the type who will undertake a tough motor adventure/expedition/rally ... and thus the halo effect spills from one iteration of the brand to the next.

What this means for magazines is that the brand, once it has been defined as such, can also be used to promise an experience replicated in other *milieux*. Journalists may detest this way of thinking about what is essentially a cultural product; but even a cursory examination of a handful of magazines from very different sectors shows the range of opportunities for brand extension:

- *Bike/Motor Cycle News*: Reclaim Our Tracks trackdays, run at various race circuits: <http://bit.ly/biketracks>.
- *CPO Agenda*: roundtable debates focusing on pressing business issues: <http://bit.ly/cporoundtable>.
- *Cosmopolitan*: Reader Evening at Debenhams with fashion designer Matthew Williamson: <http://bit.ly/cosmoevening>.
- *Country Living*: Spring Fair 2012 at the Business Design Centre Islington, 'the perfect place to stock up on new and inspiring ideas for your home and garden': <http://bit.ly/clspring>.
- *Empire*: film awards based on readers' votes: <http://bit.ly/empireawards>.
- *Glamour*: Women of the Year Awards: <http://bit.ly/glamawards>.
- *Grazia*: the weekly ran a Style Lounge at Future Fashion, in conjunction with Westfield Stratford shopping mall.
- *Huck/Little White Lies*: Church of London, the creative agency that publishes these two indy magazines, also has a gallery for exhibitions, screenings, talks and other events: <http://bit.ly/colgallery>.
- *Men's Health*: Survival of the Fittest series, an endurance contest set in a kind of obstacle course: <http://bit.ly/mhsurvival>.
- *Motor Sport*: film screenings, photography exhibitions and special reader evenings such as the Audi event with drivers and engineers from the Le Mans team: <http://bit.ly/motorsportevenings>.
- *Mslexia*: writing workshops, originally done as road shows, now delivered online: <http://bit.ly/mswriting>.
- *Peace News, Red Pepper, New Internationalist*: the Rebellious Media Conference: 'to showcase inspiring examples of radical media practice; to further develop

radical critiques of the mainstream media; to enable activists, journalists and students to engage in training and skillsharing': <http://bit.ly/rebelmedia>.

- *Psychologies*: Live in the Moment, a 'day of creative thinking, practical workshops and meditation': <http://bit.ly/psychlive>.
- *Saga*: child-free holiday offers: <http://bit.ly/sagahols>.
- *Singletrack*: mountain biking competitions: <http://bit.ly/singletrack>.
- *Top Gear*: Top Gear Live, a chance to sit in a hangar and listen to Jeremy, Richard and James, now available all over the world: <http://bit.ly/topglive>.
- *Wales Business Insider*: Aerospace Breakfast at St Athan, a chance to debate 'aviation and aerospace industries in Wales' (including Iron Maiden frontman Bruce Dickinson's plans for Cardiff Aviation): <http://bit.ly/wbibrekkie>.
- *Yours*: affordable holidays for older people <http://bit.ly/yourshols>.

These are all physical events, happenings of a material nature intended to encourage direct contact between reader and magazine and between reader and reader. They depend on a halo effect emanating from the magazine brand that will inspire in a reader the desire for self-improvement, self-discovery, meeting like-minded people, basking in reflected glory, aspiration, inspiration and even personal gain (e.g., from a business networking event). All of them can be regarded as community-building promotional exercises that simultaneously generate revenue for the publisher, thus extending Abrahamson's formula of:

reader » magazine « advertiser

into a third space (Oldenburg 1999):

reader » magazine »« event »« advertiser.

Other physical brand extensions may be more commodity-based:

- *Books* that deal with subject matter relevant to the magazine may be branded: Hearst Magazines, home of such titles as *Good Housekeeping* and *Cosmopolitan*, is very active in this field: <http://bit.ly/hearstbooks>.
- *Bookazines*: to quote from Dennis Publishing's website, a bookazine (or Magbook) is 'a perfect-bound, magazine-sized soft back book focusing on a particular subject matter': <http://bit.ly/dennisbook>. Haymarket Media came up with a conceptually interesting bookazine in 2009 when they took the 'best bits' of *Pistonheads*, which is a website that has no physical existence, and turned it into a 200-page publication: <http://bit.ly/pistonbook>. However, they don't seem to have repeated the exercise.
- *Clothing*: magazines have long offered readers logo-ed t-shirts, sweat shirts, jackets and the like, but in 2007 *Elle* put its name to a range of clothing (<http://bit.ly/brandelle>) that has now expanded into swimwear, shoes, jewellery and cosmetics: <http://bit.ly/ellekohls>.

- *Household goods*: *Elle* also offers household items, but the key *traditional* magazine for this category must be *Good Housekeeping*, which offers own-brand items as well as those recommended by the Good Housekeeping Institute: <http://bit. ly/ghgoods>. Interestingly, Hearst Magazines aggregates the online versions of its women's magazines, including *Good Housekeeping*, into the allaboutyou.com site and there is an extensive 'shop' section with its own url: allaboutyoushop. com. In the non-traditional category, *Monocle* is setting new standards of merchandising, with its shop full of desirably hip products, including clothes, travel items, fragrances, books, music and more: <http://bit.ly/monoshop>.
- *Foodstuffs*: not an extensive category but impossible to complete this section without mentioning tins of mixed nuts such as the *Men's Health* blend of almonds, peanuts and pistachios offered by Planters (<http://bit.ly/mensnuts>) and *Glamour*'s pink Krispy Kreme birthday doughnuts (<http://bit.ly/glamdo>).
- *Fragrances*: *Monocle* offers two colognes in its shop, produced in association with Comme Des Garçons, but surely no magazinophile could resist *Wallpaper**'s offering Paper Passion, which features 'the scent of freshly printed books' and book-like packaging designed by Karl Lagerfeld (<http://bit.ly/ wallpaperpong>).

Branded commodities such as those listed above lead us to a variation on, or extension of, the Abrahamson/Oldenburg formula:

> reader » magazine »« commodity »«advertiser»
>   «publisher»

where the final element may be one of the magazine's advertisers, if a commercial arrangement has been reached, or the magazine's publisher, if the commercial aspect is an in-house arrangement.

The principle behind the phenomenon of physical brand extension also accords with economic theorist Ferdinand Tönnies's principles of *Gemeinschaft* and *Gesellschaft*: seen from the reader's point of view, the magazine is a personal friend and all the other readers are potential personal friends; but seen from the publisher's point of view, the magazine is, simultaneously, a commercial entity that is expected to return a profit (Tönnies 2001; Holmes and Nice 2012: 22).

Metaphysical promotion

We do not, however, live in a purely material world and there are a number of promotional brand extensions that can be characterized as *metaphysical*. Among these we could include online multimedia magazine spin-offs; they are abstract concepts that have no physical weight and nothing more than a name to link them to the original. But it's a brand name and thus brings with it the same abstract connotations and promises first generated in the material form of print. There is a huge variety of metaphysical extensions, some of which seem quite obvious and others that stretch the connection to a magazine's brand image almost beyond breaking point.

Of the other traditional media platforms, radio is perhaps the closest to magazines in two key aspects: specialization of content and forming close bonds with the audience. It's not too much of a stretch to find many magazine brands with associated radio stations; and when the parent company is an established player in the radio industry, it's no surprise at all. Bauer is one such player and a look through its radio stations reveals among the lists of *Kiss* and *Magic*, *heat*, *Kerrang!*, *Q* and *Smash Hits*. At first sight it might seem quite easy to imagine the kind of music and presentation each magazine-radio would require; in practice, some of the playlists and presentation are surprisingly similar. *heat* and *Smash Hits* are poppy; *Q* is poppy with a rocky edge; *Kerrang!* is more obviously rocky. *heat* promises 'music and celebrity' but you have to listen for a while before getting any of the latter and the news reports seem very like every other, youth-oriented news round-up, perhaps not surprising as the news packages are supplied by ITN ON. Overall, *heat Radio* is clearly in the same general sector as the magazine but it has a very different feel. It is, however, only a part of the much larger online entity Heatworld.com, which incorporates a massive amount of multimedia material, including *heat TV* (available on Sky and Virgin) and *heat4*, a collaboration with Channel 4 that fosters links with existing C4 programmes such as US drama *Revenge* and grunge comedy *The Midnight Beast*. Links with the magazine are maintained by including editor Lucie Cave in the videos; she also has a podcast-style Saturday show on *heat Radio* that does have an obvious relationship with the print entity.

There is, of course, an inherent contradiction in the idea of a magazine-on-the-radio, especially a magazine like *heat*, because one of the most important elements in this kind of magazine is its reliance on images. *heat* is a highly visual product, making a virtue of showing celebrities looking dishevelled, or sweaty, or 'too fat', or 'too thin', whereas broadcast radio is completely non-visual (apart from the scrolling information on some digital receivers). Web-based radio does allow the 'player', the software that facilitates transmission and reception, to be surrounded by images; but it is still so different from the print pages as to be more of a brand separation than an extension. This transgression of the brand's borders is, however, accounted for in theories of intermediality and intermodality. As Lars Elleström explains:

> All kinds of sign systems and also very specific media productions and works of art must be seen as parts of a very wide field including not least the material, sensorial, spatiotemporal and semiotic aspects … the four 'modalities' of media … all forms of art, media, languages, communication and messages have some characteristics in common which make it possible … to hover between different systems and simultaneously be part of various frameworks without losing its relative stability.
>
> *(Elleström 2010: 4)*

If *heat Radio* has been derived from the print magazine in an attempt to add another modality to the brand, the reverse situation can be found in *TalkSport*, the radio station that runs brand-extending, magazine-like material on its website: news stories linked to broadcast clips, videos, slide shows, photos, polls and quizzes. *TalkSport* used to publish a fully featured online magazine (edited by Bill Borrows), which they initially promised would be free forever and although that promise was never actually broken, the 'proper' magazine extension of the brand is now freemium title *Sport* (edited by Simon Caney), which *TalkSport*'s owner, UTV Media, bought from its French owners and injected with a bit of *Shortlist*-like pizzazz. If *TalkSport* is representative of the way in which men and women chew over sport in a casual setting, *Sport* is a more reflective and, in its use of magazine craft, more sophisticated way of extending the brand (or neo-brand) into a different mode of consumption (print and iPad) and a different demographic.

Where does this leave *The Exclusives*, a reality TV show in which six would-be journalists competed for a year-long internship with Bauer by undertaking various tasks more or less related to journalism? As a promotional vehicle for *heat*, *Empire*, *Closer*, *more!* and *Kerrang!*, the programme itself did not draw a very large audience (108,000 for the final episode) and therefore perhaps fails in the most obvious result. However, Bauer's creative director Julian Linley told *Media Week*: 'It's not just about ratings for us. It's as much about the noise that the show generated around magazines and online ... . On Twitter we were the fourth most tweeted-about new show in Europe in week one ... . It's been really great to see how passionate and engaged the audience have been on Twitter' and that being able to reach its audience on this different platform was a great thing for Bauer (http://bit.ly/mwexclusives). While the overall conclusion many might draw from this is that a second series is unlikely, the importance placed on 'second screen' engagement with social media is worth noting. Bauer may be 'pleased' with it, but Hearst in both the US and the UK embraced digital back in 2006 and have developed strategies that include active management of social media communities (http://bit.ly/digihearstus; http://bit.ly/digihearstuk).

A very different kind of metaphysical extension was undertaken by *Grazia* in November 2008 when it shifted its office from Shaftesbury Avenue (London WC2) to Westfield London (Shepherds Bush, London W12) in a move that simultaneously promoted the magazine and the opening of a major shopping destination. For a week, the magazine worked out of a specially built 'office suite' on Westfield's lower floor, literally opening up the creation and production process to public scrutiny (http://bit.ly/graziawest). Although this involved a very real material presence, it also transcended lived reality by turning the magazine and its setting into a *spectacle* of the type analysed by Guy Debord (2004) in *The Society of the Spectacle*. There is multiple layering of commodity fetishism: the setting itself, Westfield London, is a temple of consumerism, its only purpose to be a location of commercial interaction; the shops within Westfield, all devising their own brands and spectaculist images; the magazine, a third space where consumer meets producer, but a third space that must, to attract the other parties, establish its own spectaculist credentials and become in and of itself a commodity to be sold and bought.

Without wishing to break a butterfly upon the wheel, it does not take a great effort to attach any of the following thoughts from Debord's theses to this promotional exercise:

- All that once was directly lived has become mere representation (*Thesis 1*).
- Understood in its totality, the spectacle is both the outcome and the goal of the dominant mode of production. It is not something added to the real world – not a decorative element, so to speak. On the contrary, it is the very heart of society's real unreality. In all its specific manifestations – news or propaganda, advertising or the actual consumption of entertainment – the spectacle epitomizes the prevailing model of social life (*Thesis 6*).
- An earlier stage in the economy's domination of social life entailed an obvious downgrading of *being* into *having* that left its stamp on all human endeavour. The present stage, in which social life is completely taken over by the accumulated products of the economy, entails a generalized shift from *having* to appearing: all effective 'having' must now derive both its immediate prestige and its ultimate *raison d'être* from appearances (*Thesis 17*).
- A use of the commodity arises that is sufficient unto itself; what this means for the consumer is an outpouring of religious zeal in honour of the commodity's sovereign freedom. Waves of enthusiasm for particular products, fuelled and boosted by the communications media, are propagated with lightning speed …. The sheer fad item perfectly expresses the fact that, as the mass of commodities become more and more absurd, absurdity becomes a commodity in its own right. Keychains that are not paid for but come as free gifts with the purchase of some luxury product, or are then traded back and forth in a sphere far removed from that of their original use, bear eloquent witness to a mystical self-abandonment to the transcendent spirit of the commodity (*Thesis 67*).

(http://bit.ly/debord1994)

The *Grazia*/Westfield promotional experiment can be categorized and explained as a *spectacle* that captures the prevailing model of social life, with the magazine lending its credibility and popularity to the temple of retail and the temple facilitating 'the [magazine] commodity's immanent presence among the faithful' (Debord 2004: *Thesis 67*). For other examples of this phenomenon, see *Grazia*'s March 2010 photo-shoot at Heathrow Terminal 5, ostensibly a big arrivals and departures hall but actually another temple of commerce (http://bit.ly/graziaheathrow); in January 2011 *Company* took a spectaculist leaf from its rival's book by relocating the editorial office to Terminal 5 for a week (http://bit.ly/companyt5).

There is, however, an even more ephemeral and intangible commodity than credibility that a magazine can offer to lease a third party: *cool*. Nothing about this is mysterious: well, nothing beyond the complex enigmatic processes that lie behind the generation of *cool*, the shifting understanding of what constitutes *cool* and the social relativity that surrounds *cool*; for some people, *Vanity Fair*'s post-Oscar party is the coolest place to be, for others the very idea of the Oscars is so totally *un*cool that the idea of holding a party to celebrate them is unthinkable. In fact, true cool may be beyond the reach of a big corporate magazine; it may exist only in the domain of the indy. *Blown* is one such cool title; produced on less than a shoestring in South Wales, it bills itself as documenting 'cultural intelligence', which turns out to mean art, music, fashion, writing, photography, theatre and music. It is a beautiful production, ticking all the haptic boxes for heft and tangibility in the way that only a print magazine can, and all the aesthetic boxes for typography, design and repro that only a print magazine can. It is the periodical equivalent of the beautiful doomed poet starving in a garret and thus is ineffably cool. But it turns out cool is a commodity that has a value because cool can be leased: worthy but dull businesses can lease some of *Blown*'s cool quotient by getting the magazine to organize and put its name to corporate cultural events. As Emma Geliot, *Blown* deputy editor, explains, the men in suits like the association while the magazine likes the sponsorship money. It's a fine tightrope to walk though because the integrity of the magazine has to be balanced on the scales against the quality of the event and the reputation of the sponsor: promotion like this is not an easy option.

Some magazines, though, not only do not have a reputation for integrity to worry about, they positively revel in giving the appearance of not caring about integrity and this allows a self-consciously 'outrageous' title such as *Nuts* to extend its brand into areas such as poker (http://bit.ly/nutspoker), cash gaming (http://bit.ly/nutsgaming), secondary ticketing (http://bit.ly/nutstickets) and dating (http://bit.ly/nutsdating). Mind you, it's not just magazines for young men which stray into the latter territory as *Yours* (http://bit.ly/yoursdating) and *Saga* (http://bit.ly/sagadating) demonstrate, although in their cases the important brand characteristics metaphysically transferred tend towards reliability and safety.

A final class of metaphysical brand extension, and one that shades into the next category of promotion, can be found in the 'webinar', web-based seminars or conferences that allow remote users to collaborate in the discussion of a specific subject. B2B publications have a long tradition of running physical conferences and webinars have become very popular among this category of magazine, allowing them to extend participation to a global audience without the need for costly and time-consuming travel and accommodation. Furthermore, webinars can be archived and accessed on a time-shifted basis, which provides continuing value for the magazine and its readers. Another advantage is that the virtual nature of the event allows a magazine to run many more events than would be possible in the physical world; *Automotiveworld*, for example, scheduled 11 webinars in the second half of 2012, two of them on the same day, (http://bit.ly/amworldweb), whereas *Building* had only one forthcoming event but a large archive to access (http://bit.ly/buildingweb). Webinars can be considered metaphysical promotions because although most participants attend virtually, there is still a central point of organization and the magazine can have a direct influence on the progress of debate and the eventual outcome.

Cyber-spacial promotion

In recent years another accessible third space has opened up between reader and magazine: cyberspace. Unlike physical or metaphysical events, the social manifestations of cyberspace are open and accessible 24 hours a day, 7 days a week, 52 weeks a year: Facebook, Twitter, Pinterest and their social media friends never close and always offer a seemingly direct channel to the magazine and its staff. That is the *Gemeinschaft* aspect: the friend we know personally, the select club we feel a part of. The *Gesellschaft* aspect (confirmed as such by the fact that companies such as Hearst employ people to *manage* these relationships) is the opportunity for promotion offered by social media: promotion of the title itself, of particular content within the title, of relationships with the editor, writers and stylists.

Take the UK version of *Glamour* as an example. For a start, when *Glamour* was launched, it was printed on a smaller than usual size of paper to make it fit easily into women's handbags. Industry mavens scoffed and predicted an early demise on the grounds that women bought fashion magazines to look at big pictures. They were wrong; *Glamour* took off like a rocket and has stayed at the top of the bestseller lists ever since, but in being wrong they gave the launch plenty of excellent promotional publicity. The magazine has also been quick to adopt social media strategies that both promote it and encourage community-building between readers, title and staff. Its Facebook page, which basically posts links to content and invites readers to comment, has gathered 95,302 Likes (the US version has 859,444 Likes). Its editor, Jo Elvin, is a prolific tweeter; in her tweets she mixes material about the magazine, perhaps hinting at the next cover star or commenting on a great photo shoot or the arrival of new fashion collections, with personal information about the school run, commuting woes or holiday packing. Whether this is a deliberate policy or a happy accident, it is clearly working as a promotional device: she has 57,390 followers (@jo_elvin, if you are interested).

In fact, most of the women's magazine editors have Twitter accounts and they all tend to adopt a semi-professional approach, so there is a double promotion going on there: promotion of the magazine brand and promotion of the personal brand. Since editors are such important and influential figureheads in the magazine world, particularly this sector, this is clearly an important development.

If Twitter encourages a directly personal connection, or at least the simulacrum of it, Facebook and Pinterest are used in a much more directly promotional way. Sticking with *Glamour* as the example of a corporate title, its Facebook page (http://www.facebook.com/glamourmaguk) is a mix of fashion titbits, celebrity catch-ups, competitions and plugs for other Condé Nast magazine brands; by contrast, its Pinterest scrapbook (http://pinterest.com/glamourmaguk/) is much more varied and lively, although perhaps a bit too neat to be mistaken for a personal project: the board showing pictures of the staff is a bit of a giveaway too.

It is perhaps in the area of cyber-spacial promotion that established magazines face their greatest challenge. The Gutenberg-era rules of publishing still protect their print forms: the resources required for production, distribution and administration are scarce and costly, forming considerable barriers to entry for rivals or start-ups; the interconnected chain of production, distribution and retail ensures that there is a network of similarly invested corporations or businesses that also benefit from stability in the system. Despite disruption caused by the global financial recession that started in 2008, the loss of advertising revenue caused by both recession and more cost-effective delivery through digital media, and the distraction of reader attention by an ever-growing amount of information flowing through people's everyday lives, the Gutenberg-era publishing model is, notwithstanding numerous noisy prophets of doom, economically resilient: current data from the Professional Publishers' Association shows the value of the UK magazine market to be £4.1 billion, with £1.9 billion of that accounted for by consumer spending on magazines (http://bit.ly/ppamarket).

But resilient only in the Gutenberg-era economy of cash; in post-Gutenberg publishing there are other factors to take into account (and the accounting). The barriers to entry are low because there is no scarcity in the means of publishing or distribution: anyone can create content and upload it to their own free blog, to free video hosting services such as YouTube or Vimeo, to free audio hosting services like SoundCloud, to their own website, constructed with free software and hosted for free by the likes of 5quidhost.co.uk. Once the content has been published or uploaded, a skilled user of Facebook and Twitter who can also write well-tuned search-friendly headlines can run her or his own marketing campaign for free; for the not so skilled, advice on how to improve is freely available online.

On the other side of the equation, a digital publisher can sign up to Google AdSense or Skimlinks and start to generate advertising revenue without the need for a sales office or expensive data-gathering; Google Analytics will freely provide all the data a publisher needs about numbers of people visiting the site, where they are from, how long they stay. If there are physical products to be sold, PayPal can handle the banking, and although this is not free, commission for the service is set at an acceptable level and the process is simple, well established and widely trusted. In fact, by becoming associated with trusted services and gaining a good feedback rating, the digital publisher can very rapidly establish trust-by-association.

Given the abundant means of publishing and distribution, we can see clearly that capital, financial capital, is not the problem for magazine start-ups in the post-Gutenberg era. Back in 1997, Michael Goldhaber identified a different kind of capital. His conference paper 'The attention economy and the Net' outlined the principles of the new paradigm: if information is ubiquitous, getting people to spend their limited amount of attention on any particular piece of information becomes increasingly important because 'economies are governed by what is scarce, and information, especially on the Net, is not only abundant, but overflowing', whereas 'Attention, at least the kind we care about, is an intrinsically scarce resource' (http://bit.ly/goldhaber).

Goldhaber considers how attention can be gained or attracted and in doing so he suggests that:

> ... since it is hard to get new attention by repeating exactly what you or someone else has done before, this new economy is based on endless originality, or at least attempts at originality. By contrast, the old industrial economy worked on the basis of making interchangeable objects in huge numbers.
>
> *(http://bit.ly/goldhaber)*

If this insight is correct, it indicates a problem for established magazine brands which thrive precisely because they offer the same thing over and over again: indeed, one does not have to look far to find readers, particularly of magazines aimed at young women, making exactly this complaint.

Perhaps as a result, new and original magazine ideas thrive online. They come and go; but many, if not most, have in common an ability to attract the attention of individuals with specific characteristics, which is what magazines have always done, of course, but in a post-Gutenberg attention economy that does not require financial capital those niches can be much smaller. Take the website www.domesticsluttery.com as an example. Its mission is to be a 'home and lifestyle blog for women who have better things to do ... . We want our homes to look good, we want damn tasty food and we want our outfits to be unusual. But we're busy and we enjoy being a little bit lazy.' The site covers most of the subjects a 'normal' woman's magazine would cover but from notably different angles; in fact, in a skewed sort of way its mix of cookery, interiors, fashion and fiercely independent reviews makes it most reminiscent of *Good Housekeeping*. The writer/editors use Twitter to promote new material and pin the lovely things they find on their Pinterest board (http://pinterest.com/domesticsluts/).

To put an objective gloss on this, we can compare the data showing traffic to the domesticsluttery site and allaboutyou.com, which provides an aggregated web presence for all Hearst magazine titles, including *Good Housekeeping*, *Country Living*, *Prima* and *Best*. Traffic measurement site Alexa.com ranks the indy site at 14,721 in the UK and the corporate at 4806; 1311 other sites link to allaboutyou and 637 to domesticsluttery. Interestingly, Alexa's demographic summaries for allaboutyou and domesticsluttery are identical: 'Compared with the overall internet population, this site's users are disproportionately female, and they are disproportionately childless users browsing from work who have postgraduate educations.' Given that the traffic for allaboutyou will include readers looking for material from a number of high circulation print magazines published by an international corporation and that domesticsluttery exists only in cyberspace and is produced by a small group of like-minded women (and a few men), the relative numbers tend to confirm Goldhaber's points about the attention economy.

One final quote from 'The attention economy and the Net' also applies to domesticsluttery and the many sites that preceded it, co-exist with it and will follow it; it also applies to *Blown*, mentioned above, and probably every niche indy magazine ever created. Most, if not all, of the writer/editors who produce the content and manage the site have other jobs that provide their main income: they all write or create in other *milieux*; they have rich cultural backgrounds. This fits exactly with Goldhaber's prediction that:

> … many of the kinds of tasks once performed by publishing company employees such as acquisition and line editors, designers, publicists, and so, will still be done, but on much more ad hoc and free-lance, eventually even unpaid basis. All of this will take place over the Web. No one will earn monetary profits from it. And this disappearance of the involvement of capital will be equally the case for attention-getting objects of just about any sort.
>
> *(http://bit.ly/goldhaber)*

Goldhaber does not mention it; but, in fact, capitalism loves disruption. There is now plenty of evidence that banks and other financial institutions can profit enormously from betting correctly on the outcome of disruptive events. On the whole, however, capitalist commercial entities prefer to engineer the disruption themselves and the disruption of media by digital technologies is simply confusing because there is no clear model for making money from it. It is not at all like an earlier example of digital disruption, which the commercial interests were able to control – namely, the almost overnight replacement of vinyl LPs and singles by CDs. That was a classic example of the music industry acting in concert to control the distribution of scarce resources; record shops that wanted to stay in business had to go along with it and the end consumer paid the final price. But what established commercial entities, like record companies or publishers, do not like is disruption that is out of their control.

Magazines should be in a good position to understand and react to this post-Gutenberg phase of disruption because of their culture of production that puts the reader's hopes, fears and needs at the centre of content creation (see Holmes et al 2012: Chapter 4). Another way of looking at this problem would be to ask: can the magazine promote its own future? The industry should be able to move towards an answer, and an understanding of the extent and consequences of the answer, by developing a framework that theorizes and attempts to unify understanding of the existing multiple modes of media consumption, and at the same time allows for future modes of consumption and the most effective ways to promote and cross-promote them. By framing the needs and conditions of consumers, this initiative could be understood as a massively expanded and problematized restatement of the traditional saying amongst magazine journalists: 'Know your reader.' This well-tried motto, despite having served so well for so long, cannot encapsulate the depth and breadth of knowledge now needed to establish preferred patterns of consumption. In the days when a magazine or newspaper was purely words printed on paper, a television programme was purely images and sounds displayed on a cathode ray tube, a radio programme was what emerged from the Bakelite wireless receiver, and a telephone was a two-part box with a rotary dial living on a table in the hallway, 'know your reader' was an adequate guide because it was relatively simple to acquire that knowledge.

The magazine industry could map the new media ecosystem as a kind of companion piece to Johan Fornäs et al's mapping of *Popular Passages: Media in the Modern Space of Consumption* (http://bit.ly/fornas). Just as *Popular Passages* started from the axiom that the culture of shopping had an unstable status, so the magazine matrix of consumption would take it as axiomatic that there is no pure 'reading' or 'writing' or 'viewing' or 'listening': each instance of media work published or broadcast is situated within an extensive network of connections. Many would call this 'convergence', and although that word has become so widely adopted and applied to so many different situations that its meaning has become diffuse, it is worth searching for a clearer meaning. Henry Jenkins is a well-practised observer of convergence, and in his 2008 essay 'The moral economy of Web 2.0 (Part Two)' he decoupled convergent *technology* (the amalgamation of devices) from convergent *cultural practice* (the amalgamation of consumption), leading to the following observation:

> Convergence is understood here not as the bringing together of all media functions within a single device but rather as a cultural logic involving an ever more complex interplay across multiple channels of distribution … . This convergence is being shaped both by media conglomerates' desires to exploit 'synergies' between different divisions and consumer demands for media content where, when, and in what form they want it.
>
> *(http://bit.ly/jenks1)*

He also added this important point about those who consume media:

> How audiences are imagined is crucial to the organization of media industries (Ang 1991; Hartley 1987), which rely on such mental models to shape their interface with their public. Convergence culture brings with it a re-conceptualization of the audience – how it is comprised, how it is courted, what it wants, and how to generate value from it.
>
> *(http://bit.ly/jenks1)*

As far as magazines are concerned, 'convergence' has wrought a considerable number of changes within the nexus of production and consumption in the recent past, causing major disruption to publishing practice. A *matrix of consumption* would map the network of publishing connections and identify key points in the nexus that may be subject to disruption. We have already seen that individual magazines and publishing corporations are willing to respond to changing material conditions; if the magazine industry can address changing cultural conditions then re-conceptualization of the audience, how it is comprised, how it is courted, what it wants, how to generate value from it and how to involve it in promotion can be effected. And such a development would be entirely appropriate within the culture of magazines because magazines have always been associated with promotion.

Bibliography

Ballaster, R., Beetham, M., Frazer, E. and Hebron, S. (1991) *Women's Worlds: Ideology, Femininity and the Woman's Magazine*, Basingstoke, UK: Macmillan.

Beetham, M. (1996) *A Magazine of Her Own*, London: Routledge.

Burrell, I. (2007) 'Interview with Ian Burrell: A Bunch of Friends and a Record Player', *The Independent*, 12 March.

Consterdine, G. (2002) *How Magazine Advertising Works IV*, London: PPA.

Debord, G. (1994) *The Society of the Spectacle*, Donald Nicholson-Smith (trans.), New York, NY: Zone Books.

Elleström, L. (ed.) (2010) *Media Borders, Multimodality and Intermediality*, Basingstoke, UK: Palgrave Macmillan.

Ferguson, M. (1983) *Forever Feminine: Women's Magazines and the Cult of Femininity*, London: Heinemann.

Fornäs, J. (undated) *Popular Passages: Media in the Modern Space of Consumption*, http://bit.ly/fornas, accessed 16 July 2012.

Friedan, B. (1963) *The Feminine Mystique*, New York, NY: Dell Publishing Co.

Goldhaber, M. H. (1997) 'The Attention Economy and the Net', *First Monday*, vol 2, no 4, 7 April, http://bit.ly/goldhaber, accessed 16 July 2012.

Hermes, J. (1995) *Reading Women's Magazines: An Analysis of Everyday Media Use*, Cambridge, UK, and Cambridge, MA: Polity Press.

Holmes, T. and Nice, L. (2012) *Magazine Journalism*, London: Sage.

Holmes, T., Hadwin, S. and Mottershead, G. (2012) *The 21st Century Journalism Handbook*, Harlow: Pearson.

Klein, J. and Dawar, N. (2004) 'Corporate Social Responsibility and Consumers' Attributions and Brand Evaluations in a Product-Harm Crisis', *International Journal of Research in Marketing*, vol 21, no 3, September, pp203–217.

Korinek, V. (2000) *Roughing It in the Suburbs: Reading* Chatelaine *Magazine in the Fifties and Sixties*, Toronto: University of Toronto Press.

Morrish, J. (2003) *Magazine Editing: How to Develop and Manage a Successful Publication*, 2nd edition, Abingdon, UK: Routledge.

Morrish, J. and Bradshaw, P. (2012) *Magazine Editing: In Print and Online*, 3rd edition, Abingdon, UK: Routledge.

Oldenburg, R. (1999) *The Great Good Place: Cafes, Coffee Shops, Bookstores, Bars, Hair Salons, and Other Hangouts at the Heart of a Community*, 3rd edition, Cambridge, MA: Marlowe & Co.

Quinn, T. (undated) *Magforum*, http://www.magforum.com/.

Reed, D. (1997) *The Popular Magazine in Britain and the United States 1880–1960*, London: The British Library.

Tönnies, F. (2001) *Gemeinschaft und Gesellschaft [Community and Civil Society]*, J. Harris (ed), J. Harris and M. Hollis (trans.), Cambridge and New York: Cambridge University Press.

White, C. (1970) *Women's Magazines 1693–1968*, London: Michael Joseph.

9

TELEVISION

The TV Ad and Its Afterlife

Jeremy Orlebar

The current paradigm

The collision of syncopated images that is the television advertising break powers commercial television in the UK and around the world. The TV ad break drives the whole economy of broadcast television, and without it non-public service television would have no credible funding base. In a postmodern, digitized, convergent media environment (Jenkins 2006), online marketing forms strive to draw revenue and influence from television advertising. Viral promotional methods via social networking sites, such as Facebook and Twitter, along with the digital video recorder (DVR) and video streaming services such as Netflix, allowing time-shifted television viewing, conspire with traditional prejudices – the ads interrupt the programmes – to destabilize the form. But as Jenkins (2006: 16) reminds us: 'convergence refers to a process, not an endpoint'.

At the start of the twenty-first century, the outlook for conventional television advertising, the TV ad break, appeared gloomy. Jenkins quotes Rishad Tobaccowala, president of the media buying group Starcom MediaVest, as sparking a panic at a gathering of television executives in 2002 when he offered 'the premature prediction that the thirty-second commercial would be dead by 2005' (Jenkins 2006: 67). As broadcast TV Britain became entirely digital in 2012, the plethora of financially viable commercial channels powered by the ad break confounds this prediction. The TV ad break is a match forged by Mammon, created in fairyland, and accepted by the public as a Faustian compromise. The current paradigm is that viewers are complicit in trading content they want to watch on television with about 12 minutes of marketing in every hour of viewing. The symbiosis between advertiser, product and viewer stimulates economic growth, entertains and provides a cosmopolitan backdrop to television schedules. It also shifts products, reinforces brand awareness and drives sales. However, MacRury confirms that convergence is changing this paradigm: 'The media-as-host and advertisement-as-parasite relationship identified by critics (e.g., Thompson 1932), or the ad-media symbiosis accepted as the default for commercial media, is being challenged by new media-advertising hybrid genres' (MacRury 2009: 227). By 2012 television advertising revenues had stabilized and given ITV, the UK's main commercial channel, a timely boost. Not only did the ad break not demise, but television commercials are the highest generator of income and initiate more sales than any other promotional form or activity (Alps 2011).

Pay TV and subscription TV generate substantial revenues for satellite TV stations such as SKY. Other ways of generating sufficient income for terrestrial TV to provide quality television content have been tried and, apart from the UK's licence fee system, do not deliver enough revenue to support the quality content viewers demand: TV drama, documentaries, professional sports, current affairs and news. TV on demand via streaming services such as LoveFilm and Netflix, launched in the UK in January 2012 for £6 a month, is gaining traction mainly for films and past quality TV content.

Convergent convulsions

Public discourse around convergence, and the wave of so-called anti-capitalist protests in 2011, led some commentators to question the moral basis of how television is paid for in the UK. The dual system of the 'compulsory tax' of the BBC licence fee and the 'hidden persuaders' of advertising on commercial television has been very successful in producing quality television content, and every so often this paradigm is questioned, this time engendered by convergence. Young people, in particular, have come to expect their musical and visual entertainment to flow at their command, and without payment, to their laptop or mobile. They watch 'free' television via catch-up services such as iPlayer, and the licence fee is paid for by their parents at home. Televised Premiership football and major international sports are available 'free' in their local pub. There is a subconscious assumption by some that Internet-led content, including broadcast television, should be free. Levine argues convincingly that quality TV content and its associate advertising revenues are compromised by convergence:

> The real issue is how to establish a functioning market for content online, whether that involves selling it or supporting it with advertising ... traditional media companies aren't in trouble because they're not giving customers what they want; they're in trouble because they can't collect money for it.
>
> *(Levine 2011: 17)*

When UK commercial television began in the 1950s, many viewers thought they were getting a free service. It was only when they looked in their fridge and saw Flora margarine, went to 'work on an egg', and had instant Smash for supper did the correlation between what they bought and what was advertised on television become apparent. The *frisson* of getting something free is never far from the consumer's consciousness. Ariely finds the incredible power of 'free' is almost too hot to handle: 'It's no secret that getting something free feels very good. Zero is not just another price, it turns out. Zero is an emotional hot button – a source of irrational excitement' (Ariely 2008: 54).

New Yorker Bill Bernbach opened the highly respected agency Doyle Dane and Bernbach during the 1960s and is credited as the inspiration behind modern TV advertising (Delaney 2008). Before it was fashionable he took an ethical stance in refusing to handle the very profitable cigarette advertising accounts of the time. Bernbach, a former political speech writer, 'identified the importance of speaking to a mass audience with a certain intellectual respect' (Delaney 2008: 10). Doyle Dane and Bernbach's greatest triumph was to introduce the diminutive Volkswagen Beetle to US car buyers brought up on rorty V8 engines and high-comfort cruising. His 'think small' campaign is interesting for a twenty-first-century audience, Delaney (2008: 14) argues, because it 'is based on a self-deprecating premise, encouraging consumers to think small'.

The 2011 to 2012 popularity of dysfunctional meerkats as an advertising phenomenon suggests that self-deprecation is still a winning formula. This campaign created by a small agency in Birmingham identifies one methodology TV advertising has used to embrace the Internet and profit from it. The meerkats seek only to alert viewers to a website. No actual product is offered; the brand is in the website URL comparethemarket.com. At the same time, another campaign was launched for a rival Internet comparison website with the brand name gocompare. com where an annoying, overweight opera singer appears from unlikely locations, such as a desert island, to sing the website brand name. In both TV ads there is no identifiable product; no specific reasons for choosing this website brand are deployed; no scientific data is extolled; there are no testimonials or celebrity endorsement; just 'go compare' or 'compare the market'. The consumer's journey to making a purchase has begun with an exhortation not to do anything until many brands have been compared on one of these websites. Choice is the new voodoo masquerading as a democratized marketplace.

The meerkats commercial works by tapping into cheeky, postmodern, ironic self-deprecation, not underestimating the consumer's intelligence, and seeking out what Hebdige (1979) describes as 'sub-cultural groups'. Resistive strategies used by such groups contribute to some of the most effective forms of advertising. Both the meerkats and the overzealous opera singer ads went viral, attracting millions of hits on YouTube. Interestingly, the more annoying opera singer ads, which for some consumers outstayed their welcome on television, had the greater success in attracting online footfall. Haig (2009: 5) suggests that it is the perception of branding that is important: 'Image is now everything. Consumers make buying decisions based around the perception of the brand rather than the reality of the product.' It may be that gocompare has a more easily perceived meaning. In the virtual universe of the Internet, advertisers struggle to get a brand imprisoned in the consumer's synapses, let alone the tricky URL of a website. These two campaigns suggest that the TV ad break does the job for them.

The TV ad break has always had to resist assaults on its hegemony. Online advertising and viral marketing have been seen as its nemesis, and it did appear that, in the convergent era, viral marketing might take revenue from television advertising. Video games, TV on demand, social networking sites, the internet and the DVD boxed set all demand viewers' attention and advertisers' concern. By 2012 the shape of the next decade of advertising looked brighter for one simple reason. Traditional linear broadcast TV with the ad break attracted the highest revenue, and delivered the most lasting brand awareness and sales. 'The real metrics that matter are what happens to a brand's sales when they advertise, and on that score, TV does very, very well indeed' (Alps 2011). The demise of the TV ad break in the digital era is not supported by research. YouGov for Deloitte reported that the ad break is the most memorable form of advertising:

> Questions over the relevance of the traditional television advert have been raised for years, yet when asked about their most favoured video format, respondents voted for the standard 30-second commercial. What television does best – display and brand building – is what online struggles with.
>
> *(Bates 2010)*

Conversely, the argument about advertising interrupting quality programming has always been of concern to liberal AB consumers. It erupted in 2011 around the popular ITV Sunday evening series *Downton Abbey*. This costume drama about the upper echelons of society during and after World War I aired on the main commercial channel ITV1, and peaked with 11 million viewers. Mark Lawson (2011) reported:

> *Downton*'s executive producer, Gareth Neame, was candid about both the necessity of the interruptions – in commercial TV, extended selling breaks are a sign of a hit show – and the practicalities of accommodating them: the creative team have around two minutes leeway for where to break each segment, and the intervals will generally be indicated in Julian Fellowes's scripts from early on.

It was at first thought that time shifting would seriously affect television advertising. Commentators predicted that by recording a programme on a DVR, the TV ad breaks could be fast forwarded and the anti-ad consumer could watch 'free' television content. Ofcom's figures show that 44 per cent of people have a DVR, but only 5.9 per cent of their viewing is time shifted, meaning that, overall, only 2.2 per cent of viewing is time shifted using a DVR (Ofcom 2010). The amount of time-shifted viewing varies by platform with Sky+ the highest at just over 16 per cent, then V+, and lowest is Freeview+ at about 13 per cent (BARB 2011). As a result, Martin Sorrel of WPP believes that commercial TV is in a much stronger position than at first thought: 'Technological advancements such as time shift, on demand and connected TV will work around broadcast TV in the future, but not replace it' (pocket-lint.com/news 2011).

Behavioural economy and neuro-marketers

Television advertising continues to attract scientific methodology to try and discover how advertising affects viewers. White (2011) observes from talking to young people that 'Authenticity and honesty have become important ingredients in today's brand communications.' Yet, there is little evidence of this approach in current TV ads. Branding of a young person's staple such as an Adidas or Nike trainer still mainlines on luxury imaging, fantasy success and celebrity endorsement – techniques not noted for gritty Ken Loach style authentic realism. They do, though, reflect the code of embedding advertising in the entertainment economy (MacRury 2009).

The TV ad break is seemingly reinvigorated and remains the most successful way to reach a mass audience. Apart from an initial wobble in the troubled economic times of 2008 when broadband and the Internet were confidently expected to kill off TV advertising, by 2012 the traditional moving image TV ad had adapted to the new convergent environment and was confidently exploiting it. The strengths of the new TV ads derive from their ability to create something that is likeable, captures attention, involves the consumer and engages in an educated dialogue. New developments in the effectiveness of advertising are driven by medical research into how the brain works and include behavioural economy. 'Behavioural economists believe that people are susceptible to irrelevant influences from their immediate environment (which we call context effects), irrelevant emotions, short-sightedness and other forms of irrationality' (Ariely 2008: 240). In its basic form, this suggests that our susceptibility is affected when we make a cup of tea during a TV ad break. This affects how we make decisions about the content of commercials that we actually do see. Ariely (2008: 167) asserts that brand expectations affect the brain: 'If we expect a brand to make us feel younger, run faster, lift our fragile self esteem, take greater care of our money, then the "higher order brain mechanisms" associate these brands with success and give them an advantage in the market place.' He 'proves' this with brain-scanning experiments to do with consumers' preferences for Coke or Pepsi. Coke wins due to its advantageous worldwide branding.

Neuro-marketing explores these areas where neuroscience and behavioural research affect advertising and consumer choice. Researchers use magnetic resonance imaging (MRI) scanning techniques to detect how the brain behaves when consumers are faced with marketing decisions, often related to TV ads. They are trying to establish what parts of the brain control the voodoo of choice. Neuro-marketing hopes to provide more accurate results than traditional focus groups and other forms of market research. Global companies such as Google, HP and Microsoft have embraced the concept, hoping to influence the subconscious responses to commercial products and to identify the most appealing brands (Penenberg 2011). Advertisers have always been interested in our subconscious and flirted with subliminal messages in TV ads before the practice was banned. Neuro-marketers aim to examine brain activity to find the brand preferences we may not even know we have. US company NeuroFocus uses three factors to determine the efficiency of a TV ad: attention, emotional engagement and memory retention. Using an electroencephalogram (EEG), it is able to measure changes in electrical fields in regions of the brain on a second-by-second basis. When a TV ad had a positive reception, this is shown in increased brain activity.

Providing a counter-cultural discourse to the hegemony of the individual, Earls (2009), acknowledging that mass behaviour is very hard to shape, believes that TV advertising can benefit from understanding the psychological imperative of the herd animal instinct. According to Earls, £2 billion is spent every year in the UK on understanding what individuals think and do, and yet: 'Most of our behaviour is … the result of our interaction with other people because we are a super social species. A herd animal if you like. We do what we do because of those around us' (Earls 2009: 11). The TV ad has always benefited from peer pressure or pester power. Postmodern ads rely on a shared *bricolage* of prompts and assumptions derived from past advertising, television shows, films and assimilated media expo-sure. Bullmore (2006: 202) takes the herd mentality trope further: 'For someone or something to be famous requires more than lots of individuals knowing about it, it entails each individual knowing that other people think and feel the same.'

If the TV ad is now part of the entertainment industry (MacRury 2009), it has attained this status partly due to British consumers' ability to put the ad break in perspective: something which David Ogilvy understood in 1985 and perhaps this is why his book was reissued in November 2011:

> There seems to be a realisation in England that maybe, just maybe, the pro-duct being sold is not the most important thing in the consumer's mind … realizing this, the British are able to present their product to the consumer in perspective. They joke about it, sing about it, and often underplay it.
>
> *(Ogilvy 1985: 173)*

This capacity for perspective plays perfectly to the postmodern consciousness of the convergent media environment. Dickason realigns inter-textuality with memory: 'Much of the complicity and connivance created by commercials is attributable to what one might loosely call popular memories, the kind of experiences which remain subconsciously within the British viewer's mind, reinforcing the impression of common identity' (Dickason 2000: 168). No self-conscious modern viewer can view a launderette without thinking of Nick Kamen taking off his Levi's, and older viewers still clunk-click their car seat belts. If the afterlife of commercials inhabited consumers' memories from pre-convergent times, then the plethora of TV ads available on the Internet should therefore reinforce this sense of common identity. Evidence from social networking sites suggests that this is happening.

Product placement

Television companies and advertising agencies have negotiated with the regulator Ofcom to incorporate new strategies within the commercial mix. These include product placement, programme sponsorship and connectivity with instant media such as Twitter. Product placement is touted as an efficient way to insinuate brands into television audiences based on widespread use in the film industry. UK politicians and regulators are wary of what they regard as underhand and devious marketing in spite of the fact that they have accepted overt product placement in Hollywood films for decades. Ofcom allowed product placement for the first time from 28 February 2011, following the government's decision to allow it on UK TV, except in relation to children's, news, religious and current affairs programmes (Ofcom 2011). The first product placement in a primetime show was in the ITV soap *Coronation Street* on Monday, 14 November 2011 (*The Guardian* 2011a). It did not appear to compromise editorial independence or to be the dawn of a new advertising era. A Nationwide cashpoint replaced an unbranded prop cash machine in Dev Alahan's corner shop, and the building society has a branded sign outside. Some forecasters estimated that the UK product placement market might be worth up to £100 million annually. Ofcom is more circumspect, suggesting it might be worth £25 to £30 million within a few years (Sweney 2011).

Veteran consumer rights warrior and documentary-maker Morgan Spurlock turned his cynical camera on to what he considers are the sinister perils of evil corporations involved with product placement and sponsorship. In his film *The Greatest Movie Ever Sold* (2011), Spurlock wants us to be concerned about advertising in films; but the bombastic nature of the film did little to convince audiences that product placement is in any way damaging. Cinema audiences seem quite undeterred that Apple had its products 'placed' in 10 of the 33 films that were number one at the US box office in 2010. Certainly, every character who opens a laptop in a Hollywood film seems to open a Mac Book. Research reported by Galician (2004) suggests that whereas product placement reinforces the ideology of consumerism, it is not in itself harmful. Scott Robert Olsen suggests that it has two main, possibly negative, effects: 'One effect is the propagation of a culture dedicated primarily to shopping, and the other is the increasing attitudes of scepticism and even cynicism with regard to veracity of information of any kind' (cited in Galician 2004: 243). Critics of product placement argue that it is distracting, can be misleading and is possibly unethical because it suggests that film stars, who may be role models for young people, are seen to 'normalize' the consumption of branded products. It has been called insidious, and it is suggested that script-writers may be forced to compromise their narratives, or characters, by incorporating unlikely products into their screenplays. The real difficulty with a critique of product placement is that it is impossible to untangle its supposed negative social effects from other signs and signifiers on screen at the time.

There are causal effects of product placement as studies show brand awareness increases after the product has appeared. In Spielberg's eponymous film, the

likeable alien E.T. gorges on an American sweet called Reese's Pieces. This product placement was credited with a 65 per cent increase in sales in three months
(Caro cited in Galician 2004: 17). For most film-goers product placement is, at
worst, a slight irritation and, at best, an extra source of entertainment. Daniel
Boorstin noticed that audiences generally enjoy the diversion of spotting products
placed in a film as a game (cited in Galician 2004: 245). Product placement in
television programmes is more subtle and less intrusive than in films and, indeed,
less distracting. This has the disadvantage that it makes for low impact. The constraints required by Ofcom, and some confusion over compliance, not public
resistance, made for a slow start to product placement on television in the UK.
Mark Wood (*The Guardian* 2011b), a partner in product placement agency Krempel
Wood, said in August 2011: 'It has not taken off, there are not the millions of
pounds, it hasn't snowballed.'

Research in Australia on product placement in reality TV found a causal effect
on consumers and on their purchasing habits. The Reality TV Insights Survey
found that although the majority of viewers do not like product placement, 94 per cent
of them have been influenced by what they have seen on a reality show. Julie
Houston (2011) of Nitty Gritty Research carried out the survey: 'With the number
of new technologies emerging in the TV sphere, it is becoming more important for
advertising messages to be embedded in the shows themselves and for these to be
creative and not heavy handed.'

The TV ad's afterlife

The most effective twenty-first-century TV advertising has evolved into an art form
within an entertainment mix, and seeks engagement at a human – not heroic –
level (MacRury 2009: 220). The role of the celebrity, laying down the tablets of
stone about what is best for us to consume, still exists, but the viral take-up is for
postmodern, ironic, often self-consciously reflective ads that stimulate the bored
office worker at his or her computer and are worthy of sharing online. The TV ad
that provokes feeling, humour or engagement, or is considered that most elusive of
concepts, 'likeable', is the one that has the greatest impact.

Viral moving image content is now viewed via mobile devices such as the iPad
or Smartphone, and not necessarily in the context of the sitting room. The 30
second TV ad is an ideal form for this technology. Consumers are looking to share
digital constructs that will authenticate their identity, transmit a simple emotional
message, or perhaps invigorate a relationship. MacRury (2009: 230) goes further:
'There is a space in the pseudo public sphere created and inhabited by advertising
to touch on a wider range of themes – including anxiety provoking areas at the
boundaries of life and death, purity and danger, the ordinary, the exotic and the
cosmopolitan.' These areas provoke engagement along with the emotions, and
when applied in a TV ad become successful promotional opportunities, as in the
John Lewis Christmas commercial of our case study. The well-crafted 30 second
TV ad that encrypts a topical value, stimulates a comment, articulates an emotion

or provokes an insight will be shared and experienced on street corners, in offices, in cafés and by groups of like-minded individuals. Viral brand awareness springs with maximum authority from the professionally produced TV ad that has already inspired a defined audience.

Martin Sorrell of global agency WPP predicts that over the next ten years people will still mainly view linear television and that:

> Advertising will still be a critical part of TV revenue but more likely 20–25 per cent, down from 31 per cent and internet connected TV will be in 50–70 per cent of households receiving such a service by 2020. The balance of power in the TV world will move further from the content providers and to the platforms instead.
>
> *(Sorrell 2010)*

The online universe is spectacularly cluttered. Blogs, mobile phone pictures and social networking sites such as Twitter contribute to the explosion of citizen-generated moving image content. The TV ad break will continue to stand out from this abundance. It is devised with care, created and produced to the very best professional standards and delivered in gorgeous widescreen HD and in 3D. Crucially, it can be first seen to best advantage on a large screen in the traditional living room, or pub/club environment. Add in Ogilvy's perspective and Ariely's susceptibility to irrationality, along with the herd instinct, and the afterlife of the TV ad on the Internet affects more consumers than any other marketing vehicle.

The cooperative venture of YouView offers another way into the afterlife of TV programmes and ads. All major TV companies have their own updated versions of on-demand TV and interconnectivity. The Freeview HD TV Guide application is a TV planner for iPhone, iPad and Android tablets; Smartphone images are shared with friends on Facebook, Twitter and by email. Where and how viewers watch TV ads will change, but not as radically as some commentators expect. Viewers may try to avoid the ad break using catch-up services; but content will still be king. The emotionally grabbing, witty 'stand-out' ads will actually be consumed more due to their availability on many digital platforms. Smart TV will be the choice of consumers of all demographics. Consumers already have the choice between watching catch-up TV on their laptop, a tablet, or a Smartphone, or via their DVR on their main TV screen. It is possible to download programmes or watch live TV not just on a laptop but on an iPhone or iPad or other mobile device. Viewers take content with them, and mobile devices are becoming the preferred device for their digital experiences. Viewers will seamlessly flip a film from DVR to tablet or Smartphone and watch on the train to work, and when they get home enjoy the dramatic finale on their big screen television. With a Smart TV all Internet services will be available simultaneously: you can tweet or check your Facebook page, read emails, book a theatre ticket seamlessly and without interrupting the film.

Research by Screen Digest in 2011 suggests that viewers will watch Internet streaming and broadcast TV on their living room Smart TV set, probably as a family or group activity, but will not be actively involved in social networking, as there is not enough privacy in the living room for those intimate tweets, Facebook updates and emails. The device of choice for personal content is Smartphone, tablet and laptop used while watching big screen television. This is known as two-screen viewing. Some consumers might try to avoid the conventional ad break by using a DVR; but group watching means the ads do get through. The ads that generate digital activity on social media sites or in the press are being actively discussed and viewed, as for example in our case study of the John Lewis Christmas campaign (2011).

The way in which viewers access television will change; but viewing patterns will change less than some commentators are predicting, according to Emeritus Professor of Management and Marketing Patrick Barwise at London Business School. Barwise also thinks that radical changes will not take place until well past the year 2020. The research group Actual Customer Behaviour carried out a study analysing viewer behaviour. It showed that live TV still accounts for 80 per cent of viewing in homes and that this percentage is actually rising slowly. Most people watch programmes live, meaning that it is still a shared social experience:

> They're all about watching regular linear TV from the regular linear schedule, either live or time-shifted. Far from heralding the death of linear TV channels, they all depend on those channels for content. ... [Television] is an extremely and increasingly well-served market which represents extraordinary value for money.
>
> *(Barwise 2011)*

This is particularly true of live sports action broadcast on television and high-impact interactive shows such as *X Factor*. Viewers cannot find 'blockbuster' experiences in full HD and surround sound week in and out on the Internet. Live TV offers content of exceptional technical quality, variety, choice and consummately professional production complemented by these same qualities in the best TV ads. Advertising around these shows will continue to be a major source of revenue for television companies and the major outlet for advertisers. Major advertising group WPP's digital CEO is Mark Read: 'We expect TV to increase in the next five years. That's because of the growth of TV in the BRICs [Brazil, Russia, India and China]. We don't expect TV to go away.' (Read 2011)

Convergence gets connected

Moving into the mature converged Smart TV viewerverse in the second decade of the twenty-first century, there are concerns as well as opportunities for advertisers.

There are concerns about the way in which TV ads are accessed, as well as the value of their afterlife. The industry is not complacent and research is still considering the value and power of the Internet on TV advertising. There are dissident voices, including US TV network CBC's head of television Kirstine Stewart:

> With [social media] it's not even that it's an extra add-on anymore, it's expected that you provide opportunities to talk about the shows, to be able to find out more. The online experience is no longer an extra extension of what you do on air, it's part of the whole delivery of what you give people.
>
> *(Stewart 2011)*

Jason Kilar, CEO of leading US pay TV video advertising service Hulu, goes further and believes that Internet TV is more powerful than traditional live TV. He is worried that there are too many TV ads per hour on live TV and that consumers are going to some trouble to avoid them:

> Consumers are demonstrating that they are the greatest marketing force a good television show or movie could ever have, given the powerful social media tools at consumers' disposal ... . In the near future, advertisers will demand the ability to target their messages to people rather than targeting their messages to TV shows as proxies for people.
>
> *(Kilar 2011)*

Hulu claims to have invented technology that: 'Has enabled us to deliver much more relevant video advertising and to do so in a manner that generates much higher recall and purchase intent than other video advertising services' (Kilar 2011). It is not at all clear how this technology works or whether it is truly effective. An annoyed blogger on the Hulu website suggests that one of Hulu's 'innovative' devices is to show ads that require user action to return to video. One disgruntled blogger wrote: 'If I don't want to choose between or take action on advertisements, then don't make me' (Andrew comment 2011). In the US viewers on live TV watch 11 minutes of ads in a 30-minute show, but they expect much less advertising when watching programmes via video-on-demand. It is certainly true that the innovative video-on-demand TV sector, paid for by targeted advertising, is another opportunity for TV advertisers.

By 2012, ownership of DVRs in the UK had reached about half the households. Research shows that the amount of viewing that people actually time shift has remained static. Households with DVRs, on average, watch about 15 per cent of their television time shifted. ITV research arm Thinkbox is not complacent but states: 'This is about the level we now expect time-shifted viewing to stay at. It would take something pretty dramatic and unforeseen to be otherwise ... nearly half of the time-shifted 15 per cent is viewed on the same day as the live broadcast … and is still watched as though it is live' (Mortensen 2012). This suggests that the ad breaks are watched at normal speed because people don't fast-forward them. Research shows that viewers with a digital recorder watch more TV, so the net result is that about 3 per cent of these viewers watch more ads at normal speed than before they owned a recorder.

Nielsen, who has researched every TV ad that has run on UK TV in the fast-moving consumer goods (FMCG) sector for *The Grocer*, has published a list of the best TV ads of 2011. The ads were measured for memorability, brand recall, band linkage, message and if they made people want to buy. The outcome reveals some not-so-new ideas for effectiveness in TV advertising:

1 Make it funny: consumers want to be entertained, not bored. (Begs the question, why are so many ads boring?)
2 Keep it simple (K.I.S.S. applies).
3 Tell a story – it engages people.
4 Use characters people can relate to.
5 Use brand icons. Practitioners of NLP [neuro-linguistic programming] will know why this works: visuality is more memorable than words.

(Arnold 2011)

A TV ad must be successful in itself if it is to have an eventful afterlife that delivers sales or footfall. Afterlife begins connectivity. Peter Sells memorably put the evolution of connectivity in perspective: 'We want connected people watching TV, not people watching connected TV' (Sells 2011). This is pertinent to the way in which a young demographic are double screening. They are watching a live edition of *X Factor* on the family TV set and at the same time texting comments on the show to Facebook or Twitter on their Smartphone or tablets. The televisual experience can be augmented via interactive apps. These can offer instant access to extra information related to the TV programme (e.g., biographical information about the contestants) and provide instant buying opportunities, or downloads to an email address. Peter Sells is excited by these developments in 2012 with one caveat: 'Broadcast television offers few demands on the viewer – an augmented TV experience should not make TV harder to watch.'

This is the exciting future afterlife of the TV ad: mobile devices that offer augmented connectivity, not to compete with linear broadcast television but to enhance the viewing experience. Zeebox is an all platforms app in partnership with E4 that brings everything together directly to your Smartphone or iPad. Zeebox links to Wiki-style knowledge, online newspapers and connects to Amazon and iTunes. Other companies such as Shazam are producing apps that make online and broadcast TV connectivity easy to use and ideal for two-screen users providing a real-time seamless connection between TV and online. This is the most promising afterlife of the TV ad although it could be said to be more of an instant extra-terrestrial life: 'This great partnership should be the most effective ever created' (Sells 2011).

Case study: *The Long Wait* – John Lewis Christmas TV ad, 2011

- *Agency:* Adam & Eve creative director: Ben Priest.
- *Writers:* Matt Gay and John Long.
- *Music:* Slow Moving Millie sings a cover of The Smiths' 'Please, Please, Please Let Me Get What I Want'.
- *Duration:* 90 seconds with 60 and 30 second versions.
- *Title:* The Long Wait.
- *Director:* Dougal Wilson at Blink Productions.
- *Cost:* including airtime, £6 million.
- *Client:* John Lewis Partnership Department Store.
- *Channels used:* ITV, C4, C5, Multichannel.
- *Media agency:* Manning Gottlieb OMD.

The campaign

This case study suggests how *The Long Wait* campaign used the emotional connection delivered by a TV ad to drive the brand forward and produce a remarkable success story. In 2011, John Lewis decided to invest 100 per cent of their budget into their Christmas TV ad, and rely on convergence with social media to enhance their message. What they called 'likeability' was identified as the key element in driving purchase intent and reinforcing brand perception. This was augmented by an iconic soundtrack which went straight into the charts. Lloyd Page, head of brand communications at John Lewis, stated: 'It has never been so important for us to emotionally connect with our customers and through television we are able to do so in such a way that has resulted in our advertising being amplified beyond all expectation' (Thinkbox 2011).

FIGURE 9.1 Still from *The Long Wait*: John Lewis Christmas TV advert, 2011 – time moves slowly
Source: © John Lewis; used by kind permission of John Lewis

The narrative is of a small boy counting down the days and minutes until Christmas morning. We see him tapping his fingers out of frustration, gazing out of the window as autumn becomes winter, dashing to bed early to will the day away. He even tries to cast a spell to speed time up. The narrative draws the viewer into believing that the boy is selfishly impatient to open his own presents on Christmas morning. The denouement in the final seconds packs a big emotional punch. The boy wakes up on Christmas Day, sees his own presents at the foot of his bed, and then searches in his wardrobe for ... what? He lifts out lovingly wrapped presents, and takes them in to his parents' bedroom. 'The theme of the ad is predicated on anticipation which is transformed into the joy of giving the right present to someone you really love' (Thinkbox 2011).

This 90-second TV ad is a classic study in the connectedness of modern TV advertising. The video launched virally on Facebook and YouTube on Friday, 11 November 2011 at 9 am. The first broadcast was on Saturday, 12 November 2011 in the high-profile ad break during the primetime *X Factor* live show on ITV1 at 8:45 pm. It immediately went viral. The agency predicted the 60 second TV advert version would be viewed by 44 million people at least once over its five-week run. It was supported by a combination of 90, 30 and 20 second versions of the advert, as well as online marketing on the retailer's social media YouTube and Facebook channels.

Created by advertising agency Adam & Eve (a start-up in 2008), the music sets the tone with a cover of The Smiths' 'Please, Please, Please Let Me Get What I Want' sung by singer-songwriter and pianist Slow Moving Millie, the performance name of 29-year-old Amelia Warner. The ad is directed by Dougal Wilson of Blink Productions, who also directed John Lewis's award-winning *Never Knowingly Undersold* advert in 2010. *The Long Wait* was filmed in July near Golders Green in London and has a resolutely ordinary, almost austere, look to coincide with the sober financial climate of 2011. The clear moral imperative is that it is better to give than to receive. This hooks into the zeitgeist of anti-capitalist protests around the world by suggesting that the John Lewis partnership approach of a more caring form of capitalism makes for a better relationship with customers. *The Long Wait* builds on the success of the 2010 Christmas advert which featured Ellie Goulding singing a cover of the Elton John classic 'Your Song'.

The Long Wait campaign is indicative of how this type of campaign could be run in the future. It topped *Campaign* magazine's Viral Chart for the week ending 18 November 2011, with more than 183,000 shares over seven days. It received 192 Facebook updates, 10,000 tweets and 190 blog posts (BBC News 2011). Ramping up the viral exposure the TV ad spawned a number of online spoofs, including a 'Shining' version with spooky organ music and the 'Se7en' version with dialogue from the 1995 thriller. James Murphy (Thinkbox 2011), partner at Adam & Eve, knew they had a good TV ad narrative that would have considerable viral impact:

> But we hadn't realised quite how much it would capture the public mood. While conventional advertising is interruptive – it comes at you

unasked – this is something people elect to watch and pass on. If you choose to watch it you pay it more attention.

The importance of the concept and delivery of the TV ad was paramount to the success of the campaign. Tess Alps (2011) from Thinkbox puts the viral aspect in perspective:

> While 2.3m viral views are valuable and are in part a barometer of the popularity of an ad ... most of them have been driven by people seeing it on normal telly and then seeking it out again or sharing it. On its very first day alone on TV the ad was seen 17.9m times. The IPA [Institute of Practitioners in Advertising] and many others have proved that the best predictor of an ad's effectiveness is not recall or awareness but likeability, so on that basis I reckon the JL [John Lewis] ad must be doing a good job.

This type of storytelling in a TV ad also attracts criticism. Charlie Brooker in *The Guardian* proclaimed:

> This year's Christmas adverts aren't adverts, they're 'events'. Ghastly events. ... reports reached me of people blubbing in front of their televisions, so moved were they by this simple tale of a fictional boy counting the hours until he can give his parents a gift for Christmas. Given the fuss they were making, the tears they shed, you'd think they were watching footage of shoeless orphans being kicked face-first into a propeller. But no. They were looking at an advert for a shop.
>
> *(Brooker 2011)*

The bottom line is all the comment, online and in the press, is just what the agency and the client predicted, planned for and anticipated would happen. The campaign was undoubtedly a success. It is a fully functional concept: movie production values, targeted TV ad, connected social networking sites, interactive feedback and clever launch day build up in the national press. It sounds so simple. Perhaps that is the secret. The fulcrum around which the campaign evolved was the distinctive narrative and high production values that imbued the film with that elusive advertising Eldorado, exceptional 'likeability'.

Analysis

Tropes of suburbia infuse *The Long Wait*. The opening shot depicts a classic 1930s semi-detached house. The appearance of a busy self-assured young boy in his own clean-cut bedroom dispels any notion this is channelling the dreamily remembered chintz and flock wallpaper of 1950s suburbia. Tropes of contemporary suburban middle-class life are connoted by laminate wooden floors, flat-pack furniture, a swivel chair in the 'home office' and homework on the kitchen table. It is a construct of modern middle-class, middle-income, middle-way, large town sub-urban living, with working parents and two young children, hinting at the 2011 political slogan of 'the squeezed middle'. Successive images build up a conceit of impatience growing out of waiting. The frustration of filling in time is emphasized with close-ups of the clock face. Time is hanging heavily on this boy's young shoulders.

The camera moves outside the suburban windows detaching the viewer from the boy's frustration. A mid shot of the boy in the window wearing his school nativity three wise men headscarf reveals a Christmas tree behind him. We realize the long wait for Christmas day is nearly over. The boy dons a homemade magi-cian's suit and tries to put a spell on the clock so that he can be instantly trans-ported to Christmas. Impatience turns to frustration. The conceit is of a happy family, but the little boy is depicted alone with his thoughts. In one five-shot sequence he is on a swing in the garden which magically turns into a snowy winter scene. Time is moving on, slowly. Childhood tropes of innocence connect with imaginary bygone Christmases.

We are gaining insight into his impatience, evoking memories and emotions of our own childhood and the build-up to Christmas day. His anxiety is almost intolerable to his family: the jigging leg, the manically consumed supper, the rushing up stairs and banging his bedroom door. Has the effort of waiting been too much? Here the ad resonates with those viewers unenthusiastic about safe suburban ethics by propositioning a counter-cultural notion that deferred gratification may be damaging and even counterproductive. This middle-class ethos carefully modulated throughout the ad insinuates itself into the viewer's mind, creating an elliptical narrative positing the notion that the denouement may not be what we expect. The hidden emotions evolving in the viewer erupt in the emotional punch of the very last shot, where the boy unfolds a genuinely innocent smile as he hands his parents Christmas gift boxes almost as big as he is. The sincerity of the moment sabotages the postmodern viewer's tendency towards knowing cynicism.

Representations are exclusively of a typically average Anglo-Saxon white family, with minimum class symbolism. The boy is ordinary and not 'cute' in the way an ad for a household product might depict him. He has his own room in a small but identifiably modern house. His suggested backstory points to a local Christian school, adequate friends and a mischievous intelligence, with a strong creative streak. We somehow know that both his nicely dressed married parents work in caring careers. This is not in any way a mawkish representation, but defiantly average and modern. The boy is every child, devoid of political correctness. The representations are absolutely spot on for the John Lewis demographic. There is a notable absence of privilege denoted by the unfussy, clean-cut furnishings that are typically bought in a John Lewis store. Tony Blair would call the father Mondeo man, although he probably runs an Audi nowadays. The soundtrack song reinforces the longing trope, and in Millie's version becomes a hymn to a better life rather than anger for past failures.

FIGURE 9.2 Still from *The Long Wait*: John Lewis Christmas TV advert, 2011 – the tag
         line is revealed
Source: © John Lewis; used by kind permission of John Lewis

The selling only starts on the pack shot right at the end, after the smile: 'For gifts
you can't wait to give', subconsciously identifying the joy of giving with a purchase. Viewers agreed: 'If you worked in advertising you'd realise this is flawlessly done.
Tugs the right emotions, makes you laugh, and then almost cry. The song choice is
great – gentle for the emotion of the ad, but lyrically it sums up the story. Better than
if it was the original Smiths track! Stop being all Grinchy' (L, YouTube 2011).

Postscript

John Lewis had 'outstanding' sales figures for the five weeks to 31 December 2011.
Total sales were £596 million, 9.3 per cent up compared with 2010. Like-for-like
sales were up 6.2 per cent. Compared with two years ago, total sales were 19.1 per cent
up while like-for-like sales grew by 14.4 per cent. The popular press was quick to
point out that it must have been due to the TV ad's little boy (John Lewis Press
Release, John Lewis Christmas trading statement – five weeks to 31 December
2011, issued Wednesday 4 January 2012).

Conclusion

In the foreseeable future of the converged digital world:

- The TV ad will continue to drive television revenues.
- Advertising opportunities will be created with TV product placement.
- In the upcoming consumer marketplace, Smart TVs, video-on-demand,
  catch-up TV with DVRs, targeted advertising, and online competition will
  proliferate.
- The TV ad will generate more income for advertisers and be more effective for
  clients than any other advertising platform.

- Connected apps will augment interactive two screen viewing.
- Exceptionally well devised and produced TV ads will head up a successful integrated campaign feeding viral, press and interactive feedback.

Bibliography

Alps, T. (2011) 'Responding to "Gordon's Republic – The John Lewis Ad: It's Only an Ad for a Shop"', *Brandrepublic*, http://gordonsrepublic.brandrepublic.com/2011/11/21/the-john-lewis-ad-its-only-an-ad-for-a-shop/#ixzz1eLoHCzuH, accessed 21 November 2011.

Andrew (2011) Comment on 'Stewart, Colbert, and Hulu's Thoughts About the Future of TV', http://blog.hulu.com/2011/02/02/stewart-colbert-and-hulus-thoughts-about-the-future-of-tv, accessed 16 January 2012.

Ariely, D. (2008) *Predictably Irrational: The Hidden Forces that Shape Our Decisions*, London: HarperCollins.

Arnold, C. (2011) 'The 2011 Most Recalled FMCG Ads', http://arnoldonethicalmarketing.brandrepublic.com/2011/12/20/2011-most-recalled-fmcg-ads-the-7-secrets-of-success, accessed 20 December 2011.

BARB (2011) 'Multi-Channel Development: 1992–2011', http://www.barb.co.uk/facts/multi-channel-development?_s=4, accessed 16 January 2012.

Barwise, P. (2011) 'Confusions and Delusions About "Non-Linear TV" and Why They Matter', http://www.guardian.co.uk/oxfordmediaconvention/patrick-barwise-non-linear-tv, accessed 22 November 2012.

Bates, J. (2010) 'New Report Reveals Television Advertising Still Packs the Greatest Punch', http://www.deloitte.com/view/en_GB/uk/industries/tmt/09dbdce6763aa210VgnVCM3000001c56f00aRCRD.htm, accessed 21 November 2011.

BBC News (2011) 'Ad Breakdown: The John Lewis Christmas Ad', 21 November, http://www.bbc.co.uk/news/magazine-15825050, accessed 21 November 2011.

Brooker, C. (2011) 'The John Lewis Commercial', *The Guardian*, 20 November, http://www.guardian.co.uk/commentisfree/2011/nov/20/christmas-adverts-john-lewis, accessed 21 November 2011.

Bullmore, J. (2006) *Apples, Insights & Mad Inventors: An Entertaining Analysis on Modern Marketing*, London: Wiley.

Delaney, S. (2008) *Get Smashed: The Story of the Men Who Made the Adverts That Changed Our Lives*, London: Sceptre.

Dickason, R. (2000) *British Television Advertising: Cultural Identity and Communication*, Luton: University of Luton Press.

Earls, M. (2009) *Herd: How to Change Mass Behaviour by Harnessing Our True Nature*, Chichester, UK: John Wiley & Sons.

Galician, M. L. (ed) (2004) *Handbook of Product Placement in the Mass Media: New Strategies in Marketing Theory, Practice, Trends and Ethics*, Philadelphia, PA: Haworth Press.

The Guardian (2011a) '*Coronation Street* Cashpoint to Mark First Product Placement in UK Primetime Show', http://www.guardian.co.uk/media/2011/oct/30/nationwide-coronation-street-placement?INTCMP=SRCH, accessed 3 March 2012.

——(2011b) 'TV Product Placement Off to Slow Start', http://www.guardian.co.uk/media/2011/aug/27/tv-product-placement?INTCMP=SRCH, accessed 2 February 2012.

Haig, M. (2009 [2005]) 'Brand Failures: The Truth About the 100 Biggest Branding Mistakes of All Time', in H. Powell, J. Hardy, S. Hawkin and I. MacRury (eds) *The Advertising Handbook*, 3rd edition, Abingdon, UK: Routledge.

Hebdige, D. (1979) *Subculture: The Meaning of Style (New Accents)*, London: Methuen.

Houston, J. (2011) The Reality TV Insights Survey, http://www.realityravings.com/2011/08/22/reality-tv-insights-survey-product-placement-in-reality-tv-shows-works, accessed 2 February 2012.

John Lewis Partnership (2011) 'Christmas Campaign: Press Release', http://www. johnlewispartnership.co.uk/media/press/y2011/press-release-11-november-2011-john-lewis-launches-6m-christmas-campaign-celebrating-the-joy-of-giving.html, accessed 11 January 2012.

John Lewis Website (2011) http://www.youtube.com/user/JohnLewisRetail#p/u/4/EosFNm78hGg, accessed 11 January 2012.

Jenkins, H. (2006) *Convergence Culture*, New York, NY: New York University Press.

Kilar, J. (2011) 'Stewart, Colbert, and Hulu's Thoughts About the Future of TV', 2 February, http://blog.hulu.com/2011/02/02/stewart-colbert-and-hulus-thoughts-about-the-future-of-tv, accessed 21 November 2011.

Lawson, M. (2011) 'TV Matters: Advertising Breaks', 19 October, http://www.guardian.co.uk/tv-and-radio/2011/oct/19/downton-abbey-advertising-breaks?INTCMP=SRCH, accessed 20 November 2011.

Levine, R. (2011) *Free Ride: How the Internet Is Destroying the Culture Business and How the Culture Business Can Fight Back*, London: Bodley Head.

MacRury, I. (2009) *Advertising*, Abingdon, UK: Routledge.

Mortensen, N. (2012) 'Thinkbox Blog', http://thinkboxblog.brandrepublic.com/2012/01/09/our-annual-graph, accessed 11 January 2012.

Ofcom (2010) 'Consumers Spend Almost Half of Their Waking Hours Using Media and Communications', 19 August 2010, http://media.ofcom.org.uk/2010/08/19/consumers-spend-almost-half-of-their-waking-hours-using-media-and-communications, accessed 21 November 2011.

——(2011) 'Product Placement Logo to Be Shown on TV Screens', 14 February 2011, http://media.ofcom.org.uk/2011/02/14/product-placement-logo-to-be-shown-on-tv-screens, accessed 21 November 2011.

Ogilvy, D. (1985) *Ogilvy on Advertising*, London: Guild Publishing.

Penenberg, A. (2011) 'NeuroFocus Uses Neuromarketing to Hack Your Brain', 8 August, http://www.fastcompany.com/magazine/158/neuromarketing-intel-paypal, accessed 16 January 2012.

Pocket-lint (2010) '10 Reasons Why Linear TV Is Here for the Long Term', 23 July 2010, http://www.pocket-lint.com/news/34503/linear-tv-is-the-future, accessed 11 January 2012.

Read, M. (2011) Cited by 'Media Briefing', http://www.themediabriefing.com/article/2011-10-25/wpp-points-to-the-media-economys-future-global-diversified-and-very-digital, accessed 11 January 2012.

Screen Digest (2011) http://www.worldtvpc.com/blog/social-networking-work-tv, accessed 11 January 2012.

Sells, P. (2011) 'TV and Mobile: A Great Partnership', *Thinkbox*, http://www.thinkbox.tv/peter-sell-tv-and-mobile-a-great-partnership, accessed 15 January 2012.

Sorrell, M. (2010) 'Shaping the Future of TV', *The Daily Telegraph*, 1 July, http://www.telegraph.co.uk/technology/news/7866219/Sir-Martin-Sorrell-Pay-TV-platforms-will-control-the-future-of-the-UK-broadcasting-business.html, accessed 11 January 2012.

Stewart, K. (2011) 'Are Television Ratings Driven by Social Networking Websites', http://www.worldtvpc.com/blog/television-ratings-driven-social-networking-websites, accessed 11 January 2012.

Sweney, M. (2011) '*Coronation Street* Cashpoint to Mark First Product Placement in UK Primetime Show', *The Guardian*, 30 October, http://www.guardian.co.uk/media/2011/oct/30/nationwide-coronation-street-placement, accessed 11 January 2012.

The Long Wait (2011) www.youtube.com/JohnLewisRetail and http://www.johnlewis.com/TV ad, accessed 11 January 2012.

Thinkbox (2011) 'JL ad Background', http://www.thinkbox.tv/server/show/ConCase Study.1705, accessed 11 January 2012.

White, R. (2011) *Communicating with Youth: WARC Best Practice Papers*, www.warc.com, accessed 14 November 2011.

10

CINEMA

A Reflection on How the Film Industry Promotes Itself

Searle Kochberg

Introduction

Cinema-going as a social phenomenon is over 100 years old. Such was its exponential growth in the first few decades that what started out as a pragmatic way of demonstrating new moving-image technologies very quickly mushroomed into a hugely popular leisure activity attracting tens of millions of people per week in the US sector alone (Balio 1976: 75). In the process, an institutional infrastructure grew up to streamline the commercial exploitation of this new mass medium of entertainment. This chapter sets out to reflect upon this exploitation by considering how the film industry has promoted itself from the 1930s to the present day; like all good yarns with plenty of twists and turns, it is always best to start with the basic 'setup'.

The challenge for all in the industry is to get films financed, promoted and put in front of a large audience. This translates as the three-branch division of the film industry, one that has remained intact since the earliest days of film exploitation. This three-branch division is made up of distribution (marketing, promotion, sales), exhibition (cinemas) and production (manufacturing). Money changes hands at every stage, with promotion focused mainly at the distribution and exhibition ends. For this reason, it is these two branches of the film industry which will be the main focus of this chapter. Today, very large distribution firms take the biggest slice of each pie. As financiers-cum-distributors, they dictate for the most part the financial details of a film's production, exploitation and rental to cinemas – namely, who gets what of the box office receipts. The chapter moves historically through three key economic phases of the US (global) and UK film industries, starting just after infancy and adolescence (1895 to circa 1925), by which time the film business had evolved a 'mature', integrated economic structure. The three phases of our study are the 'Studio Era' (late 1920s to 1950s), the 'TV Era' (1950s to 1990s) and the

'Digital Era' (1990s to present). Snapshots will be taken at key points *en route*, with case studies pulled out to highlight the salient points of each stage.

The Studio Era (late 1920s to 1950s)

By the late 1920s/early 1930s, five 'studios', known as the 'Big Five' or the 'Majors', effectively controlled the US and Canadian market. These companies were Warner Brothers, Fox (in the mid-1930s reorganized and renamed Twentieth Century Fox), Paramount, Metro Goldwyn Mayer and Radio Keith Orpheum (RKO, through which Disney distributed: see below). The Majors were vertically integrated (owning their own production facilities, marketing/promotion organizations and cinemas), and operated as an oligopoly (a group monopoly). The 1930s and 1940s were decades when up to 100 million cinema tickets were sold in North America each week. Collectively, the Majors accounted for around 75 per cent of film rentals to cinemas in the US sector, this despite owning only 15 per cent of US-sector cinemas. There are two key reasons for this.

Firstly, the cinemas that the Majors owned were deluxe single 'screens': large 1200-plus capacity houses, in the best urban and suburban locations in the US and Canada. These houses naturally had high ticket prices and in an era before TV, there was no problem filling seats. Frequent film goers were understood in that era as people going to the movies five times or more per week and films were needed to satisfy their insatiable appetites. If individual members of the 'studio' oligopoly could not supply the huge numbers of films required to fill these deluxe cinemas 52 weeks of the year, and they couldn't, the Big 5 collectively came up with a simple solution to maintain control and maximize profits. They filled their slots as much as possible with each other's films. It was a trade-off: 'You scratch my back and I'll scratch yours.'

Secondly, 'independent' owners of big-revenue deluxe cinemas (i.e., those not owned by the Big Five) had their hands tied. If they wanted the Majors' films, they were forced to take sight-unseen blocks of 'studio' films or they would be denied the films altogether (a practice referred to as block-booking). By this point along the food chain there was little left of the market to carve up, but three smaller US film companies owning no cinemas, Columbia, United Artists and Universal (known as the 'Little Three'), accounted for a further 20 per cent of cinema rentals. This left a meagre 5 per cent of rentals for even smaller domestic distributors and foreign companies (Gomery 1986: 11–18). During the 1930s, rentals of films of the Big Five and the Little Three dominated international sectors as well, particularly in Europe and Japan. The Hollywood oligopoly was very successful in setting up international marketing operations to promote their films, and because the films had usually made back their cost in the US sector already, all was profit. It is estimated that one half of the box office rentals for US films was generated in overseas markets in peace time during the Studio Era (Gomery 1986: 12). Thus, the Majors set in motion a huge revenue stream that was tightly under their control. Systems of economic control tend to be self-reinforcing and by virtue of their films beating the competition with bigger budgets and bigger star names, secured through long-term contracts, the Majors further consolidated their control of the marketplace. Simply put, their films were the ones that the public generally saw, were familiar with and wanted to see: brand loyalty through apparent consumer choice.

Yet, despite a less than crowded leisure industry at the time, film companies were not automatically assured an audience. They had to build one utilizing various marketing tools: promotion (paid advertising that is produced by the film company itself), publicity (free advertising through, for instance, the planting of stories in newspapers and fan magazines), tie-ins (mutually beneficial promotional liaisons between films and other consumer products, often filtered through personalities) and merchandising (where manufacturers pay a film company to use a film title or image on their products).

Case study 1: Warner Brothers, MGM, Twentieth Century Fox and Disney: Hollywood promotion, stars and the Studio Era

Even before the 1930s, marketing was a well-embedded procedure in Hollywood. To promote the latest production of its biggest star, the dog Rin Tin Tin, Warner Brothers distributed promotional materials for *Where the North Begins* (1923) to theatre owners, including ads, guidelines for publicity stunts (including stopping pedestrians on the street), and stories to plant in local newspapers. Merchandising, too, was piloted in the exploitation of Rin Tin Tin, with endorsement deals with Ken L-Ration, the first commercial dog food in the US (Orlean 2011: 36, 38).

By the 1930s, big money was beginning to change hands, with large contractual agreements being signed between the Majors and consumer-product manufacturers. MGM is a good example to cite because of all the Majors, it had the most to gain by effective marketing. Of all the Big Five, it had the least number of cinemas. This meant that building brand loyalty and renting its films to non-MGM cinemas were particularly important issues in MGM's corporate survival. It is no coincidence, therefore, that its marketing arm became recognized as the industry leader, both nationally and internationally, during the Studio Era. In March 1933, MGM signed a $500,000 tie-in contract with Coca-Cola, where Coke ads would employ pictures and endorsements of MGM stars, with notice of recent film releases. In the same year, Coca-Cola delivery trucks across the country carried billboards advertising the studio's biggest production, *Dinner at Eight*. It would seem that the contract also allowed for product placement in the films themselves, as evidenced in two 1938 blockbusters (or 'A' films, as they were referred to then). MGM's first Technicolor feature, the musical *Sweethearts*, uses the new colour process to mark the debut of the red 'Drink Coca-Cola' neon sign in Times Square. Elsewhere that year, in the more macho surroundings of *Test Pilot*, Spencer Tracy is heard ordering 'Two Coca-Colas please.'

The corporate logic behind branding has always been that consumers (here read filmgoers) 'attach' themselves to a brand because of what they hope it says about them, a form of fantasy or, to use a Marxist concept, a form of false consciousness, where economic and social relations in bourgeois societies are rendered false to individuals. For female spectators of the 1930s and 1940s, MGM fostered this aspirational culture through its very strong roster of female stars. To promote the MGM brand, the studio saw to it that its films became showcases for fashion, furniture design and cosmetics. An amusing example of this is related by Charles Eckert (1978: 6) who cites a story from the *Saturday Evening Post* (18 May 1935) tracking the merchandising history of a dress designed by Adrian for Joan Crawford in the 1932 film *Letty Lynton*. The MGM copyright of the design, noted for its big stiff ruffles outlining the shoulders, was marketed up and down 7th Avenue, starting with high-end manufacturers and ending with mass production firms. By 1935 the dress had reached the other side of the Pond, dominating even the cheap *prêt a porter* shops of Paris, much to the chagrin of the writer on the *Saturday Evening Post*. Eckert ends his article with the wry observation that Hollywood in the Studio Era 'did as much or more than any other force in capitalist culture to smooth the operation of the production-consumption cycle by fetishizing products and putting the libido into ... advertising' (Eckert 1978: 21).

Still, during the 1930s, the public appeal of child actress Shirley Temple, then the world's biggest star and 'the' icon of Depression America, was exploited to the full by Twentieth Century Fox, her studio, to promote its brand. A merchandising deal was struck with Ideal Toy and Novelty Company to produce the Shirley Temple doll, available in 13 different sizes. Despite the dire state of the economy in the mid-1930s, 0.5 to 1 million of these dolls were sold, launching a multi-million dollar toy bonanza. Specific tie-ins, linking consumer products with particular films, to promote both were also launched. For example, print adverts for the Packard motor car were linked to the release of Temple's *Captain January* (1936). By the following year, the Disney studio was signing 70 (merchandising) licensing agreements to coincide with the release of its first animated feature, *Snow White and the Seven Dwarfs* (1938). 'Snow White toys, books, clothes, snacks and records' were manufactured to coincide with the film's opening (Schlosser 2002: 40). To use James McNeal's term, the 'Kid Kustomer' had come of age (cited in Schlosser 2002: 44). Disney and Twentieth Century Fox had proven that allying themselves with reliable children's (and adults') consumer goods, reflecting solid American family values, only reinforced their corporate brands and paid handsome dividends to shareholders.

Case study 2: The UK's vertically integrated Rank Organization takes on the Hollywood oligopoly during the Studio Era

The only 'Major' vertically integrated film company in the UK during the Studio Era was the Rank Organization. Its attempt to break into the US market from the mid- to late 1940s is the most striking example we have of a non-US film company trying to build an American audience for its films during the Studio Era. However, Rank's attempt, despite some limited success, ultimately proved to be a failure and was all the more disappointing given Rank's economic clout in the US. The company was enormously powerful, in the same league as the US Majors. It had a controlling interest in Universal, which gave it access to the cinemas of the oligopoly. However, despite all these advantages and Rank spending enormous sums on its prestige films, few of its films found favour in the US. When they did (as did *Caesar and Cleopatra* and *Henry V*, both 1945, and *Hamlet* and *The Red Shoes*, both 1948), it was because they featured stars known to Americans, had excellent production values and were marketed carefully and at great cost as 'road show' (special event) presentations (Curran and Porter 1983: 164–178). However, these marketing strategies were too expensive and unrealistic to adopt universally and Rank's gate-crash experiment was over by the end of the 1940s.

As a footnote to the Studio Era, the construction of a 'trust' such as the Majors' oligopoly, where a group of companies operate together in the marketplace to control a commodity, was/is entirely illegal in the US. The reason usually given, however, for its resilience is the federal government's reluctance to rock the boat during the Depression (1930s) and World War II (1941 to 1945). Hollywood movies were needed to boost morale. However, by 1949 the game was up. An anti-trust suit was brought by the Justice Department against Paramount Pictures. The court found in favour of the Justice Department, against Paramount. The terms of the court order (or 'consent decree') agreed between the plaintiff and the defendant were the selling off of Paramount's cinemas and an end to block booking. Subsequently the other Majors also settled with the government. The monopoly was over.

The TV Era (1950s to 1990s)

By the mid-1950s, the film industry was struggling. The Majors had been forced to sell off their cinema chains by the US government. Competition to get films into cinemas was now rife and 'Independents' (independent production companies) were beating the Majors at their own game. They were simply quicker on their feet than the large lumbering studios, and had little in the way of fixed costs to pay for (such as a 24/7 studio infrastructure) and could therefore make films faster and cheaper. They could hire what they needed on a film-by-film basis, such as ex-'Studio' stars who had been released from their long-term Studio contracts, and pay them through incentives such as percentage-of-profit deals instead of upfront salaries. Ironically, their cost-cutting, their renting of studio space and their general flexibility made independent producers very attractive to the Majors, who by the mid-1950s were lining up to finance and distribute their films.

In the end the big bugbear was not the consent decrees but TV. It had usurped film as the leading medium of mass entertainment by the mid-1950s. The film industry went through a period of denial, trying to convince itself that the humble TV set could never compete with the majesty of cinema, particularly with an industry investing in widescreen, stereophonic sound, 3D and colour. But cinema profits continued to fall dramatically. By 1956, weekly film attendance figures in US and Canada were half what they had been at their Studio Era peak, down to 46.5 million (Bernstein 1957: 2). The Majors, whose corporate boards were largely made up of 'old boys' from a bygone era, were missing the point: the bigger picture. Social habits had changed since the war. People who had 'never had it so good' were having children, moving to the suburbs, enjoying being at home, DIY-ing. They were choosing to spend their leisure time differently.

Eventually the film industry responded accordingly and in 1956, Columbia, Twentieth Century Fox, MGM, Warner Brothers and Universal released many of their pre-1948 features to TV. In 1958, Paramount followed suit and sold 750 features to the Music Corporation of America (MCA), a major producer of (filmed) TV programming. By 1959 MCA had purchased Universal, thus setting in motion the beginning of a multiplatform marketing/distribution system for film. By the mid-1970s, new distribution windows had arrived in the form of the videocassette recorder and cable television. By the mid-1980s, cable pay-per-view and cable premium channels were added to the list of distribution windows (Balio 1990: 235–256).

Henceforth, the TV Era exploitation of film, with its increasing emphasis on new distribution windows, was marked by a shift in corporate strategy of the Majors to the role of financier-cum-distributor. Only they had the experience and money to market and promote films globally in a new cross-platform marketplace. They therefore came to reassume the dominant role in the film industry by determining a film's finance (expenditures, marketing, distribution deals with producers) and a film's exploitation.

First, in cinemas:

- determining whether a film's run was exclusive (a film screened in one theatre) or multiple (a film screened at a number of theatres simultaneously) or saturation (a film screened in upwards of 1000k screens at the same time);
- setting the agenda for the length of the film's engagement in particular cinemas, the agenda for a cinema's advertising campaign and the financial spilt of box office takings.

Then in down-the-line distribution windows:

- By 1990, the typical pattern of release for a 'blockbuster' (a big budget film), usually an adventure film genre appealing to the frequent film-goer, a 16- to 24-year-old male, looked something like this:
- theatrical window: 0 to 6 months;
- video window: 6 months + (open ended);
- pay-per-view window: 9 to 12 months;

- cable TV: 12 to 30 months;
- network TV: 30 to 60 months;
- syndicated TV: 60 months +.

The theatrical presentation would continue to remain the most important distribution window because of the prestige afforded to a film's theatrical release: premieres, press junkets (post-screening one-on-one publicity interview marathons between the media and a production's director and lead actors), critical reviews, industry awards, all increasing the value of the film with respect to other distribution windows (rental agreements, etc.).

Case study 3: *The Seven Year Itch* (1955) – Twentieth Century Fox marketing team respond to the challenge of TV: Iconic stars

By the early 1950s, the strategic advantage enjoyed by the Majors during the Studio Era was over. There was no longer a guaranteed market for their films. They had to compete with independent productions for cinema slots while at the same time having to meet huge fixed studio costs which the Independents didn't incur. Meanwhile, American audiences were staying at home and watching TV in ever-increasing numbers. In response, film companies focused their energies on promoting the difference between their screen product and the (free) TV one. Indeed, it would be a few years before the Majors changed strategy and started doing big business with TV. Twentieth Century Fox's 1952 solution to TV was its widescreen process, 'Cinemascope', accompanied for the most part by colour and stereophonic sound. Its films were now going to be events, with marketing/promotion as important as the production values. The company's big summer release of 1955, *The Seven Year Itch*, was shot in Cinemascope, colour and recorded in stereo, as one would expect. What was less expected was the astute decision by the studio to turn the location shoot into a marketing bonanza.

The script called for the film's star, Marilyn Monroe, to be photographed on location outside a cinema in Midtown Manhattan. What made this particular 15 September 1954 shoot most unusual was that several hundred press photographers were invited along to help promote the event, particularly Marilyn's white dress billowing above a subway grating. After the shoot, Fox selected its best production stills to be used for press releases or to be blown up as posters for cinema marquees. For the 1955 summer premiere of the movie, a huge four-storey version of one of the billowing-dress stills was selected as the logotype for the film (a graphic that gives 'identity' to a brand, in this case Twentieth Century Fox). The monumentality of widescreen, of poster, of star all came together as mutually reinforcing elements to create an iconic stamp for the movie. With the huge blow-up of the billowing dress hovering over many of the nation's ticket booths, the film's box office was outstanding: the gross figure in the US/Canada sector alone was $12 million (IMDb).

Critics at the time were quick to put the enormous popularity of *The Seven Year Itch* down to Marilyn's performance/star image. That image, which was greatly enhanced by the billowing-dress photo, was marked by the sociocultural context of its making: a mixture of the new liberated female subject, borne out of the experience of young women during World War II, and a hyper-feminine persona/ body-object of the 1950s, a product of the censure of the Eisenhower Era. Already, in 1953, the publication of Alfred Kinsey's candid 'scientific' report on American female sexuality had appeared. That same year, a nude photo of Marilyn, taken in 1948, was used as the centrefold in the first edition of *Playboy* magazine. The billowing-dress Marilyn logotype taps into this zeitgeist. In marketing terms, Twentieth Century Fox was consciously building its brand on 'pillars', branding strategies, values and audience demographics that exploited tensions evident in the social discourse of the age. As 'the' female body image of the 1950s, Marilyn's figure moves across film and print media, seemingly free to express itself, while at the same time encoded by the censure of post-war patriarchal advertising. This logotype is truly an American myth in the making, apparently reconciling social dilemmas that cannot be reconciled in real life (Dyer 1987: 19–66).

Over time the billowing-dress logotype has been reproduced so much that its meaning bleeds way beyond the film that generated it. As a linguistic sign, its meaning is at once very dense and very diffuse. To some it clearly denotes Monroe, to others it connotes aspects of 1950s American media and advertising, and to others broader aspects of gender politics. The list goes on and on. It might be useful here to refer to Baudrillard's notion of the simulacrum, where in his analysis of postmodern consumer society he argues that 'endless networks of media and advertising images. … precede any reality to which they might be said to refer' (Childers and Hentzi 1995: 280). Applied to this example, an online search today for the Marilyn logotype will likely take us on any number of digital 'journeys' to a huge variety of sites. Very quickly, a search for the billowing dress can generate almost 'endless networks' of signification, with no obvious beginning or end, no clear point of source and no end point. Networks of signifiers are generated that have no clear referent.

Case study 4: *Jaws* (1975) – Hollywood film promotion and distribution: The dawn of a new era

In 1973, two independent producers working out of Universal Pictures, Richard Zanuck and David Brown, acquired the screen rights to *Jaws*. By early 1975, Universal (the financier-cum-distributor of the film) was collaborating with Bantam (the publisher of the paperback version of the book) on a highly innovative promotion to accompany the imminent publication of the paperback and the release of the film. Both film distributor and paperback publisher immediately recognized the mutual benefits of a joint promotion strategy. For both, the end goal was the exploitation of the *Jaws* brand to the full. To achieve this, a cross-media logotype was developed, designed to appear on the cover of the paperback and on all the film's advertising. Later, producers Zanuck and Brown 'embarked on a 6-city tour sponsored by Bantam Books' to promote the publication of the paperback and to build audiences for the soon-to-be released film (Daly 1980: 114).

It is difficult to label *Jaws* a blockbuster exactly, as it wasn't funded as such from the onset; but once the book was established as a bestseller, the film's release was handled as if it were. What Universal came up with for the film's release in June 1975 was to mark the dawn of a new era in the promotion and distribution of Hollywood's 'big' films. For the first time the exploitation of a movie incorporated a 'wide' release pattern in cinemas, opening in 464 theatre screens on 20 June 1975 across the US and Canada. This was accompanied by a nationwide media campaign on a massive scale: in the days leading up to the film's release (specifically 18 to 20 June 1975), Universal funded a media blitz of approximately 25 30-second ads per night on primetime TV. The logic behind the strategy was to create maximum visibility for the film as quickly as possible in order to recoup production/ distribution costs as soon as possible. It is clear that the strategy paid off handsomely. '*Jaws* made 14 million dollars its 1st week in release ... [and] as of September 5, 1975, Universal declared *Jaws* the all-time box-office champion' (Daly 1980: 124–125).

The *Jaws* figures in summary are as follows:

- production costs: $8 million;
- pre-opening marketing/promotion costs: $1.8 million (including $700,000 for 18 to 20 June TV blitz);
- opening weekend: $7,061,513 (US: IMDb) (22 June 1975) (464 screens);
- theatrical gross: $430,510,134 (worldwide: IMDb).

Universal also exploited tie-ins and merchandising to increase profits:

> In eight weeks over a half million *Jaws* t-shirts, 2 million plastic tumblers, and 2 hundred thousand soundtrack record albums were sold. *The Jaws Log*, a quickly produced paperback about the making of the film, sold over 1 million copies in the first month ... .
>
> *(Daly 1980: 137–138)*

Even allowing for the fact that not all of the promotion strategy was new, what is clear from this case study is that *Jaws* marks the birth of the Modern Era in film marketing and promotion. What was truly innovative about the strategy was the combination of pre-opening cross-media branding, TV blitz marketing and saturation booking. Previously 'big' films had opened in exclusive runs in deluxe locations only – for example, Times Square, New York, and Leicester Square, London. This basic structure has remained the cornerstone for blockbuster promotion campaigns ever since.

Case study 5: *The Crying Game* (1992) – Miramax promotion strategy and the art of building an audience

The marketing/promotion strategy for *The Crying Game* is a classic example of how to build an audience for a low-budget 'off-centre' film (mainstream film but not 'blockbuster') in the pre-Digital Era. *The Crying Game* was a Miramax 'pick-up', a film that it did not finance, but one for which it acquired the US distribution rights after the production was completed. In the spring of 1992, this largely UK pack-of-cards co-production, where each source of funding depends on the participation of the others, was picked up by Miramax for US distribution. The difficult themes of the picture, race, cross-dressing, transgressive sexuality, IRA 'terrorist' cells meant that this was a film that was not going to be a straightforward marketing campaign. Miramax had to find the film's 'natural' audience first and then build on that. The UK distributors of the film, Mayfair, had failed to do this by rushing too quickly to a wide release pattern. The net result: the film failed at the UK box office. Miramax would not make the same mistake. The strategy it came up with was to prove so effective that even today elements of it are used as 'the' classic model for an off-centre film promotion.

To garner critical interest and to create a buzz around the film, Miramax screened the film at the Telluride, Toronto and New York Film Festivals. It then released it to a limited number of US cinemas at the end of November 1992. To promote the film, Miramax borrowed the one successful element from the UK marketing campaign, enlisting the media in a conspiracy of silence, not to give the film's secret away. But Miramax added an extra twist: the audience was also involved in the conspiracy. The film was promoted using the slogan: 'The movie everyone is talking about, but no one is giving away its secrets.' This both fired the imagination of the film-going public and neatly avoided the problem of drawing too much attention to the difficult themes of the film. The release pattern started very modestly, the film opening in only six screens in the US. But as audience interest mounted, the release pattern went 'wide': by early February 1993, the film was playing on 239 US/Canada screens. Later that month, the film received six Oscar nominations: it was now playing on 500 screens. By the week preceding the Oscars, the number of US/Canada screens showing the film was in excess of 1000, such was the momentum of the campaign.

Miramax had originally picked up the US distribution of *The Crying Game* in the spring of 1992 for a paltry $1.5 million. By 1997, the total gross US box-office figure was around $68 million (Giles 1997: 50). However, the film's US success was a hollow victory for the UK producers. None of the monies found their way back to them. Only the US based distributors, Miramax, were the winners.

Case study 6: *Trainspotting* (1996) – building a UK youth audience for an off-centre film

Leaving the miseries of the UK marketing strategy of *The Crying Game* behind, a classic UK/Euro marketing success is the campaign for the low-budget UK co-production *Trainspotting*. As the film's UK theatrical and video distributor, Polygram, a multimedia Dutch entertainment group, set itself the challenge of widening the film's 'natural' appeal beyond the cult status of the Irvine Welsh book on which the film was based. If the budget of the film was typically low for a UK TV-financed film (Channel 4 and co-producers had spent £1.5 million), the marketing budget was atypically high. Polygram spent £800,000 marketing the film in the UK.

The challenge was to tap the mass youth audience, the 16- to 24-year-old multiplex audience, and a marketing campaign was designed to do just that. Polygram utilized its expertise in the music industry, marketing the film like a record album release. A graphic design team was brought in to create the film's (now) distinctive look, the *Trainspotting* logotype, bright orange graphics/typesetting mixed with black-and-white portraits of the cast. This logotype was ubiquitous in the cross-media exploitation of the film: for cinema release, for the CD, for print-media advertising (e.g., youth 'style' magazines) and for video. By supporting the brand the way it did, it gave *Trainspotting* a strong brand identity. Then the promotional trailer brought the 'accent-on-youth' pillar of the marketing campaign to a crescendo, with its emphasis on the film's humour and Britpop music track. The strategic emphasis on a broad youth market paid off handsomely. The film found its audience and became a major domestic and international hit. The UK box office alone was £12.3 million (IMDb).

The Digital Era (1990s to the present)

Looking back it is easy to see that the Hollywood of the 1950s made the near-fatal error of misreading its business. It wasn't only in the business of making films, but also in the business of providing entertainment and it needed to follow its customers. Had it done so, it might have embraced TV earlier, reconfigured itself as 'multi-media' and seen profits rise. Instead, it stuck rather doggedly to a policy of 'we make movies' (investing in 3D, widescreen and stereophonic sound) and saw profits fall for years (Levitt 2011: 42–43).

By the mid-1990s, however, the Majors as financiers-cum-distributors again dominated the industry. Distribution windows for film ran from theatrical release, through the video home system (VHS), to pay-per-view cable/satellite, to standard cable/satellite, to network TV and finally to syndicated TV. The year 1996 saw the arrival of the latest tier in home film distribution, the digital versatile disc (DVD). This new digital system was designed to compete with VHS, which it very quickly superseded. As early as 2001 the DVD market was growing at ten times that of the VHS market. Digital technology offered vastly superior image and sound, and increased storage capacity; and DVD was cross-platform, that is to say it could run on multiple types of hardware systems.

Such was the economic importance of DVD that it soon led to a rethinking of the exploitation strategy behind the Majors' distribution of their films. Henceforth there was a closing of the (time) gap between the theatrical release date and the next, DVD, window. Today the typical distribution cycle for a studio film in the US is as follows:

- theatrical window: 0 to 4 months;
- DVD window: 4 months + (open for an indefinite period);
- video-on-demand (VOD)/pay-per-view window: 5 months +;
- VOD is followed by a premium cable/satellite channel window (for approximately one year), which precedes free-to-air television, etc.

1999 to 2004 proved to be the golden years of DVD marketing and sales, with the DVD release of the blockbuster *Gladiator* (November 2000) marking a major watershed. The DVD two-disc set included audio commentary, deleted scenes, a behind-the-scenes documentary, a theatre trailer and a history of gladiatorial games. In anticipation of huge sales, prior to its release date, 2.6 million copies of the DVD were shipped to retail outlets in the US/Canada sector. Eventually, DVD sales reached 4.5 million units worldwide, the best-selling DVD up to that point.

From the vantage point of 2012, pundits now forecast the future of film exploitation with only two main distribution windows: the theatrical window and VOD. DVD sales are falling every year. If the theatrical release continues to be paramount in a film's commercial exploitation strategy, due to the status and prestige associated with a theatrical premiere, its publicity and its critical reviews, it is the wider picture of converging digital entertainment technologies that is the focus of attention for most companies.

The industry more than understands that it is in the entertainment business, all of it: at home, out of the home, in film, TV, games, digital design, animation, digital print, music, merchandising, tie-ins, online, offline, Smartphone, PC and MAC. Financing-cum-distribution occurs across the media technologies, of which (digital) film is but one. Seen in this light, the recent interest in digital 3D technology is not just a re-tread of the 1950s all over again. It is a logical, in many senses ideal, cross-platform technology, equally at home across a range of hardware devices. Today, multi-media conglomerates put big money into attracting their main customer base to the local multiplex, the 12- to 24-year-old male customer segment, who it turns out is also the main customer for any down-the-line associated digital software (Rust et al 2011: 2–3). Any media corporation worth its salt must build a relationship with this viewer-cum-user or 'viewer'. As the courtship progresses, corporate marketing personnel push products and brands, theirs and tie-ins, using the 'nudge factor' or 'leverage'. Much of this is done online. A recent example of such a strategy was the collaboration between Twentieth Century Fox and Rovio, an entertainment media company based in Finland specializing in games for touch-screen Smartphones. The two corporations collaborated on the animated feature *Rio* (2011), with Rovio producing a new version of its popular mobile game *Angry Birds*, now christened *Angry Birds Rio*, to promote the feature film and its own social-gaming business. A tie-in was thus established to the mutual benefit of both corporations, with Rovio's social gaming proving an ideal digital marketing tool to promote *Rio* to a viewser generation of movie-goers. *Angry Birds Rio* was launched in March 2011 and the film, *Rio*, released one month later. *Angry Birds Rio* hit 10 million downloads in the first ten days of its launch (nma.co. uk, posted 26 May 2011) and by September 2011 *Rio* grossed $143,618,384 at the US/Canada box office alone (IMDb).

In the new converging media marketplace, branding and promotion experts have seen their control over the construction of meaning of a film increase. In this panacea of endless media and advertising images, it is the marketing team that has the most to say about modes of viewing and target audiences. This is reflected in rising marketing budgets: in 2008, Hollywood Majors were said to be spending approximately one third of a film's budget, around $36 million, on marketing a big budget film, more in the case of huge blockbusters.

In his book *Show Sold Separately*, Jonathan Gray argues that in the cross-platform digital age, marketing para-texts, the online and offline promotion and publicity materials, the tie-ins, the merchandising, increasingly 'create [film] texts, they manage them, and they fill them with many of the meanings that we associate with them' (Gray 2010: 6). If there is a triangular relationship between the film, the audience and the industry, Gray argues, then it is the para-texts that 'fill the space between them ... negotiating or determining interactions' (Gray 2010: 23). A case in point is the humble trailer. In a world of converging technologies, the trailer of old is no more. It now occupies a very central role in the promotional packaging of a film. Besides film companies setting up individual websites to promote any new releases, many digital TV providers now offer free VOD movie trailers. The social network sites (e.g., YouTube and Facebook) also circulate trailers and previews. However, Gray goes on to propose a rather depressing scenario for the filmmaker: that with an ever-increasing viewing of para-texts on/offline comes an ever-increasing dissolution of the meaning of the film itself, with the marketing texts replacing it. This is bound to consolidate power even more in the hands of marketing persons who 'pre-purpose and repurpose' the endeavours of directors (Gray 2010: 71–72).

Yet, fans also create their own para-texts: 'criticism and reviews, fan fiction [associated with particular films/ genres], fan film and video (vids) ... fan art, spoilers, fan sites' (Gray 2010: 143). These audience-generated para-texts can either be 'on message' or not, for audiences are very creative when it comes to the business of subverting the meaning of studio product. They can create 'their own genres, genders, tones and styles', carving out for themselves and others alternative paths through movie texts (Gray 2010: 143). Eventually, however, financial power tends to win out. Any audience para-texts that find a wider audience will eventually get assimilated by the industry. This has happened time and time again, particularly with fan sites. Mainstream culture has an uncanny knack of absorbing marginal 'voices' to reinvigorate itself, to make itself more acceptable to its target audience. And when that audience, by and large, is young, this is particularly important for credibility. This is how hegemonic power works: ideological control by consent, not through force. Ideas that are generated outside tend to be absorbed as fully integrated creative technologies by the industry very quickly (Huyssen 1986: 15).

Case study 7: *Harry Potter and the Deathly Hallows Part 2* (2011) – Harry Potter as the quintessential contemporary brand

1997 saw the UK publication of the first Harry Potter book by J. K. Rowling, *Harry Potter and the Philosopher's Stone*. By 1999, and the publication of the second in the series, *Harry Potter and the Prisoner of Azkaban*, the Harry Potter cult was born. 'By the third book you had queues [at booksellers], and by the fourth it was starting to feel like those stories of people lining the docks in New York for the next instalment of Dickens's *David Copperfield*. Harry Potter was a game changer. It changed publishing' (Jon Howells of Waterstone's Booksellers, cited in Hoyle 2011: 4). Harry Potter changed more than publishing: the promotion of the books, the film franchise and now the e-books have been an object lesson in cross-platform branding in an era of convergence, with its storytelling myths going viral seemingly 'at the click of a mouse' (Aspden 2011: 11).

By 2001, the film rights to the books had been acquired by Time Warner and the first in a planned series of films was released, *Harry Potter and the Sorcerer's Stone* (US title). To promote the film, Time Warner set up a 'marketing council' with AOL, at the time under the same corporate umbrella, to facilitate a synergy of marketing talents across the multimedia conglomerate. Lateral integration of different corporate entities, such as Time Warner and AOL, can extend the global reach of production/marketing/sales/distribution systems of multi-media conglomerates. By definition, it casts a much wider net of power and control over the marketplace than vertical integration, as witnessed in the Studio Era. For *Harry Potter and the Sorcerer's Stone*, Time Warner companies handled US TV/cable/ satellite promotion (HBO and Warner's networks), the music (issued on Warner Music's Atlantic Records label) and print media promotion (Time Warner's print media empire). AOL, in turn, handled online merchandising (with 90 licensing partners and 700 products), ticket promotions and giveaways (linked to AOL subscriptions) (Grimes 2001: 17).

Since 2001, the further film adaptations and the Time Warner branding have helped to spur on book sales, and Harry Potter has grown to become one of the world's most widely recognized brands. Stephen Brown in his book *Wizard! Harry Potter's Brand Magic* (2005), identifies the answer to this success in the pillars which drive the brand: the stories themselves. In the branding of Harry Potter, marketing persons have exploited the fundamental power of the parables themselves, the myths. This world of Harry Potter is full of 'hocus pocus, good versus evil, a wizard with a big white beard, a baddie, the game of Quidditch, a hairy funnyman on a flying motorbike. And to top it all, a troll ... "snotting" all over Harry's wand' (Barbara Ellen cited in Hoyle 2011: 5). These story elements act as a catalyst for any developing brand story, stories feeding off stories again and again. The

Time Warner marketing machine has always been sensitive to this. From 2001 to 2011, the cross-platform promotional strategy was designed to promote the films as a developing series and with it a brand that was growing and changing at the same time in the minds of the public. This avoided audience *ennui* early on in the series.

For the eighth, and final, film in the series, *Harry Potter and the Deathly Hallows Part 2* (2011), the promotion shifted away from the developing-story strategy of previous movies to a focus on the one central marketing point of this last film: to 'move' the audience towards the conclusion of the tale, the final duel between Harry and Voldemort. To this end, ubiquitous in the marketing materials, was one tag line: 'It all ends 7.15', referencing the release date of 15 July 2011. The official website also included a link to an iPhone app that consumers could use to trade spells with each other. This isn't to say that marketing materials for the campaign didn't also refer to earlier campaigns. Posters and banners (released from 28 March 2011), trailers (from 27 April 2011), TV commercials and online promotion all referred back to the logotype of the first film, the Harry Potter lightning flash.

Such was the success of the promotion campaign that the film took more money than any other in its opening weekend, $168.8 million in the US/Canada sector and $307 million elsewhere, including $36.6 million in the UK (Kaufman 2011). But the Harry Potter promotion story doesn't end there. One month before the release of *Harry Potter and the Deathly Hallows Part 2*, J. K. Rowling announced a move to e-books with the launch of a website *Pottermore* to handle distribution. She had sensibly retained the digital rights to her books and hence was now free to exploit them as e-books. As a strategist, J. K. Rowling has been brilliant. The multimedia conglomerates helped to build up and sustain her brand. Now she leaves them behind. She has even excluded other online stores, such as Amazon and Apple, from selling her e-books. Are we witnessing a successful assault on the power brokers of the media entertainment sector? Maybe, but a word of caution: global media conglomerates have a long history of acquiring successful 'Independents' to expand operations and to knock out the competition. One is left wondering if *Pottermore* will be one more corporation to add to that statistic.

Case study 8: *Paranormal Activity* (2007) and no-budget marketing

Earlier I mentioned the nudge factor, leverage, where film companies try to drum up excitement to build an audience. Social media sites are the main conduit for facilitating this nudge factor today and the marketing history of *Paranormal Activity* makes that point very clearly. This digital film had virtually no budget ($10,000) but was eventually picked up by Paramount, who thought that audiences might respond to the film if they could only see it. The promotion budget was kept very low, with marketing directed online.

Amy Powell, Paramount's executive vice president of interactive marketing strategies, was given the film to market. Everything about the campaign was designed to cost as little as possible but to affect the best possible result (Keane 2010). The website featured video comments by horror fans, rather than established critics, so that punters could dialogue with their peers. Written quotes from the vox pops were then targeted at colleges, a likely audience base for such an independent, no-budget horror film. In no time at all the talking-heads videos and the quotes went viral, since each piece of content had a social sharing element. Twitter was also used to post the latest 'sound bite' info on the film, at the time the longest on-going Paramount posting on Twitter. Here Amy Powell's team really excelled because the Paramount postings occurred late at night, after general Twitter activity had trailed off and on-line insomniacs were looking for something to engage with. As the excitement for the film mounted, audiences were nudged online to 'demand' that the film be screened in such-and-such a theatre. The campaign was neatly summarized by the film's sales agent, Stuart Ford, as follows: 'You like it so much? You want it? Then demand it! Tell us where you want it and we'll play it there!' (cited in Maher 2009: 3).

Paramount listened keenly to its online audience, and the subsequent roll-out exhibition strategy, starting with a limited US run on 25 September 2009 at 12 screens in college towns, followed by a wide national release on 16 October 2009, worked brilliantly. The film went on to gross $193 million worldwide at the box office (IMDb).

Case study 9: Gwyneth Paltrow – celebrity lifestyle guru for the Internet age?

In an age of information overload, consumers appear to be cutting to the chase and aligning themselves 'with a personality who thinks like them and can make recommendations' (Jacobs 2011: 1). Now, more than ever, 'the "real world" becomes constituted in terms derived from the "star world"' (Tudor 1974: 83). In his book *Stars*, Richard Dyer (1979) postulates that the star-persona is constructed by the industry through four categories of 'text': the films in which they appear, the critical reviews, the promotional materials and free publicity. If this remains generally true, in recent years celebrities have been afforded a space to break free somewhat of the constraints imposed on them by media conglomerates. Social media sites that they set up themselves offer them more control over their personae and afford them a more 'direct' connection with their audiences.

Gwyneth Paltrow is a case in point. In 2008 she set up www.goop.com to offer advice under the tagline 'Nourish the inner aspect'. To date, Goop.com has signed up 150,000 subscribers who log on for advice under the headings: Make, Go, Get, Do, Be and See. The game plan would appear to be for Paltrow to make money from her online brand by 'transform[ing] followers into customers, through product lines, advertising and e-commerce' (Jacobs 2011: 1). In the far-off days of the Marilyn logotype, such (relative) economic control was unimaginable for a star due to the industry's stranglehold over promotion and publicity. This is all well and good; but at the end of the day, the website is still about making money at the consumers' expense, feeding our fantasies in a culture where a premium is placed on lifestyle and 'self-improvement'.

Case study 10: *The Guardian* newspaper in 2011 – building a UK audience through cross-platform state-of-the-art applications

(Based on an interview with Robert Ingram-Smith, head of international business development at *The Guardian*, London, 5 July 2011)

This case study has been chosen because it neatly summarizes recent convergence strategies by a media organization whose fingers are in many pies and whose website, *Guardian Online*, now has 52 million unique users per month, one third in the UK, one third in the US and one third in the rest of the world. The strategic moves made by *The Guardian* in recent years are clear evidence of a shift to cross-platform exploitation, to a move beyond a news perspective, and to engage with young audiences for whom the pecking order is the mobile phone first, then digital (PCs/ MACs), then print. As I write, *The Guardian* is working on a consortium 'film' pilot project called *Interesting Stuff*. The project is based in Cornwall and south-west England, and harnesses digital technologies to deliver combinations of film, arts and editorial content to audiences in social venues, on mobile phone devices and in the home. Some research and development funds have been made available through the European Union Media Programme. *The Guardian* partners for *Interesting Stuff* are Twofour (based in Plymouth), working in TV/film production, broadcast media and educational resources; media interests in Italy, Denmark and the Czech Republic, providing film content for the pilot; and Golant Media Ventures (London based), the engineers of the project, responsible for knitting together all the parties involved. The heart of the project is exploring solutions for delivering film and ancillary content cross-platform.

The editor of *The Guardian* has coined the term 'mutualisation of content' to describe *The Guardian*'s policy of collating content in the era of convergence. Each *Guardian* journalist is effectively a content curator, collating, for example, the most interesting blogs and Facebook pages in their subject for *Guardian* readers and audiences online. In many senses, *Interesting Stuff* is best understood as a manifestation of this curatorial role. *The Guardian*'s function in the pilot is to bundle up packages of content from inside or outside the organization that are essentially supplementary reading either ahead of, or after, watching the film. A film set in Cornwall, for instance, might be assembled as a package with a whole raft of content that is about Cornwall, or about the author of the book on which the film is based, or interviews with actors who have appeared in the film. *The Guardian* might arrange to screen the film in a social venue and, ahead of time, direct punters to a portal page who will then pull down content that sits outside the film. It's rather like a tie-in, but taken to the next level. And what are the commercial advantages to be had for *The Guardian*? Firstly, if the audience is large enough for

Interesting Stuff, *The Guardian* can charge higher advertising rates; secondly, the corporate marketing people can then make capital from the increased visibility of *The Guardian* brand.

Conclusion

This chapter has been a reflection on how the film industry has promoted itself since the Studio Era. During the 1930s and 1940s, power was consolidated around five vertically integrated Majors who largely controlled the marketing of film. Later, in the TV Era, the Majors maintained a grip on film promotion through their reconfiguration into financiers-cum-distributors and by eventually linking up with other media, especially TV. In fact, by the 1980s, the concept of the autonomous film company was a thing of the past, with the Majors by now absorbed into much larger, laterally integrated, multi-media empires. This is the point at which we see the explosion of multi-platform marketing and distribution of film.

In the Digital Era of online technologies, the opportunities afforded by cross-platform marketing and promotion have increased exponentially. In this new digital world, marketing has gone 'viral'. Much is made of the democratization that the Internet has brought. This may be true in terms of audience interactivity and agency, but at the same time lifestyle ideals have moved from the movie theatre, to the TV, to the DVD, to the PC, to the Smartphone.

The mainstream film industry has always been driven by an ethos of spinning dreams for profit; but now ego-ideals are fed to us through a plethora of marketing avenues undreamed of a few decades ago. If 'ethical' multi-media groups such as *The Guardian*, owned by a charitable trust, can be relied upon to keep in check the worst excesses of promotional culture, others cannot. In those cases, consumers are ever vulnerable to the new digital onslaught of viral commodity fetishism.

Bibliography

Aspden, P. (2011) 'The Fable Maker Who Left Books for Brand Management', *Financial Times*, 9/10 July, p11.

Balio, T. (ed.) (1976) *The American Film Industry*, Madison, WI: University of Wisconsin Press.

——(1990) *Hollywood in the Age of Television*, Cambridge, MA: Unwin Hyman Inc.

Bernstein, I. (1957) *Hollywood at the Crossroads: An Economic Study of the Motion Picture Industry*, Los Angeles, CA: Hollywood Film Council.

Brown, S. (2005) *Wizard!: Harry Potter's Brand Magic*, London: Cyan Books.

Childers, J. and Hentzi, G. (eds) (1995) *Columbia Dictionary of Modern Literary and Cultural Criticism*, New York, NY: Columbia University Press.

Curran, J. and Porter, V. (eds) (1983) *British Cinema History*, New Jersey: Barnes and Noble Books.

Daly, D. (1980) *A Comparison of Exhibition and Distribution Problems in Three Recent Feature Motion Pictures*, New York, NY: Arno Press.

Dyer, R. (1987) *Heavenly Bodies*, London: Macmillan.

——(1979) *Stars*, London: British Film Institute.

Eckert, C. (1978) 'The Carole Lombard in Macy's Window', *Quarterly Review of Film Studies*, vol 3, winter.

Giles, J. (1997) *The Crying Game*, London: British Film Institute.

Gomery, D. (1986) *The Hollywood Studio System*, London: Macmillan.

Gray, J. (2010) *Show Sold Separately*, New York, NY: New York University Press.

Grimes, C. (2001) 'Harry Potter and the Sales Team', *Financial Times*, 16 November, p17.

Hoyle, B. (2011) 'Wooosh! The End of an Era Conquered by a Boy Wizard', *The Times*, 6 July, pp4–5.

Huyssen, A. (1986) *After the Great Divide*, Bloomington and Indianapolis: Indiana University Press.

Jacobs, E. (2011) 'At Home with the Stars', Life and Arts section, *Financial Times*, 23/24 July, p1.

Kaufman, A. (2011) 'Harry Potter Makes Box-Office Magic', http://articles.latimes.com/2011/jul/18/entertainment/la-et-0718-box-office-20110718, accessed 1 March 2012.

Keane, M. (2010) 'Case Study: *Paranormal Activity* Takes Over Twitter', 8 June, http://econsultancy.com/uk/blog/6047-case-study-paranormal-activity-takes-over-twitter, accessed 1 March 2012.

Levitt, T. (2011) 'Marketing Myopia', *Harvard Business Review on Reinventing Your Marketing*, Boston, MA: Harvard Business Review Press.

Maher, K. (2009) 'A Scream Made for a Song', Times 2, *The Times*, 6 November, p3.

Orlean, S. (2011) 'The Dog Star', *The New Yorker*, 29 August.

Rust, R. et al (2011) 'Rethinking Marketing', *Harvard Business Review on Reinventing Your Marketing*, Boston, MA: Harvard Business Review.

Schlosser, E. (2002) *Fast Food Nation*, London: Penguin.

Tudor, A. (1974) *Image and Influence*, London: Allen and Unwin.

Data sources

http://www.imdb.com

http://www.nma.co.uk/

INDEX

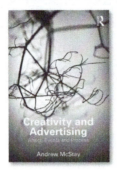

Made in the USA
Monee, IL
07 October 2022

15422261R00142